The Complete Planning Guide
for Microsoft® Project

For Windows 95 and Windows 3.1

The Complete Planning Guide for Microsoft® Project

For Windows 95 and Windows 3.1

Thomas C. Belanger

Butterworth-Heinemann
Boston Oxford Johannesburg Melbourne New Delhi Singapore

Copyright © 1996 by Butterworth–Heinemann

A member of the Reed Elsevier group

All rights reserved.

No part of this publication may be reproduced, stored in a retrieval system, or transmitted in any form or by any means, electronic, mechanical, photocopying, recording, or otherwise, without the prior written permission of the publisher.

Recognizing the importance of preserving what has been written, Butterworth–Heinemann prints its books on acid-free paper whenever possible.

Illustrations by Gary Kirby

Microsoft, MS, MS-DOS, FoxPro, PewerPoint, Visual Basic and Windows are registered trademarks, and IntelliSense and Windows NT are trademarks of Microsoft Corporation in the United States of America and other countries.

Screen shots reprinted with permission from Microsoft Corporation

Lotus and 1-2-3 are registered trademarks of Lotus Development Corporation
dBASE, dBASE III, dBASDE III PLUS, and dBASE IV are registered trademarks of Borland International, Inc.

Library of Congress Cataloging-in-Publication Data
Belanger, Thomas C.
    The complete planning guide for Microsoft Project : for Windows 95 and Windows 3.1 / by Thomas C. Belanger.
      p.   cm.
    Includes bibliographical references and index.
    ISBN 0-7506-9777-6 (pbk.)
    1. Microsoft Project for Windows. 2. Industrial project management---Computer programs.   I. Title.
HD69.P75B437   1996
658.4'02855369—dc20   96-24393
                                                                                               CIP

British Library Cataloguing-in-Publication Data
A catalogue record for this book is available from the British Library.

The publisher offers special discounts on bulk orders of this book.
For information, please contact:
Manager of Special Sales
Butterworth–Heinemann
313 Washington Street
Newton, MA 02158–1626
Tel: 617-928-2500
Fax: 617-928-2620

For information on all Business Books available, contact our World Wide Web home page at: http://www.bh.com

10 9 8 7 6 5 4 3 2 1

Printed in the United States of America

Contents

Preface xiii
Techniques and Conventions xiv
Fast Lane Tips—Quick Reference xv

CHAPTER 1: PROJECT PLANNING AND THE PROJECT TEAM 1

Introduction 2
What Is a Project? 2
A Case for Detailed Planning 3
Project Requirements 4
A Project Planning and Control Model 5
The Planning Team 6
Putting Together a Quarterly Newsletter 6
The Work Environment 7
Starting a New Project File 11
The Kickoff Meeting and the Project Description 17
The Project Goal 18
Companion Products Related to this Chapter 21

CHAPTER 2: MICROSOFT PROJECT FUNDAMENTALS 23

Introduction 24
The Menu Bar 24
   The File Menu 25
   The Edit Menu 27
   The View Menu 29
   The Insert Menu 31
   The Format Menu 33
   The Tools Menu 36
   The Window Menu 38
   The Help Menu 39
Help in Version 4.1 39
   Answer Wizard 40
   Screentips 41
   Quick Preview 41
   Tip of the Day 42
   About Microsoft Project 42
Help in Version 4.0 42
The Toolbar 47
Views and Tables 50
   Choosing a Table or View 50
   Inserting Columns 51
   Customizing a Column Head 53
   Creating a New Table 53
   Deleting a Task 54
   Editing a Task 55

CHAPTER 3: SCOPING OUT YOUR PROJECT — 57

- Introduction — 58
- Project Phases or Objectives — 58
  - *Project Standards and Guidelines* — 59
  - *Top-Down Approach* — 60
  - *Bottom-Up Approach* — 62
  - *The Second Team Meeting* — 62
- Constructing an Outline (WorkBreakdown structure) — 68
  - *The Third Team Meeting* — 68
  - *Outline Levels: Expanding and Collapsing* — 72
  - *Summary Tasks, Parent Tasks, and Children Tasks* — 73
  - *Display WBS Codes* — 73
  - *Customizing WBS Numbers* — 75
- Time Estimating — 77
  - *Entering Work Hours* — 77
  - *Adding Duration* — 78
- Task Analysis — 82
  - *The Task Analysis Worksheet* — 83
- Companion Products Related to this Chapter — 89

CHAPTER 4: COMMUNICATION AND RESOURCES — 91

- Introduction — 92
- The Communication Plan — 92
  - *Stakeholders and Information Needs* — 93
  - *Gathering Information and Updating Project Status* — 93
  - *Vacations* — 96
- The Resource Management Toolbar — 97
  - *Resource Management Toolbar Icons* — 98
  - *The Resource Allocation View* — 98
  - *The Task Entry View* — 99
- Resources and Costs — 103
  - *Identifying Resource Needs and Fixed Costs* — 104
  - *Developing a Resource Pool* — 105
  - *Assigning Resources and Fixed Costs* — 109
  - *Managing and Reassigning Resources* — 111
  - *Changing Resource Data* — 112
- Resource Leveling — 113
  - *Reassigning Resources* — 114
  - *Delaying or Lengthening NonCritical Tasks* — 114
  - *Instructing Microsoft Project to Level Resources* — 115
  - *Resource Graph* — 116
  - *Replacing a Resource* — 118
- The Project Funding and Budget — 119
- Companion Products Related to this Chapter — 121

CHAPTER 5: SCHEDULING THE PROJECT — 123

- Introduction — 124
- Project Scheduling — 124
  - *Newness* — 125

    Size......125
    Colluboration......125
    Team Experience......125
    Permanence......126
  The Calendar View......126
    Creating a Task......129
    Editing Task Information......130
  The Gantt Chart......134
    Editing the Gantt Chart......135
    How to Use the Gantt Chart Wizard......141
    The Planning Wizard......141
  Types of Predecessor-Successor Task Relationships......142
  The PERT Chart......145
    The Fourth Team Meeting......146
    Creating the Task Network with Stickies......147
    Establishing Predecessor-Successor Relationships......148
    Modifying the PERT Task Network......149
  Finalizing the Schedule......152
    Resolving Resource Overallocations......152
    Reducing Duration......154
    When Planning Is Complete, Set the Baseline......155
  Companion Products Related to this Chapter......157

CHAPTER 6: MANAGING A GREAT MANY PROJECTS   159

  Introduction......160
  Managing One Project......160
    The Tracking Toolbar......162
    The Workgroup Toolbar......166
    The Tracking Table......167
    The Variance Table......169
    The Cost Table......171
    The Work Table......174
  Managing Many Projects......176
    Creating Project Templates......177
    Saving Several Projects as a Workspace......179
    Sharing Common Elements as Global Files......180
    Sharing Resources with Other Projects......182
    Creating Subprojects......183
    Linking Master Project and Subproject Dates......185
    Consolidating Projects......186
    Links Between Any Projects......189
  Companion Products Related to this Chapter......190

CHAPTER 7: DO IT YOUR WAY REPORTS AND FORMS   191

  Introduction......192
  Defining Information Requirements......192
  Overview Reports......193
    Project Summary......194

vii

  Top-Level Tasks 195
  Critical Tasks 196
  Milestones 197
  Working Days 198
 Current Activity Reports 198
  Unstarted Tasks 199
  Tasks Starting Soon 200
  Tasks in Progress 200
  Completed Tasks 200
  Should Have Started Tasks 201
  Slipping Tasks 202
  Cost Reports 202
  Weekly Cash Flow 203
  Budget 203
  Overbudget Tasks 204
  Overbudget Resources 204
  Earned Value 205
 Assignment Reports 206
  Who Does What 207
  Who Does When 207
  Weekly To-do List 208
  Overallocated Resources 208
 Workload Reports 209
  Task Usage 210
  Resource Usage 210
 Custom Reports 210
  Task 211
  Resource 213
  Monthly 214
  Crosstab 215
 Sorting and Filtering 216
  Sorting 216
  Filtering 218
 Print Preview 220
 Page Setup 221
 Printing 222
 Creating Custom Forms 224
  The Dialog Editor 225
 Companion Products Related to this Chapter 230

CHAPTER 8: ADVANCED FEATURES   231

 Introduction 232
 Customizing Menus, Toolbars, and Toolbar Buttons 232
  Changing the Menu 232
  Deleting Items from the Menu 237
  Customizing Toolbars and Buttons 238
  Creatomg a New Toolbar Button 240
 Working with Macros 242
  Available Macros 243

Importing and Exporting 259
   Importing 260
   Exporting 262
Object Linking and Embedding 263
   Linking and Embedding Objects from Another Application in Microsoft Project 264
   Linking or Embedding Objects from Microsoft Project in Another Application 266
Companion Products Related to this Chapter 267

Appendix 269
Appendix A 271
Appendix B 273
Glossary 277
Bibliography 283
Index 285

FIGURES

Figure 1-1. Welcome to Version 4.1 8
Figure 1-2. Welcome to Version 4.0 8
Figure 1-3. Version 4.1 Up and Running Tutorial 9
Figure 1-4. Up and Running Main Menu 10
Figure 1-5. Cue Cards 11
Figure 1-6. Version 4.1 Project Info 12
Figure 1-7. Version 4.0 Summary Info 12
Figure 1-8. Version 4.1 Save As 14
Figure 1-9. Version 4.0 Save As 14
Figure 1-10. Change Working Time 15
Figure 1-11. Create New Base Calendar 16
Figure 1-12. Summary Task Information 19
Figure 1-13. Save Baseline Planning Wizard 20
Figure 2-1. The Menu Bar 24
Figure 2-2. Secondary Mouse Button Minimenu 25
Figure 2-3. More Tables 30
Figure 2-4. Table Definition 30
Figure 2-5. More Views 31
Figure 2-6. Column Definition 32
Figure 2-7. Insert Object 33
Figure 2-8. Timescale 34
Figure 2-9. Gridlines 34
Figure 2-10. Bar Styles 35
Figure 2-11. Resource Leveling 37
Figure 2-12. Options 38
Figure 2-13. Version 4.1 Microsoft Project Help Topics 40
Figure 2-14. Answer Wizard 41
Figure 2-15. Help Contents 43
Figure 2-16. Project Planning Process 44
Figure 2-17. Version 4.0 Search 45

ix

Figure 2-18. Help Index..46
Figure 2-19. Available Toolbars 48
Figure 2-20. Blank Gantt Chart with Standard and Formatting Toolbars......................49
Figure 2-21. Icon Function...50
Figure 2-23. Column Definition...52
Figure 3-1. Entry Table...64
Figure 3-2. WBS Outline Part I..70
Figure 3-3. WBS Outline Part II...71
Figure 3-4. WBS Outline Part III..71
Figure 3-5. Inserting a WBS Column...74
Figure 3-6. Showing WBS Numbers..75
Figure 3-7. Task Details Form..76
Figure 3-8. Outline with WBS Numbers and Duration Part I..79
Figure 3-9. Outline with WBS Numbers and Duration Part II......................................80
Figure 3-10. Outline with WBS Numbers and Duration Part III...................................81
Figure 3-11. Right Mouse Button...82
Figure 3-12. Summary Task Information...82
Figure 3-13. Task Analysis Worksheet 84
Figure 3-14. Completion Example #1..85
Figure 3-15. Completion Example #2..86
Figure 3-16. Risk Example #1..88
Figure 3-17. Risk Example #2..88
Figure 4-1. Change Working Time 97
Figure 4-2. Version 4.0 Resource Management Toolbar..98
Figure 4-3. Version 4.1 additional Resource Management icons...................................98
Figure 4-4. Resource Allocation View...99
Figure 4-5. Task Entry View...100
Figure 4-6. Using Resource..101
Figure 4-7. Create Pivot TablesMacro..102
Figure 4-8. Pivot Tables from Microsoft Excel..103
Figure 4-9. Changing The Default Rate...108
Figure 4-10. Resource Form...109
Figure 4-11. Resource Assignment...110
Figure 4-12. Resource Information Dialog Box, R Version 112
Figure 4-13. Resource Information Dialog Box, Task Version 113
Figure 4-14. Resource Leveling Dialog Box..116
Figure 4-15. Resource Graph..117
Figure 4-16. Zoom on Resource Graph 118
Figure 4-17. Removing and Replacing a Resource Assignment..................................119
Figur 5-1. Calendar View with Seven-Day Week..127
Figure 5-2. Calendar Timescale Dialog Box..128
Figur 5-3. Calendar View with Five-Day Week...128
Figure 5-4. Calendar View Daily Tasks List..129
Figure 5-5. Calendar Gridlines Dialog Box 131
Figure 5-6. Calendar Text Styles Dialog Box 131
Figure 5-7. Calendar Bar Styles Dialog Box 132
Figure 5-8. Calendar Layout Dialog Box...133
Figure 5-9. Reengineering Gantt Chart..135
Figure 5-10. Gantt Font Dialog Box...136
Figure 5-11. Gantt Format Bar Dialog Box..136

Figure	Page
Figure 5-12. Gantt Timescale Dialog Box	137
Figure 5-13. Gantt Gridlines Dialog Box	138
Figure 5-14. Gantt Text Styles Dialog Box	138
Figure 5-15. Gantt Bar Styles Dialog Box	139
Figure 5-16. Gantt Bar Layout Dialog Box	140
Figure 5-17. Gantt Chart Excerpt from the Newsletter Project	144
Figure 5-18. PERT Task Network Excerpt	145
Figure 5-19. Task Node	150
Figure 5-20. Box Styles for the PERT Task Network	151
Figure 5-21. Resource Usage View	152
Figure 5-22. Resource Leveling for Jim Mulligan	154
Figure 5-23. Save Baseline Dialog Box	156
Figure 6-1. Tracking Toolbar	162
Figure 6-2. Project Statistics Box	162
Figure 6-3. Update Project Dialog Box	163
Figure 6-4. Update Tasks Dialog Box	164
Figure 6-5. Resource Update Options Dialog Box	165
Figure 6-6. Update Resource Work Timesheet	165
Figure 6-7. Workgroup Toolbar	166
Figure 6-8. Software Selection and Installation Project (Excerpt)	178
Figure 6-9. Save Workspace as Dialog Box for Version 4.1	179
Figure 6-10. Organizer Dialog Box	181
Figure 6-11. Share Resources Dialog Box (Active Window)	182
Figure 6-12. Consolidate Projects Dialog Box	188
Figure 7-1. Report Categories	193
Figure 7-2. Overview Reports	194
Figure 7-3. Current Activity Reports	198
Figure 7-4. Cost Reports	203
Figure 7-5. Assignment Reports	206
Figure 7-6. Workload Reports	209
Figure 7-7. Custom Reports Dialog Box	211
Figure 7-8. Define New Report Dialog Box	211
Figure 7-9. Task Report Dialog Box	212
Figure 7-10. Resources Report Dialog Box	213
Figure 7-11. Monthly Calendar Report Definition Dialog Box	214
Figure 7-12. Crosstab Report Dialog Box	215
Figure 7-13. Sort Dialog Box	217
Figure 7-14. Page Setup Dialog Box	221
Figure 7-15. Print Dialog Box	223
Figure 7-16. Custom Forms Dialog Box (Resources)	224
Figure 7-17. Custom Forms Toolbar (Version 4.1 only)	225
Figure 7-18. Entry Form Dialog Box	225
Figure 7-19. Cost Tracking Dialog Box	226
Figure 7-20. Work Tracking Dialog Box	226
Figure 7-21. Earned Value Dialog Box	227
Figure 7-23. Task Relationship Dialog Box	227
Figure 7-24. Tracking Dialog Box	228
Figure 7-25. Custom Forms Dialog Box (Tasks)	228
Figure 7-26. Task Analysis Worksheet Created with the Dialog Editor	230

Figure 8-1. Menu Bars Dialog Box 234
Figure 8-2. Menu Bar Definition Dialog Box with Communication Menu 235
Figure 8-3. View Definition Dialog Box 236
Figure 8-4. Box Styles Dialog Box 237
Figure 8-5. Customize (Toolbars) Dialog Box 240
Figure 8-6. Customize Tool (Button) Dialog Box 241
Figure 8-7. (Toolbar) Button Editor Dialog Box 242
Figure 8-8. Available Macros 243
Figure 8-9. Adjust Dates Dialog Box 245
Figure 8-10. Batch Printing Dialog Box 246
Figure 8-11. Batch Definition Dialog Box 247
Figure 8-12. Save Print Batch File Dialog Box 247
Figure 8-13. Date Range from Today 249
Figure 8-14. Duration Display Dialog Box 250
Figure 8-15. Introduction to Microsoft Project Analyzer 252
Figure 8-16. Microsoft Project Analyzer Dialog Box 252
Figure 8-17. PERT Entry Form 254
Figure 8-18. PA PERT Weights Form 255
Figure 8-19. Record Macro Dialog Box 258
Figure 8-20. Expanded Record Macro Dialog Box 258
Figure 8-21. Task Form Prepared for New Object 265
Figure 8-22. Insert Object Dialog Box 266

TABLES

Table 1-1. Kickoff Meeting Agenda 17
Table 3-1. Program Phases 61
Table 3-2. Task List 66
Table 3-3. Outline Levels 69
Table 3-4. Outline Levels for a Small Project 69
Table 3-5. Project Summary Task 72
Table 3-6. Icons for Developing a Project Outline 73
Table 4-1. Stakeholder Information 93
Table 4-2. Project Directory 95
Table 4-3. Tasks Assigned to Jim Mulligan 102
Table 4-4. Resource Sheet 106
Table 4-5. Cost Table 120
Table 5-1. Changes to the Calendar View 130
Table 6-1. Tracking Table Excerpt 169
Table 6-2. Variance Table Excerpt 170
Table 6-3. Task Version of the Cost Table (excerpt) 172
Table 6-4. Resource Version of the Cost Table 173
Table 6-5. Task Version of the Work Table (excerpt) 175
Table 6-6. Resource Version of the Work Table 176
Table 8-1. PERT Analysis Sheet 255

PREFACE

Those who work on projects in engineering, marketing, manufacturing, human resources, finance, customer service, or other departments can all predict that their responsibilities will be different a year from now. Because the needs of customers change rapidly, meeting these needs requires a unique work effort. The development of new products and the delivery of customized services now mandate the use of detailed project planning and conscientious project management.

Those who work in the public sector at the local, county, state, or federal levels also provide many success stories that are the direct result of applying the art and science of project management.

Reengineering, downsizing, mergers, rightsizing, and other changes dictated by a rapidly changing environment are all carried out best when the discipline of project management is applied.

This guide provides new and experienced project management practitioners with a straightforward and logical process for detailed project planning—as well as a methodical system for project communication, tracking, and monitoring.

The **Complete Planning Guide for Microsoft Project** attempts to meet the needs of those new practitioners who have minimal training or experience in project management. It does this by providing "basic training" in project planning and management while training new users in sophisticated techniques for streamlining project management.

Those who are experienced with project management and with Microsoft® Project can quickly get the information they need by driving in the **Fast Lane**. The **Fast Lane** renders quick, to-the-point instruction by skipping over basic training and identifying "cut to the chase" suggestions and techniques. Each Fast Lane Tip is indicated by the symbol shown below to the right of the tip as shown below.

Fast Lane TIP

A table that lists all fast lane tips is located after the Table of Tables in this section.

Microsoft Project provides extensive on-line help to users of both Versions. Version 4.1 for Windows® 95 has an intelligent Answer Wizard based on IntelliSense™. It enables you to type questions using your own words, and receive answers in the form of a list of related topics. Version 4.0 for Windows 3.1 provides "cue cards" that display step-by-step instructions that remain on the screen while you work. This guide is intended to be a companion to the on-line help system in both Versions and to the user manuals.

The guide is made up of eight chapters. Chapters 1–5 provide a step-by-step process for planning a project and the essential Microsoft® Project features to be used. Chapter 6 provides guidelines for managing one or more projects, focusing on the features that enable you to manage multiple projects. Chapter 7 introduces you to the variety of standard and customized reports that are available and guidelines for creating customized forms. Chapter 8 provides ideas for streamlining your work, for example by using macros; it also provides additional ways to customize Microsoft Project to your personal work style.

TECHNIQUES AND CONVENTIONS

Every user of Microsoft Project is likely to have personal preferences about the way he or she accomplishes work. Some prefer to use a mouse; others prefer to use the keyboard. For this reason, most instructions contained in this guide are provided with instructions to click on icons or buttons, and their keyboard equivalents.

For example, many **Fast Lane Tips** begin with the instruction "Click on **Insert**, or press **Alt/I**." The word "click" instructs you to point to an icon or checkbox and click the left mouse button (for most right-handed users). Two keys separated by a slash (/) indicate that you should depress both keys at the same time. Bold menu items and keys, as shown above, indicate actions that you take to perform a desired function.

Version 4.1 for Windows 95 and Version 4.0 for Windows Version 3.1 are explained in this guide. For easier reading, Version numbers are typically used throughout this guide to make distinctions. Most operations in Versions 4.0 and 4.1 are identical. Where there is a difference, it will be clearly marked. Most dialog boxes in Versions 4.0 and 4.1 are also virtually identical.

I would like to thank my wife, Pat Lamoureux for her empathy and support during the many evenings and weekends that were consumed by this project.

FAST LANE TIPS—QUICK REFERENCE

Tip #	What It Does	Page
1	To start a new file	13
2	To change working hours in the standard project calendar	15
3	To change working days in the standard project calendar	16
4	To perform functions using the keyboard	25
5	To identify dialog boxes from a submenu	26
6	To see a display of all buttons/icons and their titles	47
7	To return a toolbar to its original format	49
8	To examine tables and views	51
9	To insert a new column in a table	52
10	To customize a column heading	53
11	To create a new table	53
12	To edit a task	55
13	To open the Microsoft Project template library	60
14	To plan team meetings	62
15	To open the most recently used files	63
16	To increase (or decrease) row height	65
17	To create a project summary task that summarizes and accumulates project data from all tasks	72
18	To show outline numbers beside the task name in the task name column	74
19	To enter customized WBS numbers	76
20	To enter work hours (as opposed to automatic calculation based on duration)	77

21	To manage risks	86
22	To develop a communication plan consider these elements	93
23	To change hours or days for a particular resource	96
24	To display the resource management toolbar	97
25	To view and remove constraints from a task view	100
26	To change one of the views in a combination view	101
27	To create a list of resources and fixed costs	105
28	To replace or customize a column heading in the resource sheet	106
29	To change standard default rates for resources	107
30	To assign a resource or fixed cost to a task	110
31	To enter a fixed cost from the Gantt View	111
32	To delay the start of work by a resource on the task form	114
33	To locate a resource overallocation	117
34	To see cost estimates (and actual costs and variances after the project begins)	120
35	To change the calendar display from seven days to five days	127
36	To display all tasks scheduled for a particular date using a mouse	128
37	To create a task in the calendar view using a mouse	129
38	To change and format data in the calendar view with a mouse	133
39	To change the format of the Gantt bar section	140
40	To establish predecessor-successor relationships in the Gantt bar section	142
41	To change task duration on the Gantt bar using the mouse	143
42	To display free slack beside task bars	144
43	To establish a predecessor-successor relationship in a Gantt	148

	table or task sheet	
44	To change a dependency relationship in the PERT chart to reflect lead or lag time	149
45	To save the project baseline	155
46	To update percent complete on Gantt chart bars	161
47	To enable Microsoft Project to calculate work hours and schedule based on duration	166
48	To save a project file as a template	178
49	To save several files as a workspace	179
50	To save a common element as a global file	181
51	To share resources among several projects	183
52	To create a subproject from several tasks in the active project	184
53	To create a subproject by inserting an existing project	185
54	To enable the subproject to control its start date	186
55	To consolidate projects	187
56	To link start and finish dates from tasks in different projects	189
57	To sort tasks by critical path, then by start date	217
58	To apply the same sort order again	218
59	To apply the same filter again	220
60	To add headings for tables, views and reports from the menu bar	222
61	To print all columns (even those not showing)	223
62	To create a new custom form for task analysis	229
63	To add a new menu to the menu bar	231
64	To add a new PERT task network to the menu bar	233
65	To change box contents in the PERT task network	237

66	To remove a view from the View menu	238
67	To remove a toolbar button using the mouse	239
68	To add a toolbar button	239
69	To create a new toolbar button	241
70	To run the Accept All Updates macro	244
71	To run the Adjust Dates macro	244
72	To run the Batch Printing macro	245
73	To run the Date Range From Today filter macro	248
74	To run the Effort-Driven Scheduling macro	249
75	To run the Format Duration macro	250
76	To run the Project Analyzer macro	251
77	To install the PERT Schedule Analysis macro	254
78	To record a macro to switch to the summary table	257
79	To import a file	261
80	To add imported information to the end of a destination file	261
81	To export a file	262
82	To link or embed a picture object in the resource form or task form	264

1

Project Planning and the Project Team

In this chapter you will learn how to:

1. Standardize project management terminology

2. Create a new file

3. Enter task notes

4. Establish the project goal and objectives

5. Change working days on the standard project calendar

6. Save a file

INTRODUCTION

This chapter introduces you to the language of project management and to Microsoft Project. For those with much project experience, this will be a brief refresher. For those new to project management, this chapter provides essential project management terminology and direction.

The chapter also introduces a sample project, the development of a quarterly newsletter. This project will be used throughout the guide to illustrate project planning and management techniques.

WHAT IS A PROJECT?

A *project* is a set of interrelated tasks designed to accomplish a specific goal. The development of a manufacturing process for a new product is an example of a project. Other examples include:

- Developing a software solution
- Installing a computer system
- Renovating a building
- Building a prototype
- Moving an office
- Conducting market research
- Publishing a newsletter

Projects are unique work efforts, and often require you to do something that has never been done before in exactly the same way, with team members who may not have worked together before. Projects are finite; they have a beginning and an end.

The term *program* is generally applied to a larger endeavor, such as a collection of related projects. The design, development, and production of a new product is commonly referred to as a program.

Some projects are planned and accomplished by one person who may rely on a few other people to provide data, supplies, or administrative support. Other projects are planned and managed by a project team with as many as several hundred team members.

The project *sponsor* is typically a manager or a formal committee that has commissioned and approved the project. The sponsor often helps to define the scope of the project, as well as financial and scheduling limits. A *stakeholder* is an individual or group who has an interest, or "stake", in the project. Your management, customers, and project team members are all project stakeholders. Different stakeholders may have vastly different information requirements for the level of detail required and reporting intervals.

Project management is the process of defining, scheduling, tracking, controlling, and reporting on the activities and tasks that make up the project. Reports, e-mail, voicemail, videoconferencing, teleconferencing, telephone calls, meetings, and other forms of communication keep the project on track, and the stakeholders informed. This will be discussed in more detail in Chapter 4.

Projects typically begin when an idea is approved. This can happen when a simple suggestion is given a verbal "OK." It can also happen when a formal, written proposal is approved or when one or more contracts are generated.

A CASE FOR DETAILED PLANNING

When projects are begun using the "ready, fire, aim" technique, and are then managed without specific requirements and a detailed plan, not too many good things are likely to happen. Most likely, undesirable things will happen. Here are a few:

- Important work will be overlooked
- Unnecessary work will be done
- Rework will be necessary
- Quality will be reduced
- Scrap and rejections will be increased
- Changes will expand the scope of the project
- Project work will be delayed
- Team members will become frustrated

PROJECT REQUIREMENTS

A successful project meets requirements in four dimensions:

- Technical
- Quality
- Schedule
- Cost

The technical dimension establishes that all items produced by the project meet established customer and technical requirements. Examples include tolerance, endurance, environment, size, and weight requirements.

The quality dimension provides specific metrics by which the quality of the product or service can be measured. For a software development project, this may mean that the finished software solution can perform a certain function in three seconds.

The schedule dimension requires that activities, tasks, or milestones must be completed within a certain span of time, or before a certain date.

The cost dimension requires that individual tasks and the project as a whole be completed within specified financial limits. Depending on the type of project, the cost dimension may also be related to revenue management, return-on-investment, or other indicators.

To manage your project, you can document these requirements in many ways. You can record all of the requirements as part of a project plan on a word processor, record them in Microsoft Project, or use spreadsheet software. However you choose to do it, ensure that you and your team have clearly written requirements and specifications before entering into a contract or agreement. When the project begins, this information will provide direction and a yardstick to measure results.

A PROJECT PLANNING AND CONTROL MODEL

Planning and managing a project represents an investment. For many projects, the consumption of time and other resources represent an investment of thousands if not millions of dollars. When the total value of all of an organization's projects carried out in one year are considered, it is easy to see the importance of detailed project planning.

By following the sequence shown below, you will help to ensure that your project is planned and scheduled in sufficient detail to meet all requirements.

1. Gain a clear understanding of the project—define specific requirements and quality metrics, as well as cost and schedule constraints.

2. Identify the requirements for a planning team—determine the skills and knowledge necessary to plan all project work.

3. Assemble a planning team—schedule team members, space, materials, and equipment to create a project plan.

4. Create a project description, goal, and objectives.

5. Build a WBS outline. See Chapter 3.

6. Identify the resource requirements necessary to implement the project—in most cases, this should include the planning team. See Chapters 3 and 4.

7. Develop time estimates for each task, work package, or activity. See Chapter 3.

8. Identify and assess risks—for each task and the overall project. See Chapter 3.

9. Plan for risk prevention and contingencies. See Chapter 3.

10. Estimate costs. See Chapter 4.

11. Identify sequential and concurrent work, predecessors, and successors. See Chapter 5.

12. Create a task network (referred to as PERT in Microsoft Project). See Chapter 5.

13. Analyze the critical path and other paths, seeking opportunities to reduce duration. See Chapter 5.

14. Save the baseline—this will be compared to actual results as the project is implemented. See Chapter 5.

15. Gather and update project status—implement the communication plan. See Chapter 6.

16. Modify assignments and schedule as necessary. See Chapters 4, 5, and 6.

17. Report results. See Chapter 7.

THE PLANNING TEAM

In many projects, the planning team is also the team that performs project work. This is the preferable process for planning projects. It means that the people who will actually do the work also plan the work. Some may be part time. Some may be located at different sites. Although this ideal scenario is not always possible, attempt to recruit as many likely team members as possible to be part of the planning team.

PUTTING TOGETHER A QUARTERLY NEWSLETTER

> Chris Tomathy, a Communications Manager, has been asked to establish a quarterly newsletter for her organization. She works in the communications department for Handy Universal Products, Inc. (HUPI). HUPI is an international supplier of products made from recycled paper, including envelopes, boxes, napkins, and party supplies.
>
> Early discussions have indicated that the newsletter may include columns and articles on company direction, new product information, news about new sites, acquisitions, promotions, partnerships with other companies, information on company policy, and financial results.

To produce each newsletter, Chris believes that the following skills are needed on the project team:

- Project manager (Chris's job)
- Writer/editor
- Desktop publisher
- Graphic designer

Project Planning and the Project Team

- Paste-up artist
- Printer

In producing each newsletter, input may be obtained from company correspondents at any of eight international locations. Chris plans to use electronic mail and fax to communicate with foreign offices. In the near future, the company may begin to use videoconferencing.

THE WORK ENVIRONMENT

Chris has chosen Microsoft Project to plan and manage the premier issue, and will learn to use the software as she plans the project. She intends to start her project by scheduling a project kickoff meeting on Monday afternoon from 1:00–3:00. After several phone calls, it appears that the following people will be working on the project, and will be at the meeting:

- Chris, project manager
- Jim Mulligan, writer/editor
- Jane Parker, desktop publisher
- Forrest Boles, graphic designer
- Cynthia Kraft, paste-up artist
- Jack Boucher, manager of the printing department

To prepare for the kickoff meeting, Chris reserves a room and arranges to have the following equipment and materials available to plan the project:

- A flip chart and markers
- Her personal computer, loaded with Microsoft Project
- A projector and screen to display results as the team works

Several days before the meeting, Chris installs Version 4.1 of Microsoft® Project on her PC. After the installation is complete, she starts Microsoft Project and sees the Welcome box shown below.

7

The Complete Planning Guide for Microsoft® Project

Figure 1-1. Welcome to Version 4.1 Box

The Welcome box for Version 4.0 is very similar, as shown below.

Figure 1-2. Welcome to Version 4.0 Box

After you become familiar with Microsoft® Project, you may choose not to display this screen each time you use the tool. When that happens, simply check the box at the bottom left that says "Don't display this startup screen again," and this screen will not be displayed again when you re-start the program.

Project Planning and the Project Team

Chris decides to click on **Take a Short Guided Tour**. Advancing through the tour, she sees the following project views:

- Gantt chart—a chart that shows tasks and their corresponding bars
- Calendar view—a monthly calendar much like a typical wall calendar
- PERT chart—a task network that displays the flow of all project work
- Task form—a form that can be used to enter and edit task information
- Resource graph—a histogram that displays peak allocation levels and overallocations
- Task sheet—a sheet that displays a number of columns of task-related data, such as date and duration

After the tour Chris feels that she has a pretty good preview and understanding of the software. She doesn't expect to remember everything, but feels that with a little practice it will come easily.

She then decides to choose Create Your First Project to get a head start on the upcoming meeting, and sees the box shown below.

Figure 1-3. Version 4.1 Up and Running Tutorial Box

The Complete Planning Guide for Microsoft® Project

Chris first chooses **Learn about how to use this tutorial**, and sees a screen that shows how to use procedure cards. Procedure cards provide step-by step instructions for performing a wide variety of functions. They actually remain on the screen while you work.

After the quick tutorial, she returns to the box shown in Figure 1-3 and chooses **Create a schedule**. The box shown in Figure 1-4 appears.

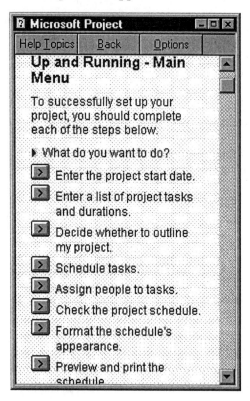

Figure 1-4. Up and Running Main Menu

Since she is not exactly sure of most of the project details at this point, she decides to leave the tutorial for now.

In Version 4.0, the equivalent of procedures are known as cue cards. Version 4.0 also has an Up and Running Tutorial. If you choose the box beside Up and Running Tutorial in the Welcome box. you will see the following:

Project Planning and the Project Team

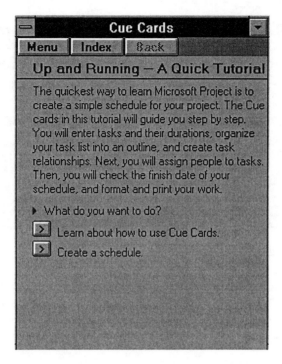

Figure 1-5. Cue Cards Screen

You can learn about cue cards quickly because the information is shown in one screen. Using the tutorial in both versions, you can work through the steps necessary to enter preliminary project data.

STARTING A NEW PROJECT FILE

To start a new project file in either version, click on this icon located beneath the word **File** on the menu bar in the top left corner of your screen. You can get the same result from the keyboard by pressing the **Ctrl** key and the letter **N** at the same time.

When you start a new file in Version 4.1, the Project Info dialog box shown in Figure 1-6 appears. If your project is starting on the same day that you create the new file, you can leave the default setting—that day's date—as the start date for the project. Otherwise, you will need to enter the starting (or finish) date for the project.

Chris notices that the file name for the project (near the top) is Project 2. She makes a mental note to give the project a name.

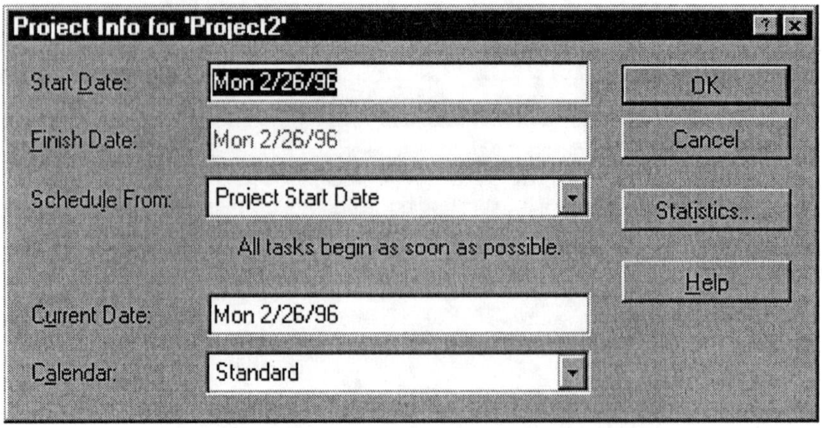

The Complete Planning Guide for Microsoft® Project

Figure 1-6. Version 4.1 Project Info Dialog Box

> Note: Throughout this guide, you may see dialog boxes for Versions 4.1 and 4.0 of Microsoft Project. A dialog box with buttons in the top right corner indicates Version 4.1.

In Version 4.0, the dialog box appears slightly different and is named the Project Summary Info Box.

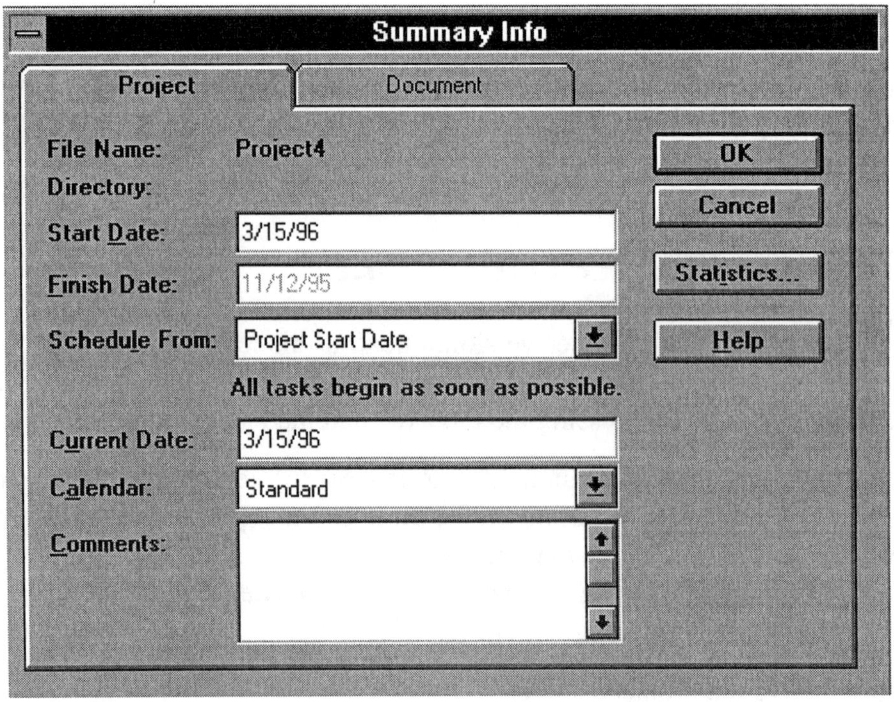

Figure 1-7. Version 4.0 Summary Info Dialog Box

This dialog box asks you to make a key decision about scheduling your new project:

Project Planning and the Project Team

Do I want Microsoft Project to **schedule this project from the start date**? or from the finish date?

The default setting is Schedule From: **Project Start Date**. If that is your preference, use the **Tab key** to move down to **start date** and enter the date on which the project starts. Microsoft® Project will schedule accordingly, based on the durations, predecessors, and successors that you enter in the file.

Fast Lane Tip #1

To start a new file

1. Click the ▯ icon, located beneath the **File** menu item on the standard toolbar, or press **Ctrl/N**.

2. When the Project Info or Summary Info box appears, choose to schedule the project from the start or from the finish date. (The start date is recommended, since it provides more scheduling flexibility.)

3. (Version 4.0 only) Enter any comments about the project, such as project number or the relation of this project to other projects.

4. Click on **OK**.

Chris decides that this is a good time to save the new file. She clicks on the word **File**, then chooses **Save As**. You may also do this by pressing **Alt/F**, then choosing **Save As**. When the Save As box appears, she enters waytogo1, since this is the first issue of the newsletter. The dialog box shown in Figure 1-8 appears.

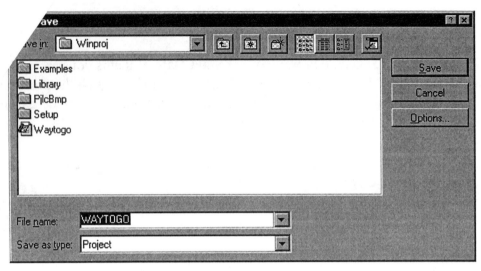

Figure 1-8. Version 4.1 Save As Dialog Box

The dialog box used in Version 4.1 has a variety of folders that can be used to store files. Chris chooses the Winproj folder, and clicks on **Save**. The dialog box for Version 4.0 is similar, as shown below.

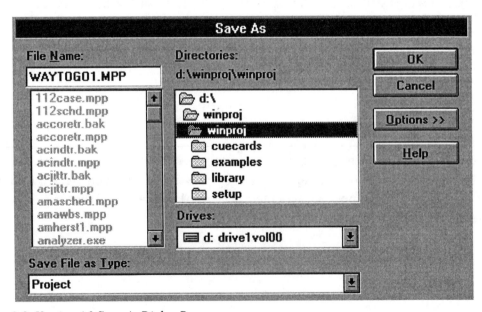

Figure 1-9. Version 4.0 Save As Dialog Box

After saving the file, Chris remembers that she needs to set the working hours and days for the team. She tries the **Tools** menu, and notices that one of the choices reads Change Working Time. She chooses it and changes the working hours to read 8:30 to 12:15 and 1:00 to 5:00, with forty-five minutes for lunch.

Project Planning and the Project Team

> ## Fast Lane Tip #2
>
>
>
> To change working hours in the standard project calendar
>
> 1. Click on the **Tools** menu, or press **Alt/T**.
> 2. Choose **Change Working Time**. The dialog box shown in Figure 1-10 appears.
> 3. Use the Tab key or cursor to move to the **Working Time**: From and To cells.
> 4. Make changes to working hours as necessary to reflect normal shifts and business hours.

While she is there, she decides to check the working days for the project. She knows that there will be holidays, and that people will probably not be working on those days. She clicks on **January 15**, then clicks on **Nonworking** to indicate a holiday for Martin Luther King day. Next she clicks on the down arrow at the bottom of the vertical scroll bar beside January, moves to February, and continues to indicate nonworking days for the company for 1996.

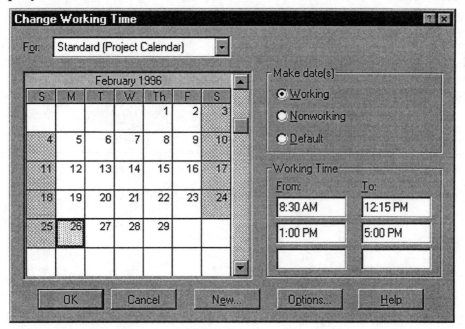

Figure 1-10. Change Working Time Dialog Box

The Complete Planning Guide for Microsoft® Project

To add another shift, click on **New** at the bottom of the box, and you will see the dialog box shown in Figure 1-11. The dialog box for Version 4.0 is virtually identical. In most cases it is a good idea to start with a copy of the base calendar, and then make changes as necessary.

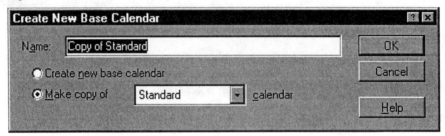

Figure 1-11. Create New Base Calendar Dialog Box

Fast Lane Tip # 3

To change working days in the standard project calendar

1. Click on the **Tools** menu, or press **Alt/T**.

2. Choose **Change Working Time**. The standard project calendar will appear.

3. Point the cursor to a date that will be a nonworking day such as a holiday.

4. Click on the button beside **Nonworking**. A shadow will appear in the nonworking day.

5. Click on the down arrow beside the calendar dates to move to the next month.

Project Planning and the Project Team

THE KICKOFF MEETING AND THE PROJECT DESCRIPTION

Several days before the kickoff meeting, Chris develops an agenda for the meeting as follows, and sends a copy to all stakeholders.

Table 1-1. Kickoff meeting agenda

Agenda Item	Output	Time Estimate
Overview and question and answer (Chris)	All questions from team members are answered	30 minutes
Develop name for newsletter	Newsletter name	30 minutes
Write project description and goal	Description and goal entered into Microsoft Project	30 minutes

At the kickoff meeting, Chris explains what she knows about the newsletter to the group. She then asks the group for additional ideas. Next, Chris asks for suggestions to name the new newsletter. After about thirty minutes, the group agrees on **Way To Go** as a name for the newsletter. She will have to get the name approved before it's official.

17

She and the group then turn to project planning. They decide that the first step in planning the project is to develop a project description. In some quarters, its equivalent is the *statement of work*. After brainstorming, the team develops a brief project description:

Chris will record the description in Microsoft Project later.

Project Description

The Way To Go newsletter will be designed and produced quarterly for an English-speaking international audience. The newsletter will be between 16 and 20 pages, two-color plus black, and saddlestitched. It will be used as an internal communications document.

The newsletter will be designed, produced, and managed by internal staff members that will include communications staff, graphic design and desktop publishing staff, printing and bindery staff, and the shipping department. On occasion, external freelance writers will be used.

THE PROJECT GOAL

After developing the description, the team collaborates to develop the goal statement. The project goal is the project's ultimate endpoint. All project effort is intended to move the project team closer to its goal. The project goal for the newsletter appears below.

Project Goal

To distribute 1,000 copies of the premier issue of Way To Go on July 8.

Chris creates a task in Microsoft® Project to represent the goal. She then enters the description and project goal as a note to the project summary Task. To do this, she types Newsletter#1 on the top line of the newly created file, and clicks on the ▦ icon, then enters the project description and goal as shown above. Using the keyboard, you can reach task notes by pressing **Alt/I**, and then pressing **N**.

Project Planning and the Project Team

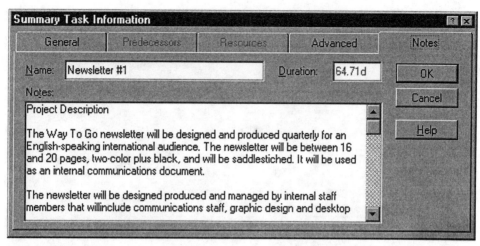

Figure 1-12. Summary Task Information Dialog Box

After the project description and goal are developed, the team agrees that the next step is to develop a list of tasks necessary to complete the project. They will use brainstorming. However, Chris realizes that almost two hours have passed, which was the amount of time that everyone allotted for the kickoff meeting.

Forrest suggests that they schedule another meeting next Monday at 1:00, and for everyone to block out 1:00–4:00 to develop the list of tasks. Everyone but Cynthia and Jack will be able to make it, but they agree to give Chris their ideas by Friday afternoon. In between meetings, the others will all write down their ideas about necessary tasks. Chris adjourns the meeting. The team will reconvene for its second planning meeting in Chapter 3.

Chris decides to save the file with the new data, and clicks on the icon that looks like a floppy disk. She could have also used the **F12** function key, or **Ctrl/S** to save the file. When she saves the file, she sees the Planning Wizard, shown below.

The Complete Planning Guide for Microsoft® Project

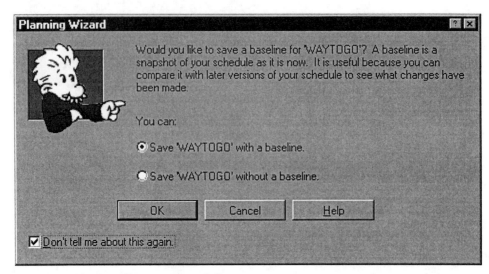

Figure 1-13. Save Baseline Planning Wizard Box

When you save your file, you will be asked by the Planning Wizard if you would like to save the file with a baseline. Since the team has not completed its planning work, she clicks beside Save <u>Way to Go</u> without a baseline. She then clicks on the box that says "Don't tell me about this again." By doing this Chris will not have to waste her time responding to this box every time she saves her file. (Saving the project baseline will be discussed in Chapter 6.)

COMPANION PRODUCTS RELATED TO THIS CHAPTER*

The following products can be used to help you get your project started.

DOORS for Microsoft® Project, software tool for managing project requirements; Zycad Corporation Fax: 1-(201)-989-5959.

How To Plan Any Project: A Guide for Teams, 2nd Edition, softcover workbook; Belanger, T. C., The Sterling Planning Group, 1995, ISBN 0-9631465-1-3; $29.95 1-(508)-422-6611.

Project Kick*Start* for Windows 3.1, software tool for building new projects; Experience in Software, Inc. 1-(510)-644-0694.

*Not all of these tools have been designed for Version 4.1.

2

Microsoft Project Fundamentals

In this chapter you will learn how to:

1. Use the menu bar and toolbars

2. Access all menu items in the fastest way

3. Use help

4. Change the appearance of views and tables

5. Delete and edit information

INTRODUCTION

This chapter is designed to be a quick reference source for all of the menus and submenus that can be used while you are working in the Gantt chart or other task view.

In this chapter you will learn more about other submenus and commands under the File menu and the other standard menu items shown on the menu bar. Each submenu item and command that is displayed is briefly explained here. You will also learn how to make changes in the appearance of several tables and views. In addition, you will learn about many of the functions that can be performed by pointing and clicking on icons located in toolbars.

THE MENU BAR

The Menu Bar is very similar to other Windows applications, and displays available menus. It appears as shown below in Figure 2-1. You can also add and remove menu items. This will be explained in Chapter 8. Some submenus change when you change from one view to another, for example, when you move from a Gantt chart to a PERT chart.

| File   Edit   View   Insert   Format   Tools   Window   Help |

Figure 2-1. The Menu Bar

> Note: All of the descriptions contained in this chapter refer to submenu items that are displayed in a Gantt view.

To see a list of choices for any item on the menu bar, click on the word, such as **Edit**, or press the **Alt** key and **E** (**Alt/E**) for the Edit menu. You can always use the underlined letter of the menu item together with the Alt key to see the list of choices for items on the menu bar, and for dialog boxes. On the submenu, press only the underlined letter to make a selection.

The menu bars in both Versions are identical with one exception. Version 4.1 displays an icon beside File on the menu bar. This icon provides several functions for working with the file and window.

Microsoft® Project Fundamentals

If you use a mouse, try to get into the habit of clicking the secondary mouse button, normally located on the right (if you are right-handed). Do this by first pointing and clicking on a section of the screen about which you need information, or would like to change. You will immediately see a context-sensitive minimenu that will access many functions. For example, if you are working in the Gantt chart, you can quickly access many editing functions, as shown in Figure 2-2, by clicking the secondary mouse button.

Figure 2-2. Secondary Mouse Button Minimenu

Fast Lane Tip #4

To perform functions using the keyboard

1. If you prefer to use the keyboard to make choices from the menu bar, you can quickly access any menu item shown on the menu bar by pressing **Alt** and the underlined letter; For example, **Alt/O** to see the Format menu.
2. When you see a submenu, you can choose an item by pressing only the underlined letter.

The File Menu

Every time you work in Microsoft Project, you will use the File menu. You will need to perform many important functions using the File menu. In addition to creating a new file, the File menu is also used to:

- **Open**—click on ![open icon], or press **Ctrl/O** to open an existing file.

Fast Lane Tip #5

To identify dialog boxes from a submenu

Every menu item followed by an ellipsis (...) takes you to a dialog box to make choices about the command.

- **Close**—click on **File**, or press **Alt/F** then choose **Close** to close a file that is currently displayed, referred to as the <u>active file</u>.

- **Save**—click on ![save icon], or press **Ctrl/S** to save the active file.

- **Save As**—click on **File** or press **Alt/F**, then choose **Save As** to name a new file or to change a file name. The Save As dialog box is displayed.

- **Save Workspace**—click on **File**, or press **Alt/F**, then choose **Save Workspace** to save several open files as a group.

- **Properties (Version 4.1 only)**—click on **File**, or press **Alt/F**, then choose **Properties**. Several tabs provide file information such as name, file type, title, keyword, notes, project start and finish dates, duration, total work, total cost, percent complete, and user-defined object linking and embedding (OLE) properties.

- **Find File (Version 4.0 only)**—click on **File**, or press **Alt/F**, then choose **Find File** to locate a misplaced file. The Search dialog box is displayed.

- **Project Info (Version 4.1) Summary Info (Version 4.0)**—click on **File**, or press **Alt/F**, then click on **Project Info** or **Summary Info** to find out the project start date, whether scheduling is calculated from start or finish, and other information.

Microsoft® Project Fundamentals

- **Page Setup**—click on **File**, or press **Alt/F**, then click on **Page Setup** to choose page orientation, margins, header, footer, legend, and other information.

- **Print Preview**—click on ![icon], or press **Alt/F**, then choose **Print Preview** to see how the document will appear when printed.

- **Print**—click on ![icon] to print the active file as is, or press **Ctrl/P** if you would like to use print preview, or change the header or other information.

- **Send**—click on **File**, or press **Alt/F**, then choose **Send** to send a copy of the current file via Microsoft Mail or other MAPI-compliant electronic mail program.

- **Add Routing Slip**—click on **File**, or press **Alt/F**, then choose **Add Routing Slip** to send a file to a member of your team or another stakeholder. (You must have Microsoft Mail or another MAPI-compliant electronic mail program to use this workgroup feature.)

- **Post to Exchange Folder** (Version 4.1 only)—click on **File**, or press **Alt/F** to display a dialog box. The dialog box can be used to post a project file to a subscribed public folder that allows other users on a network to access the file. Related to Properties submenu item.

The Edit Menu

The Edit menu performs many useful functions. However, there are many hotkey combinations and icons that perform these functions, so you may not be using this menu too often. Here are the many functions that can be performed here. Most can be performed very quickly.

- **Undo** (or **Can't Undo**)—click on ![icon] to reverse the previous action, or press **Alt/E** and choose **Undo**. This is a very useful icon. You can increase the number of actions that will be reversed in the Tools menu under Options.

- **Cut** (cell)—press **Ctrl/X**, or click on ![icon] to remove the contents of one or more selected cells.

The Complete Planning Guide for Microsoft® Project

- **Copy** (cell)—press **Ctrl/C**, or click on ![icon] to copy the contents of one or more selected cells.

- **Paste**—press **Ctrl/V**, or click on ![icon] to paste data, pictures, or objects that were cut or copied.

- **Paste Special**—click on **Edit**, or press **Alt/E**, then choose **Paste Special** to paste information from another application, or to create a link.

- **Fill Down**—press **Ctrl/D** to copy data from the top cell to all cells in a selected column.

- **Clear**—click on **Edit**, or press **Alt/E**, then choose **Clear** to see the submenu. Clears formatting, data, and other information from sheets and the Gantt chart.

- **Delete Task**—select the data to be deleted and press the **Del** key.

- **Link Tasks**—press **Ctrl/F2** or click on ![icon] after selecting two or more tasks to establish a predecessor-successor relationship.

- **Unlink Tasks**—click on ![icon] after selecting two or more tasks to disconnect a predecessor-successor relationship.

- **Find**—press **Ctrl/F** to see the Find dialog box, which will help you to find a specific task, resource, or word.

- **Go To**—press **F5** to see the Go To dialog box, which will help you to quickly go to a specific task ID number or date.

- **Links**—click on **Edit**, or press **Alt/E**, then choose **Links** to change the properties of linked objects.

- **Object**—click on **Edit**, then **Object** to see the Object submenu. The menu differs according to the object selected. It is used to work with linked and embedded objects, and displays the server application name.

The View Menu

The View menu and its submenus provide you with many choices about the appearance of the Microsoft Project window. The default view is the Gantt Chart, which is capable of showing a number of columns of data at the left and horizontal bars to represent the durations of project phases and milestones at the right.

The first three choices focus on tasks; the next three, as their names indicate, are resource-related. The last four choices under View can be used for both. You will need to use this menu to switch between the Gantt chart, the calendar view, and the PERT chart. Each choice is briefly explained below.

- **Calendar**—click on **View**, or press **Alt/V**, then choose **Calendar** to see the calendar view. It can display the task name in a bar and a variety of other fields.

- **Gantt chart**—click on **View**, or press **Alt/V**, then choose **Gantt Chart** to show a window with a table on the left and bars that represent duration on the right. This is the default view.

    PERT chart—click on **View**, or press **Alt/V**, then choose **PERT Chart** to see the task network as drawn by Microsoft Project. You can click and drag the boxes to move them to a preferred location, create new tasks, and connect predecessors and successors here.

- **Resource graph**—click on **View**, or press **Alt/V**, then choose **Resource Graph** to see which resources are underallocated, fully allocated, or overallocated.

- **Resource sheet**—click on **View**, or press **Alt/V**, then choose **Resource Sheet**. You can add and remove resources here, and modify resource data, such as number of units, rates, accrual method, and other data.

- **Resource usage**—click on **View**, or press **Alt/V** then choose **Resource Usage** to display the number of hours each resource is scheduled on any given day.

- **Table**—click on **View**, or press **Alt/V**, then click on **Table** to see several format choices. The last table used is shown beside the word "table". Click on **More Tables** to see the dialog box shown below.

The Complete Planning Guide for Microsoft® Project

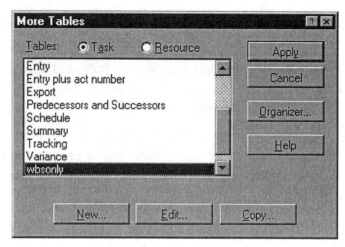

Figure 2-3. More Tables Dialog Box

The dialog box for Version 4.0 is virtually identical. For a task-related table, click on any of the choices shown. To see resource-related choices, click on **Resource**, near the top of the box.

To make a new table that is similar to one of the standard tables, choose **Copy** to see the Table Definition dialog box, shown below in Figure 2-4.

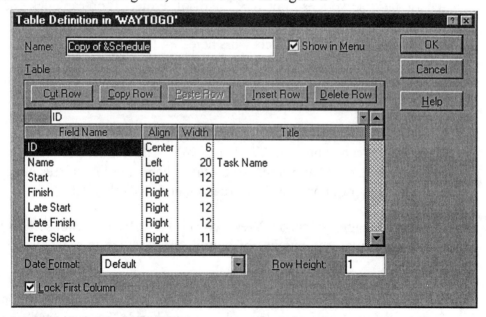

Figure 2-4. Table Definition Dialog Box

Microsoft® Project Fundamentals

Using the Table Definition dialog box, you can add, remove, or modify the fields used in any table.

- **More Views**—click on **View**, or press **Alt/V**, then choose **More Views** to see the choices of charts, forms, graphs, and sheets shown below and others. You can also create a new view or make changes to existing views by using the New, Edit, and Copy buttons.

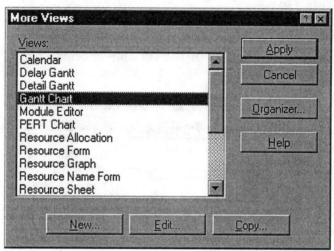

Figure 2-5. More Views Dialog Box

- **Reports**—click on **View**, or press **Alt/V**, then choose **Reports** to see the categories of standard reports that are available, or to create your own customized Version. See Chapter 7 for more information.

- **Toolbars**—click on **View**, or press **Alt/V**, then choose **Toolbars** to add, remove or customize a toolbar. You can also use click and drag to move individual icons from any toolbar into the current toolbar section. These functions are also available under Options on the Tools menu.

- **Zoom**—click on **View**, or press **Alt/V**, then choose **Zoom** to change the amount of time displayed in the Gantt bar section.

The Insert Menu

The Insert menu contains important commands for inserting new tasks, and for inserting recurring tasks such as "update schedule" or "build prototype" when many are required. You can also insert a page break, drawing, picture, or object using this menu.

- **Insert Task**—position the cursor on the task located immediately after the insertion point, and press the **Ins** key, or press **Alt/I**, then choose **Task** to insert a task. You can also insert more than one task cell by selecting two or more blank cells first.

- **Insert Recurring Task**—click on **Insert** or press **Alt/I**, then choose **Recurring Task**.

- **Insert Column**—click on **Insert** or press **Alt/I**, then choose **Column** to add a new column to the left of the column selected. The Column Definition dialog box appears.

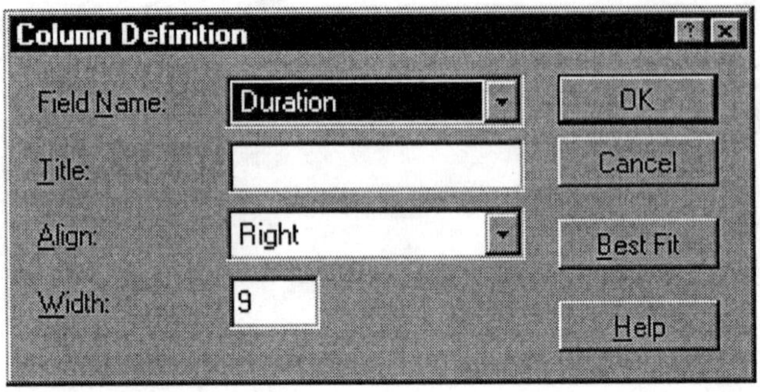

Figure 2-6. Column Definition Dialog Box

- **Task Information**—click on [icon], or press **Shift/F2** to change task information, such as predecessors, duration, constraints, dates, and other information. This takes you to the Task Information box, as does the Task Notes choice below, but with a different active tab.

- **Task Notes**—click on [icon], or press **Alt/I**, then **N** to see the Task Information box, and to change task information such as predecessors, duration, constraints, dates, and other information. To conserve space on the toolbar, you may want to remove either this icon or the Task Information icon.

- **Resource Assignment**—press **Alt/F8**, or click on **Insert**, then choose **Resource Assignment** to add, remove, or assign a resource, or the proportion of a resource's time.

- **Page Break**—click on **Insert** or press **Alt/I**, then choose **Page Break** to begin the selected task or resource on the next page. If you decide later to remove the page break, return to the selected task. When you reopen the Insert menu, the menu displays **Remove Page Break**. Make this choice to remove the page break.

- **Drawing**—click on **Insert** or press **Alt/I**, then choose **Drawing** to insert the drawing toolbar. The drawing toolbar can be used to insert a drawing that you create by using the drawing icons.

- **Object**—click on **Insert** or press **Alt/I**, to see the Insert Object dialog box shown below. You can create a new object or insert an object from a wide variety of files. See Chapter 8.

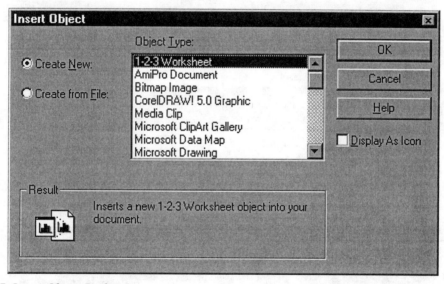

Figure 2-7. Insert Object Dialog Box

The Format Menu

The Format menu contains useful functions for changing the appearance of all views, tables, and charts. You will probably use it frequently. Some of these choices may be good candidates for macros. See Chapter 8.

- **Font**—click on **Format**, or press **Alt/O**, then choose **Font** to change the font, font style, color, or size of selected tasks.

- **Bar**—click on **Format**, or press **Alt/O**, then choose **Bar** to modify the shape or text. Bars can also be modified using Bar Styles below.

The Complete Planning Guide for Microsoft® Project

- **Timescale**—double-click on the Gantt timescale, or press **Alt/O**, then choose **Timescale** to see the Timescale dialog box. With this box, you can change the major and minor scales shown above task bars on the Gantt chart, such as quarter, month or week, alignment of data, enlargement percent, and other display choices.

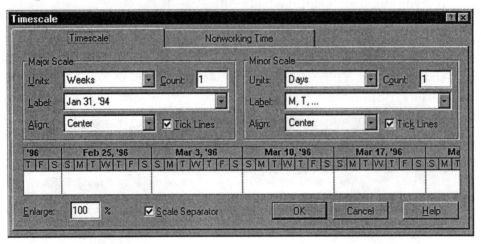

Figure 2-8. Timescale Dialog Box

- **Gridlines**—click on **Format**, or press **Alt/O**, then choose **Gridlines** to add certain vertical and horizontal gridlines to views and tables.

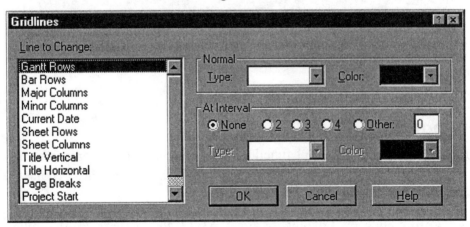

Figure 2-9. Gridlines Dialog Box

- **Gantt Chart Wizard**—click on **Format**, or press **Alt/O**, then choose **Gantt Chart Wizard**, which prompts you with several questions about the types

Microsoft® Project Fundamentals

of bars, and fields of information to accompany bars, link lines and other data.

- **Text Styles**—click on **Format**, or press **Alt/O**, then choose **Text Styles** to change the type, size or color of fonts for certain types of tasks.

- **Bar Styles**—click on **Format**, or press **Alt/O**, then choose **Bar Styles** to make changes to the start shape, bar and end shape for tasks, milestones, and other items.

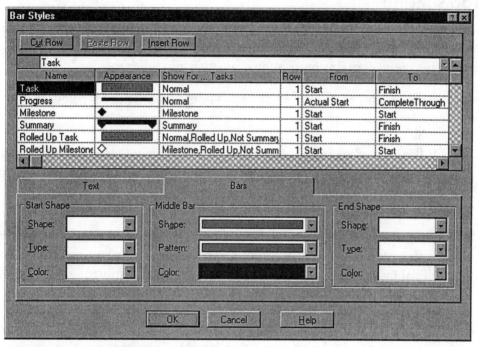

Figure 2-10. Bar Styles Dialog Box

- **Details**—click on **Format**, or press **Alt/O**, then choose **Details** to see the submenu, which provides choices that examine a wide variety of resource information and some task information. This submenu is available only from resource forms, the resource graph, and resource allocation, resource usage, and task form views. The active view determines the available commands.

- **Layout**—click on **Format**, or press **Alt/O**, then choose **Layout**. This dialog box displays different choices for the calendar, Gantt, and PERT views.

- **Layout Now**—click on **Format**, or press **Alt/O**, then choose **Layout Now** to change the layout of the PERT chart or calendar view. (Not available for the Gantt chart.)

- **Drawing**—click on **Format**, or press **Alt/O**, then choose **Drawing**. This item is available only from the Gantt chart, and then only when a drawing or text box is selected.

The Tools Menu

Items on the Tools menu perform many useful and time-saving functions. Included on this list are spellcheck, filtering, sorting, resource leveling, macros, and a wide variety of options. This menu contains more submenus than any other menu.

- **Spelling**—press **F7** or click on **Tools**, then choose **Spelling** to check spelling in the active file.

- **Outlining**—click on **Tools**, or press **Alt/T**, then choose **Outlining** to indent, outdent, show, or hide one or more tasks. These functions can be performed faster when you use these icons from the Formatting toolbar.

- **Filtered For**—click on **Tools**, or press **Alt/T** and choose **Filtered For:** to display standard filtering choices; for example, filtering out everything but critical tasks, or only those tasks using a specific resource.

- **Sort**—click on **Tools**, or press **Alt/T**, then choose **Sort** to change the order of display. The default setting is to sort by ID number. You may sort by cost, start date, priority, and other standard choices, or other methods that you devise.

- **Change Working Time**—click on **Tools**, or press **Alt/T**, then choose **Change Working Time** to change working hours or working days on a calendar for a specific resource or on the standard project calendar.

- **Resource Leveling**—click on **Tools**, or press **Alt/T**, then choose **Resource Leveling** to instruct Microsoft® Project to level resources. Microsoft Project does this by delaying tasks until the necessary resources are available. Use this with caution, and consider choosing the box that says Delay Only Within Slack.

Microsoft® Project Fundamentals

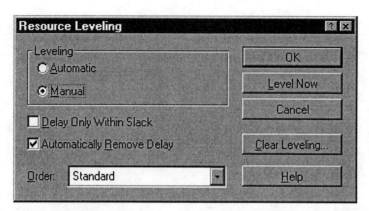

Figure 2-11. Resource Leveling Dialog Box

- **Tracking**—click on **Tools**, or press **Alt/T**, then choose **Tracking** to make more choices about updating certain tasks, updating the entire project, or saving the project baseline.

- **Multiple Projects**—click on **Tools**, or press **Alt/T**, then choose **Multiple Projects** to consolidate projects, share resources among projects, open a project file from a database, or save a file to a database. You can use the Multiple Project commands across a network or on a standalone computer. See Chapter 6.

- **Workgroup**—click on **Tools**, or press **Alt/T**, then choose **Workgroup** to open a submenu. The submenu provides choices for sending and receiving scheduling information via electronic mail.

- **Macros**—click on **Tools**, or press **Alt/T**, then choose **Macros** to create, edit, or run macros. See Chapter 8.

- **Record Macro**—click on **Tools**, or press **Alt/T** and choose **Record Macro** to begin recording macro steps. See Chapter 8.

- **Customize**—click on **Tools**, or press **Alt/T**, then choose **Customize** to modify the menu bar, toolbars or forms. See the View menu for another way to customize toolbars.

- **Options**—click on **Tools**, or press **Alt/T**, then choose **Options**. You will see the following options tabs which can be used to make hundreds of choices about preferences in the way you use Microsoft Project.

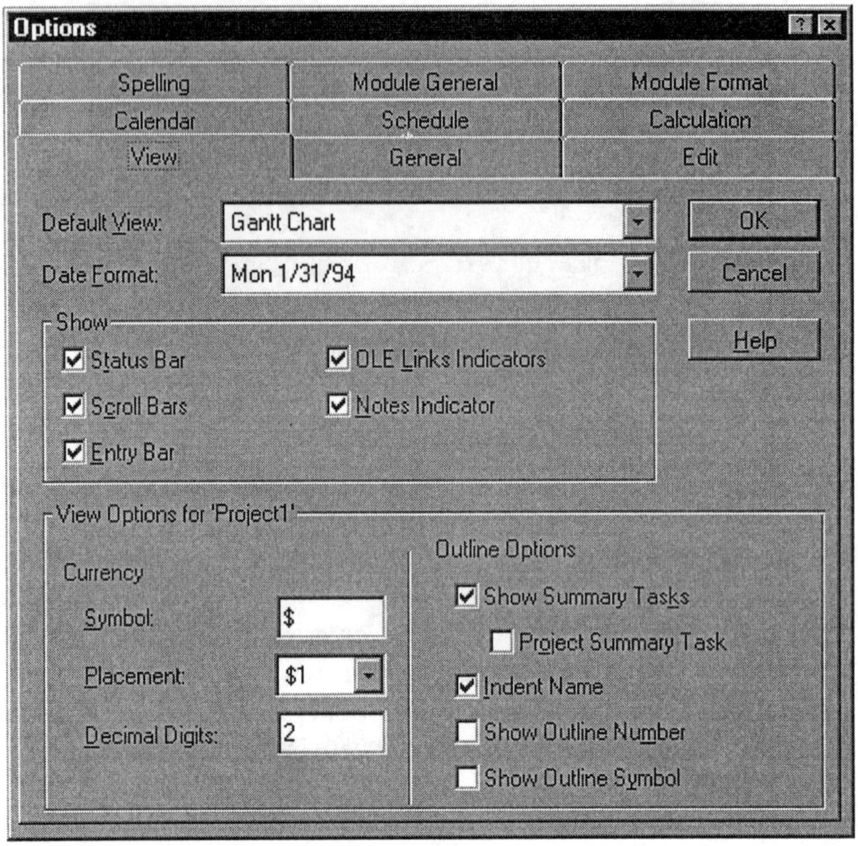

Figure 2-12. Options Dialog Box

The Window Menu

The Window menu provides choices about which window to display, whether to show all active files, and whether or not to use a combination view. It is similar to the Window menu in many other Windows® applications.

- **New Window**—press **Shift/F11** or click on **Window**, then choose **New Window** to add an active file to the screen. You can show the current file using a different view, show a different active file with the same view, and make other choices.

- **Arrange All**—click on **Window** or press **Alt/W**, then choose **Arrange All** to display all opened files simultaneously.

Microsoft® Project Fundamentals

- **Hide**—click on **Window** or press **Alt/W**, then choose **Hide** to hide the active project.

- **Unhide**—click on **Window** or press **Alt/W**, then choose **Unhide** to reveal hidden files.

- **Split**—click on **Window** or press **Alt/W**, then choose **Split** to display a combination view with the task form in the lower pane if you are in a task view, or, to display a resource form in the lower pane if you are in a resource view.

- **Currently Open Files**—click on **Window** or press **Alt/W**, then view the files that are currently open.

The Help Menu

The on-line help that is available in Microsoft® Project has never been so extensive. In Version 3.0 of Microsoft Project, the user manual had seven hundred and six pages. The new user manual for Versions 4.0 and 4.1, is now only two hundred and seventy—less than half of what used to be required because of the expanded on-line help system!

You can seek and find help in so many ways that the next section of this chapter is devoted exclusively to showing you a wide variety of approaches. After trying some of these approaches, you can develop your own personalized system for quickly getting answers.

HELP IN VERSION 4.1

Every person who learns to use Microsoft Project will, over time, develop preferences in seeking help to do his or her work more efficiently. You can get help in many ways, whether you are using Windows 95 and Version 4.1, or Windows 3.1 and Version 4.0.

Version 4.1 for Windows 95 has added the Answer Wizard, which responds to questions that begin with "How do I (you fill in your question)", or "Tell me about (you fill in your question)." The Answer Wizard uses IntelliSense to interpret and respond to your question. After you complete the question, you will see a list of related topics to choose from.

There are several ways to get help while working in Version 4.1 of Microsoft Project for Windows 95. The Help menu for Project in Windows 95 is structured differently

The Complete Planning Guide for Microsoft® Project

than Version 4.0. All help topics, including access to the Answer Wizard, can be accessed from Microsoft Project Help topics, which is the first help topic. The first time that you seek help, you will need to load help topics. You will be prompted to do this.

To get help on any topic, press **F1**, click on **Help** or press **Alt/H**, then choose **Microsoft Project Help Topics**. You will see the box shown below.

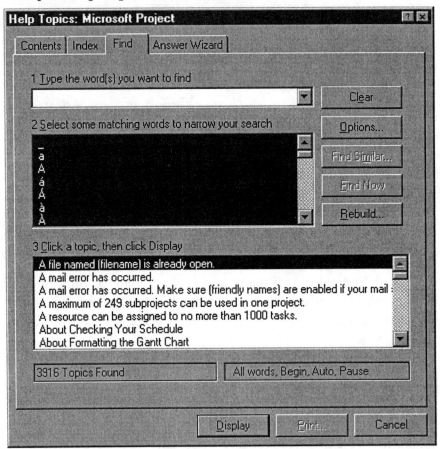

Figure 2-13. Version 4.1 Microsoft Project Help Topics Dialog Box

Answer Wizard

The Answer Wizard is the primary method for getting help in Version 4.1 of Microsoft Project. To go directly to the Answer Wizard, click on ![icon] or press **Alt/H**, then choose **Answer Wizard**. You will see the dialog box shown in Figure 2-14.

Microsoft® Project Fundamentals

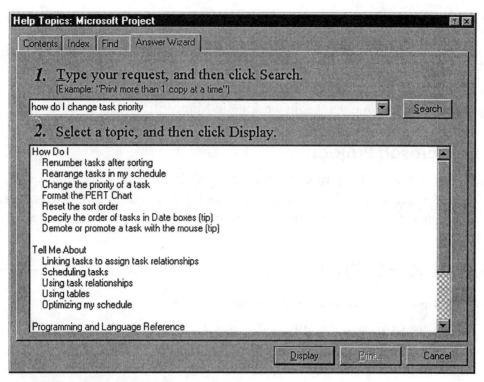

Figure 2-14. Answer Wizard Dialog Box

When this dialog box appears, simply type in your question, such as "tell me about linking tasks,, or "how do I change task priority?", shown above. Microsoft Project provides a list of topics from which to choose.

Screentips

Screentips provide a brief explanation of the functions of buttons and dialog box sections. To display a screentip for an icon or button, click on [icon], then click on the icon or button that you want to find out about.

Quick Preview

The Quick Preview selection provides a quick overview of Microsoft® Project. Make this selection if you want an overview or refresher on fundamentals. Click on **Help** or press **Alt/H**, then choose **Quick Preview**.

Tip of the Day

You can use this feature to get one or more brief tips. If these tips are not currently displayed when you open Microsoft® Project, you can activate them from the **Tools** Menu under **Options,** behind the **General** tab. Choose **Show Tips at Startup** to see one or more tips each time you begin working in Microsoft® Project.

About Microsoft Project

You can find out system information, such as available memory and disk space, swap file size, and other system information, by making this selection. Click on **Help,** or press **Alt/H**, then choose **About Microsoft Project**.

HELP IN VERSION 4.0

To obtain assistance in Version 4.0 for Windows 3.1, do any of the following:

- Press the **F1** key. You'll see the contents of the help system in a category as shown below, with a brief explanation for each.

Microsoft® Project Fundamentals

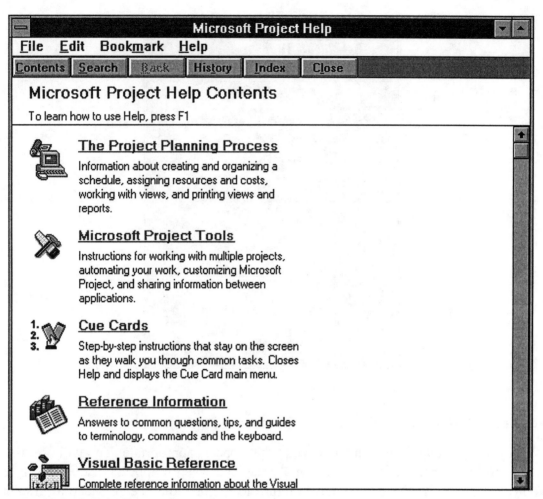

Figure 2-15. Help Contents Screen

The final item on the list (not shown above) is Technical Support.

When you see this box, examine and consider the choices. If necessary, use the vertical scroll bar and arrows that are located to the right of the box to see other selections.

When you have made your choice, click on the green underlined category, or on the icon to its immediate left. In most cases you will find your answer.

For example, if your confusion is about the project planning process, click on the **Project Planning Process** or on the icon and you'll see the following choices:

The Complete Planning Guide for Microsoft® Project

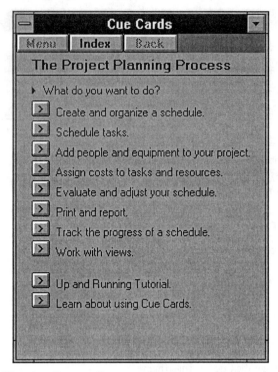

Figure 2-16. Project Planning Process Screen

See Appendix A for a list of cue card topics (for version 4.0).

When you see the list, click on the heading that appears appropriate. You will normally see helpful information. If you click on a topic, and when it appears, it does not meet your needs, click on the word **Back** to return to the previous menu. Make a different choice.

- A second way to seek help is to click on **Help**, and choose **Search**. As you begin to type, Microsoft® Project takes you to its help topics that begin with that letter, and continues to filter out topics that do not have those letters as you type.

  For example, imagine that you want to find out how to add a new column to the Gantt chart. Near the top of the dialog box, you begin to type **ad**.... As you type, choices beginning with the letters ad appear, and suddenly you see "adding columns". That appears to be a good choice, so you point and click on **adding columns**, then you click on **Show Topics**. Information appears at the bottom of the screen, as shown in Figure 2-17.

Microsoft® Project Fundamentals

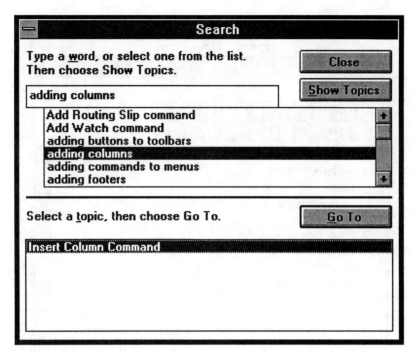

Figure 2-17. Version 4.0 Search Dialog Box

You see the words Insert Columns: Command, and click on **Go To**. A box appears with the information that you need, and you learn how to insert a new column.

- Another way to find help is to click on **Help**, then choose **Index**. You will see the screen shown in Figure 2-18. You can click on a letter, for example **I** for inserting.

The Complete Planning Guide for Microsoft® Project

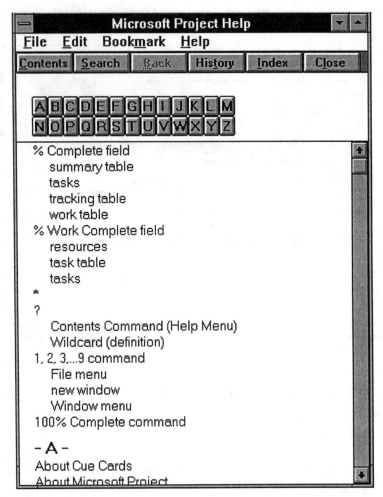

Figure 2-18. Help Index Screen

- To get help with an object on the screen, or areas of the screen, click on [icon] , to the far right of the toolbar, then point and click to the appropriate area. This is the same icon used in other Microsoft applications.

- Cue cards (Version 4.0) Cue cardsare probably the "ace in the hole" for new and experienced Microsoft Project users. For performing infrequent tasks, a familiarity with the structure of cue cards provides just-in-time learning. See Appendix A for a list of cue cards that are available in Version 4.0.

Microsoft® Project Fundamentals

Click on the ![icon] Cue Card icon, or press **Alt/H**, then choose **Cue Cards**. On the standard toolbar, it is located at the far right of the screen, to the left of the help pointer. You will see the Cue Cards box, as shown in Figure 2-16.

On your first visit to cue cards, you may want to begin by clicking on the last option, **Learn about using Cue Cards**. Take a few minutes to get acquainted. After reading that page, return to cue card choices by clicking on **Next**.

When you return to the Cue Cards box, read the list. If you see what appears to be the desired topic, point and click. You will then see an expanded list of cue cards, each containing detailed instructions. There are hundreds of MS project functions available using this method.

Once you have chosen a cue card, you can resize the cue card or move it to any part of your screen. It stays there until you close it.

THE TOOLBAR

As you have seen earlier, the fastest way to do many jobs is to click on an icon. Icons, also referred to as <u>buttons</u>, are shown in the toolbar section of the Microsoft Project window beneath the menu bar. Many of these icons were shown in the menu bar section earlier in this chapter.

Fast Lane Tip #6

To see a display of all buttons/icons and their titles

1. Click on **Help** or press **Alt/H**.

2. (Version 4.1) Choose **Microsoft Project Help Topics**. (Version 4.0) Choose **Search for Help on**.

3. Type **Button Index**.

4. (Version 4.1) Click on **Display**, or press **Enter**. (Version 4.0) With **Button Index** selected, choose **Show Topics**, then **Go To**. You will see a list of all buttons/icons in Microsoft® Project.

The Complete Planning Guide for Microsoft® Project

The toolbar section of the window displays buttons that will quickly perform a wide variety of tasks. For example, clicking on either of these icons 🗐🗐 allows you to change virtually any task detail except those related to costs. It can be used to add a note to a task such as that task's completion criteria, approvals necessary, or other important information. Consider removing one of these buttons if your toolbar section is getting crowded. Both take you to the same tab choices.

There are various other toolbars that you can choose to display either temporarily or permanently. To see a list of other available toolbars, click on **View**, or press **Alt/V**, then choose **Toolbars**. You'll see the following box:

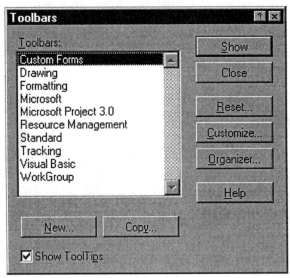

Figure 2-19. Toolbars Dialog Box

When you see this dialog box, you can choose to show, hide, or customize any existing toolbar. You can also create an entirely new toolbar by using the **New** button at the bottom.

Modify one of the existing toolbars by using the **Copy** button to copy a toolbar that is similar to the one that you want, and then making the desired changes.

Microsoft® Project Fundamentals

Fast Lane Tip #7

To return a toolbar to its original format

1. Select the toolbar.

2. Click on **Reset** or press **Alt/R**.

Throughout this guide, you will see suggested icons/buttons for performing many jobs. To learn about customizing a toolbar, see Chapter 8. Figure 2-20 shows an empty Gantt chart with the Standard toolbar and the formatting toolbar. The entry bar, where you can place your cursor and make changes, is located just beneath the toolbar section.

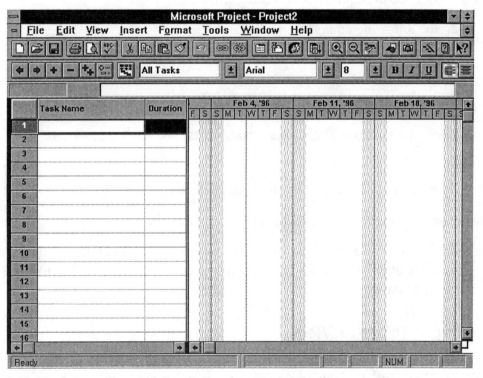

Figure 2-20. Blank Gantt Chart with Standard and Formatting Toolbars

49

To find out what any icon will do, place your cursor (do not click) on the icon and its function will appear in yellow, as shown below for the Attach Note icon.

Figure 2-21. Icon Function

VIEWS AND TABLES

The type of information needed to plan and manage a project will vary from one project to another, and from one team to another. To plan and manage your project, you will probably need to change the type of information that is displayed while you work. Some teams will need cost data, some will not. If you are working on a one-person project, you may not have a need to plan the use of resources.

To help in changing the appearance of the Microsoft® Project window, you can choose from more than 100 available data columns, or fields.

You can do the following and much more:
- Choose from more than twenty standard views and tables
- Add and delete columns
- Customize column headings, giving them a shorter or more familiar name
- Create a column heading such as "comments" and enter textual data
- Modify column height and width
- Choose to align the column at the left, center or right

Each of these functions is discussed below.

In this section we will discuss various ways to change the columns of data that are displayed. In Chapter 7 you will learn more about how to work with Microsoft Project views, tables and reports.

Choosing a Table or View

Before modifying any columns, examine the standard views and tables that are available in Microsoft® Project. To do this:

Microsoft® Project Fundamentals

Fast Lane Tip #8

To examine tables and views

1. Click on **View**.

2. Click on **Table: Entry**. You will see several other choices.

3. Choose each table, one by one, then press **Enter** or click on **OK** to see the type of data displayed in each one.

4. Choose **More Views**, located just beneath Tables, and select each of these one by one to see the type of data displayed in each one.

5. Select the table or view that is closest to your current need.

Since the team will be developing time estimates and establishing dependency relationships at the next meeting, Chris plans to use the entry table. An excerpt is shown below in Figure 2-22.

ID	Task Name	Duration	Start	Finish	Predecessors	Resource Names
	Newsletter #1	1	11/6/9	11/6/9		
1	Budget Requirements	1	11/6/9	11/6/9		

Figure 2-22. Entry Table

Inserting Columns

After looking at the Entry table, Chris decides that she would also like to add a column for successors. To insert a new column, do the following:

The Complete Planning Guide for Microsoft® Project

Fast Lane Tip #9

To insert a new column in a table

1. Click anywhere in the column to the immediate right of the desired location for the new column.

2. Click on the **Insert** menu, or press **Alt/I**, then choose **Column**. You will see the dialog box shown in Figure 2-23 below.

3. Use the scrolling arrow beside the Field Name section, and choose **Successors**.

4. Choose whether to have the data in that column aligned at the left, right, or center. (Since this particular field is likely to have many items for some tasks, the left is recommended.)

5. Click on **Best Fit**" to instruct Microsoft Project to automatically adjust the size of the column to accommodate the data. You can also type in a number; this number represents the number of characters that can be horizontally displayed.

Figure 2-23. Column Definition Dialog Box

Microsoft® Project Fundamentals

Customizing a Column Heading:

You may want to change column headings for many reasons. If, for example, you are working on a large project, and you want to change the heading of the Task Name column to read "Objectives, Activities, and Tasks", do the following:

Fast Lane Tip #10

To customize a column heading

1. Double-click on the column heading that you would like to change. You will see the Column Definition dialog box, as shown in Figure 2-23.

2. Press the **Tab** key on your keyboard. Your cursor will be placed beside the word Title.

3. Enter the new heading that you would like to appear above the column. This will become the new column heading.

4. Click on **OK**, or press **Enter**.

Creating a New Table

On many occasions, particularly when you begin to use Microsoft Project you will want to create a new table for your needs or for another stakeholder. To create a new table, follow the steps shown below.

Fast Lane Tip #11

To create a new table

1. Click on **View**, or press **Alt/V**.

2. Choose **Tables**, then choose **More Tables**.

3. Choose **New**.

4. To begin entering fields, click on the scrolling arrow with a horizontal line just beneath the **Delete Row** button. When you do this, you will see a list of possible **Field Name** columns.

5. Scan the **Field Name** columns and click on the columns you would like to choose.

6. If you know you want certain columns, and you know their titles in Microsoft® Project (or would like to guess), begin typing the title. When you type the first letter you will see a list of choices beginning with that letter. Continue typing until you have highlighted the desired column—then click on that column. It will appear under the Field Name column and will have default info under the Align(ment) and Width columns.

7. Continue until you have all the desired columns. Customize column headings as desired, using information from the "Customizing a Column Heading" section earlier in this chapter.

8. Edit the **Align** column by clicking in that column and using the same downward-pointing arrow used above to choose from left, center, or right alignment.

9. Edit the **Width** column by clicking in that column and then clicking on the same downward arrow, then choosing from the numbers presented; or type in a number to represent column width.

10. When finished, click on **OK**, or press **Enter**.

Following these steps, you can create a very wide variety of tables that are likely to meet the informational needs of virtually all stakeholders. This will be discussed in more detail in Chapters 4, 7, and 8.

Deleting a Task

When you are constructing a file, there will be instances when you would like to delete one or more tasks. If you attempt to delete a summary task, the Planning Wizard will caution you that the component tasks will also be deleted.

The fastest way to delete a task is to place your cursor on the task or tasks that you want to remove, then press the **Delete** key. You can also delete a task by clicking on **Edit**,

Microsoft® Project Fundamentals

then **Delete Task**. After you have deleted one or more tasks, Microsoft® Project removes the task and the line, and automatically renumbers remaining tasks.

Note: If you cut a task, the text and other information is deleted, but a blank task remains.

Editing a Task

Making changes to a task can be accomplished in several ways. As discussed earlier, you can make changes in the Task Information dialog box or on the task form. To make quick changes to displayed information, follow these steps:

Fast Lane Tip #12

To edit a task

1. Click on the cell that you want to edit.

2. Move the cursor to the entry bar, located <u>above</u> the tasks.

3. Make the correction by placing the cursor to the left of the character(s) and pressing **Del**; or by placing the cursor to the right of the character(s), and then pressing the **backspace** key.

4. Click on the checkmark (✓), or press **Enter** or the down arrow key. The change will be made.

55

3

Scoping Out Your Project

In this chapter, you will learn how to:

1. Construct a WBS Outline

2. Make changes to the outline

3. Estimate the time required to accomplish project work

4. Analyze task details

5. Assess risks and plan for contingencies

INTRODUCTION

Now that you have gained much more familiarity with Microsoft Project, it is time to continue planning your project. To guide you, the newsletter team will try to "get their arms around the project" by developing a Work Breakdown Structure outline.

Chris and the newsletter team will hold their second and third meetings in this chapter. They will be leading you through the construction of a WBS outline, time estimating, task analysis, risk assessment, and contingency planning for your project.

PROJECT PHASES OR OBJECTIVES

To reach the project goal, you must usually accomplish major categories of work. Most often, these major categories of work are referred to as *phases*, *objectives*, *major milestones,* or simply *milestones*, depending on the size of the effort and local practices.

In increasing numbers, organizations are developing formal project management methodology, standards, guidelines, and templates. When this is done, the project experience of the organization can be archived and made available to improve efficiency on new and future projects. Templates and other guidelines and documentation can guide you in choosing a project life cycle, and in using the organization's common terminology, standards, and practices.

There are many benefits to standardizing project management practices and terminology. By standardizing project management, you can:

- Improve quality
- Meet or exceed customer requirements
- Save time
- Reduce costs
- Reduce rework
- Reduce duplication of effort
- Improve the quality of communication among employees, partners, and customers

Project Standards and Guidelines

In many organizations, standard project templates are available to plan and manage similar efforts, such as those needed for new product development projects or capital projects. In these environments, standard project templates and standard lifecycles are often used as a starting point for project planning.

When standard templates or standard life cycles are used, members of the project team typically begin project planning by customizing the standard model. Customizing or scaling a model consists of eliminating tasks, combining tasks, and adding new tasks. If your organization does not use standard templates or life cycles, but many of your projects are very similar, you may want to consider developing one or more standard templates.

By using a standard template to assist you in project planning, you are likely to save time and prevent many different teams from "reinventing the wheel" again and again. This method of project planning is considered a "top-down" approach. (See the Top-Down Approach section later in this chapter.)

The Template Wizard

Both Versions of Microsoft® Project contain a Template Wizard to help you in setting up and using a template. It consists of a series of help screens that advise you when you are starting to plan a new project that is based on a template. See Chapter 6 for more information about templates in a multiproject environment.

Available Templates

Versions 4.1 and 4.0 provide several templates that can help you start quickly in scoping out many projects. The list is slightly different in the two versions, as indicated below. Available templates include:

- audit.mpt
- eventpln.mpg
- iso9000.mpt (Version 4.1 only)
- isoaudit.mpt (Version 4.1 only)
- laninst.mpt
- lansub.mpt

The Complete Planning Guide for Microsoft® Project

- mktplan.mpt
- rollout.mpt
- rollup.mpt
- softdev.mpt (Version 4.0 only)

Fast Lane Tip #13

To open the Microsoft Project template library

1. Click on  or press **Ctrl/O**.
2. In **File of Type** (Version 4.1) or **List Files of Type** (Version 4.0), choose **Templates** (*.mpt).
3. From the Winproj folder or directory, choose **Library**.
4. Double-click on **Library** to see a list of sample project templates.
5. Choose one that appears to be appropriate for your project.
6. Save the template under a new project file name (*.**mpp**).
7. Make changes as necessary to the new file.

When it is time to publish the next newsletter, Chris and the team can save time by saving their current file as a template, since it is likely that changes will be made in the newsletter project as it unfolds. Therefore, save the template after the project is substantially complete.

Top-Down Approach

You can begin project planning in one of three ways:

- Top-down approach

Scoping Out Your Project

- Bottom-up approach
- A combination of Top-Down and Bottom-up

The top-down approach is used in many environments in connection with one or more life-cycle models. The top-down approach provides improved efficiency by taking advantage of standard project life cycles, phases, activities and tasks. In new product development programs, for example, you may begin program and project planning with a proven structure. The standard phases for this type of program could be similar to the ones shown in Table 3-1.

Table 3-1. Program phases

Phase 1	Concept
Phase 2	Definition
Phase 3	Prototype Engineering
Phase 4	Development
Phase 5	Production
Phase 6	Product Support
Phase 7	Product Retirement

Some of these phases may overlap. In certain life-cycle models, such as evolutionary, spiral, or incremental, a phase or part of a phase may be repeated. In software development, these life-cycle models allow developers to write and install systems, kernels, or segments in increments, while collaborating with customers.

When using some of these life-cycle models, the team does not attempt to plan *all* project details up front. Rather, plans are developed incrementally. Many other life-cycle models exist. See the Bibliography for sources of information on different life-cycle models.

When using the top-down approach to project planning, a common error is to stop breaking down the work before reaching a satisfactory level of granularity. To help ensure that you have broken down tasks sufficiently, consider using a rule of thumb, such as forty hours, at the lowest subtask or work package level. This number can be higher or lower, depending on the familiarity with the task. Another general rule of thumb is to break down new, untried tasks to finer granularity than familiar tasks.

Bottom-Up Approach

If a project has never been planned and managed by the project team, you will want to ensure that the team thinks broadly and creatively when attempting to define all project tasks. The newsletter project fits this description. Another example would be a project to move the office space for a group of people from one location to another. Since a standard model may not exist for this project, the team will usually benefit by using the bottom-up approach and by brainstorming.

Fast Lane Tip #14

To plan team meetings

If possible, hold team planning meetings off site to minimize interruptions and to maintain focus. If available, arrange to use a different facility owned by the organization, a conference center, or a team member's home.

The Second Team Meeting

To prepare for the second meeting, Chris reserved a room with a flip chart easel and pad. The team should have enough time at this meeting to scope out the project and prepare an outline.

Scoping Out Your Project

On Monday, Chris arrives about fifteen minutes early for the meeting and hooks up her PC, the projector and the screen. She then turns on the PC and starts Microsoft® Project.

Next, she opens the Waytogo1 file.

Fast Lane Tip #15

To open the most recently used files

1. Click on **File**, or press **Alt/F**.
2. Look at the bottom of the **File** menu to see if the file you want to open appears there.
3. Select the appropriate file by clicking once on the name of the file or by pressing the number beside the file. The file will open.

With the WayToGo1 file opened, Chris chooses the **Entry** table, which is the default table. This table is automatically displayed the first time that you choose **View** on the menu bar. See Figure 3-1. The entry table displays seven columns of data:

- ID number
- Task Name
- Duration
- Start (date)
- Finish (date)
- Predecessors
- Resource Names

To the right of the columns of data are the Gantt chart bars. Use the mouse to move the divider bar to the left when you need to see the Gantt bars, and when you want to print.

The task form is displayed at the bottom of the window in this combination view. The task form shows:

The Complete Planning Guide for Microsoft® Project

- Task name (of the selected task)
- Duration or elapsed duration
- Fixed—whether or not the task's duration is fixed
- Buttons—to move to the previous or next task
- Start (date)
- Finish (date)
- Percent complete
- Id
- Resource Name
- Units
- Work
- Predecessor Name
- Type
- Lag

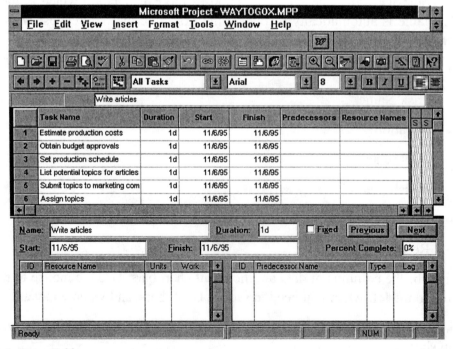

Figure 3-1. Entry Table

Scoping Out Your Project

Jane arrives shortly after Chris and they clarify their roles in the meeting. As the team members arrive on Monday afternoon, Chris and Jane welcome them. They start the meeting promptly at 1:00. Chris announces that management has enthusiastically approved the name Way To Go for the newsletter. Everyone seems pleased. Chris then sits at the PC and enters the tasks while Jane facilitates the discussion and writes responses on a flip chart.

Jane begins the discussion by asking the planning team:

What are the tasks necessary to complete the project?

In response to this question, team members make suggestions about the necessary tasks. As the suggestions are made, Jane records them as given on the flip chart. Chris enters data into Microsoft® Project.

While she is entering activities and tasks, Chris discovers that many of the names of activities and tasks require several words. A wider column is needed, and she wants to try to make the rows large enough to accommodate two lines of text.

She decides to seek help about having the columns word wrap. She clicks on **Help**, clicks on **Index**, then **w**. There is no listing for "word wrap". She decides to try looking under "rows." Aha! There it is under "rows: height".

Fast Lane Tip #16

To increase (or decrease) row height:

1. Place the cursor between any two rows in the ID column until you see a symbol that looks like this ‡

2. Holding down the mouse button, drag that arrow downward, making the row higher until the activity or task name wraps to a second row.

After solving that problem, Chris enters tasks as the team works. After about an hour and a half the team has developed the list of tasks shown in Table 3-2.

The Complete Planning Guide for Microsoft® Project

Table 3-2. Task list

Estimate production costs
Obtain budget approvals
Set production schedule
List potential topics for articles
Submit topics to marketing committee
Assign topics
Brainstorming session of design ideas
Create three preliminary designs
Compare designs and select best design
Develop final design
Obtain approval
Select staff to write articles
Recruit freelance writers
Set deadlines
Write articles
Make revisions
Approve final copy
Submit diskette to desktop publisher
Develop preliminary layout
Edit copy to fit layout
Revise layout
Incorporate graphic elements
Prepare and submit diskette to paste-up artist
Choose or develop graphics
Obtain and prepare photography
Prepare and submit diskette to desktop publisher
Download file and run out linotronic films
Paste-up signatures

Scoping Out Your Project

Strip-in photos
Submit mechanicals to printer
Print newsletter
Distribute newsletter

After about two and a half hours, the team has run out of ideas. They look over the list one last time but no new tasks are added. This seems like a complete list. Chris saves the file to her hard disk by clicking on the 🖫 icon. Then, to back up the file, she clicks on **File**, then **Save As**; and saves the file to a floppy on drive A.

Jane continues the meeting by asking the team:

What else needs to be planned?

The team responds with the following list:

- An outline
- Time estimates
- Dependency relationships
- Materials and supplies
- Costs
- Resource assignments
- Risks and contingency plans
- Deadlines

The team decides to use the list of tasks that they generated to develop an outline. Looking at their watches, the team sees that it is time to adjourn the meeting. They will need to continue planning at the next meeting. After checking their calendars, they agree to get together again on Wednesday morning at 8:00 a.m. and work until noon to develop a WBS Outline and time estimates for the project. They also agree to do some thinking about how long it will take to accomplish their tasks. Chris agrees to call Cynthia and Jack to see if they will be able to make it. When she returns to her office, she checks around to find a small meeting room for the meeting on Wednesday morning, and reserves one.

CONSTRUCTING AN OUTLINE (WORK BREAKDOWN STRUCTURE)

The Third Team Meeting

On Wednesday morning, Chris arrives early, sets up the PC and projector and opens the WAYTOGO1 file and displays the list of tasks they developed. Jane had told her that she would be arriving late, so Jim agrees to facilitate the group while Chris enters the data.

Now that the team has a list of tasks that seem to represent all project work, they decide to organize the tasks into categories and develop an outline. In project management, an outline is a form of work breakdown structure. A *work breakdown structure* (WBS) is a hierarchy of project work.

In general, a work breakdown structure can be created in two ways: the WBS outline, which is the method used by Microsoft® Project, and a graphic method. The graphic WBS appears much like a standard organization chart, except that in most organization charts each box represents a person and a job title with broad responsibility over an indefinite time period. On a graphic-style WBS, the boxes are used to represent a finite amount of work, whether or not a resource has been assigned.

When the goal is broken into major categories of work, these major categories are often referred to as *phases*, *objectives* or *major milestones*, depending on the size of the project. For a large project or program, the levels of work in a WBS outline may look like the ones shown below in Table 3-3.

In very large projects and programs, there can be twenty or more levels of work! For many reasons, the lower levels of work may be managed as separate projects. The terminology may vary from one organization and industry to another. Many

Scoping Out Your Project

organizations have found it helpful to standardize project management terminology by giving names to the levels of project work.

In Microsoft Project, a *milestone* is usually a task with zero duration. It normally signals the beginning or end of an important task. The term "task" is a generic term that is used to identify a specific work element at any level.

For programs or large projects, the levels of work can include those shown below.

Table 3-3. Outline levels

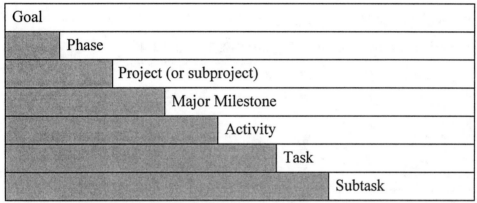

Note: There can be many additional levels.

For small projects such as the newsletter project, only a few levels of indentation may be needed. See Table 3-4 below.

Table 3-4. Outline levels for a small project

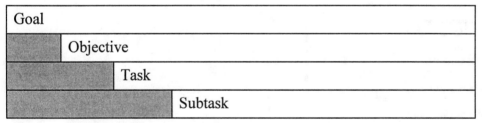

This is the terminology that the newsletter team will use.

The newsletter team completes the WBS outline. It groups the listed tasks under larger categories of work that they will call objectives. This type of organization will help in assigning responsibilities. It will also help in preparing summary reports for management as the project gets underway. The project objectives for the newsletter project are as follows.

1. Define Budget Requirements
2. Schedule Production

The Complete Planning Guide for Microsoft® Project

3. Create Layout and Masthead Design
4. Write Newsletter Content
5. Edit and Revise Layout and Copy
6. Integrate Graphic Elements
7. Prepare Mechanicals
8. Print Newsletter
9. Distribute Newsletter

The entire WBS outline is shown below in Figures 3-2, 3-3, and 3-4.

ID	Task Name	Duration
	Newsletter #1	1d
1	Define Budget Requirements	1d
2	Start project	0d
3	Estimate production costs	1d
4	Obtain budget approvals	1d
5	Schedule Production	1d
6	Set production schedule	1d
7	List potential topics for articles	1d
8	Submit topics to marketing committee	1d
9	Assign topics	1d
10	Create Layout and Masthead Design	1d
11	Brainstorming session of design ideas	1d
12	Create three preliminary designs	1d
13	Compare designs and select best design	1d
14	Develop final design	1d
15	Obtain approval	1d
16	Write Newsletter Content	1d
17	Select staff to write articles	1d
18	Recruit freelance writers	1d
19	Set deadlines	1d
20	Write articles	1d
21	Make revisions	1d
22	Approve final copy	1d
23	Submit diskette to desktop publisher	1d

Figure 3-2. WBS Outline Part I

ID	Task Name	Duration
24	Edit and Revise Layout and Copy	1d
25	Develop preliminary layout	1d
26	edit copy to fit layout	1d
27	Revise layout	1d
28	Incorporate graphic elements	1d
29	Prepare and submit diskette to paste-up	1d
30	Integrate Graphic Elements	1d
31	Choose or create graphics	1d
32	Illustrations	1d
33	Photography	1d
34	Sidebars, quotes, excerpts	1d
35	Obtain and prepare photography	1d
36	Prepare and submit diskette to desktop p	1d
37	Prepare Mechanicals	1d
38	Download file and run out linotronic films	1d
39	Paste-up signatures	1d
40	Strip-in photos	1d
41	Submit mechanicals to printer	1d

Figure 3-3. WBS Outline Part II

ID	Task Name	Duration
42	Print newsletter	1d
43	Do camera work	1d
44	Obtain materials	1d
45	Print color #1; dry	1d
46	Print color #2; dry	1d
47	Print black; dry	1d
48	Collate and bind	1d
49	Deliver to mailroom	1d
50	Send samples to Project Manager	1d
51	Distribute Newsletter	1d
52	Schedule mailing and order envelopes	1d
53	Prepare and send mailing labels to mailr	1d
54	Attach labels, stuff envelopes, apply post	1d
55	Premier Party	0d

Figure 3-4. WBS Outline Part III

Notice that the duration for every task at this point is one day. This is the default setting. Later in the meeting they will be adding time estimates for tasks. Chris has also created a milestone task, "Start project," which she placed under Define Budget Requirements. Later, she will connect beginning tasks to this milestone.

At the highest level in the outline is the project goal. Chris and the team would like to have all project details "roll up" to the project goal. She recalls that while becoming familiar with the Tools menu in Microsoft Project, she saw a choice in the Options submenu under Views for creating a project summary task. The project summary task (which is the goal) is listed first in the project and is positioned at the far left. So that all costs, percentage complete, and project duration information can be accumulated here, she establishes the project summary task.

Fast Lane Tip #17

To create a project summary task that summarizes and accumulates project data from all tasks

1. Click on **Tools**, or press **Alt/T**.
2. Choose **Options**.
3. Choose **View**.
4. Click in the checkbox to the left of **Project Summary Task**.

After you create a project summary task, a newly created task with the file name of the project appears at the top. You can of course change this to reflect the project goal by clicking on the cell, then typing in the editing box just above the column headings. When finished, click on the checkmark to record the change. Chris changes the summary task to read Newsletter #1, and for the time being plans to number each subsequent newsletter.

Microsoft Project will now automatically roll up and accumulate data to show the scheduled end date for the project and other data.

Table 3-5. Project summary task

					April		
ID	Task Name	Duration	3/24	3/31	4/7	4/14	4/21
	Newsletter #1	1d					

Outline Levels: Expanding and Collapsing

In Microsoft Project you can have as many as ten outline levels, or levels of indentation. Some call these *WBS levels*;, others refer to them as *outline levels*. In Microsoft Project you can choose either name as a column heading or field. The structuring and numbering are identical for both.

For some audiences, such as the project team, you may want to display all of the levels of work for a project. At other times you may only need to see the objectives. You can quickly move from expanded view to collapsed view for the entire outline or component phases by double-clicking on a task or summary task.

Summary Tasks, Parent Tasks, and Children Tasks

The buttons used for indenting, outdenting, expanding or collapsing the WBS outline are part of the formatting toolbar, and are normally located on the second row of icons beneath the View menu item.

Table 3-6. Icons for developing a project outline

←	The left-pointing arrow will move a task or group of tasks to the left. This function is known as *outdenting*" or *promoting*".
→	The right-pointing arrow will move a task or group of tasks to the right. This function is known as *indenting*", or *demoting*".
+	The plus sign is used to expand a summary task and show the subtasks. To expand a task to reveal the component subtasks, place your cursor on the phase and click on the icon with the plus sign. You can also do this by double-clicking on the summary task.
−	The minus sign is used to hide or collapse subtasks. Simply click on a summary or "parent" task. Double-clicking works here too.
++	The double plus sign will expand the outline to show all tasks. To expand the entire project schedule, if you can only see one line or some portion of the outline, place your cursor at the highest level of the outline shown, then click on the icon with two pluses. The entire schedule appears.
⊕⊖	Use the icon that contains the white plus and green minus sign if you would like to quickly see which tasks contain subtasks. A task with a plus sign to its left indicates that there are subtasks.

Management will normally wish to see only summarized information. To show a brief overview of a large project, or to prepare a summary report for management, you may want to hide subtasks. To reveal only a summary task and hide its subtasks, select that task, and double-click. The subtasks or "children" are hidden.

Displaying WBS Codes

Microsoft® Project automatically assigns identical WBS codes and outline numbers to all tasks. If you would like to display WBS codes, insert a column where you would like to see the codes. To do this, position your cursor in the column to the right of the

The Complete Planning Guide for Microsoft® Project

desired location (default setting), then click on Insert, or press Alt/I. Next, choose Insert. You will see the Column Definition dialog box, as shown below.

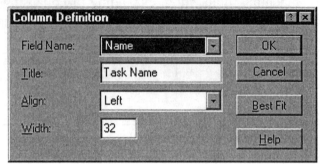

Figure 3-5. Inserting a WBS Column

When the box appears, you will be in the Field Name field. Type a **W** or use the scroll bar to locate WBS. Choose **WBS**. If you would like to change the title, alignment, or width of the column, do that here. Use the down arrow beside the **Align** field to choose either left or center alignment. Click on **Best Fit** or press **Alt/B** to let Microsoft Project calculate the column width. Click **OK** or press **Enter**. A WBS column will be inserted.

If you would like to display WBS codes in the task name column, do the following:

Fast Lane Tip #18

To show outline numbers beside the task name in the Task Name column

1. Click on **Tools**, or press **Alt/T**.
2. Choose **Options**, then the **View** tab.

   Beneath **Outline Options**, in the lower right-hand section, click on the check box beside **Show Outline Number**, or press **Alt/M**. See Figure 3-6.

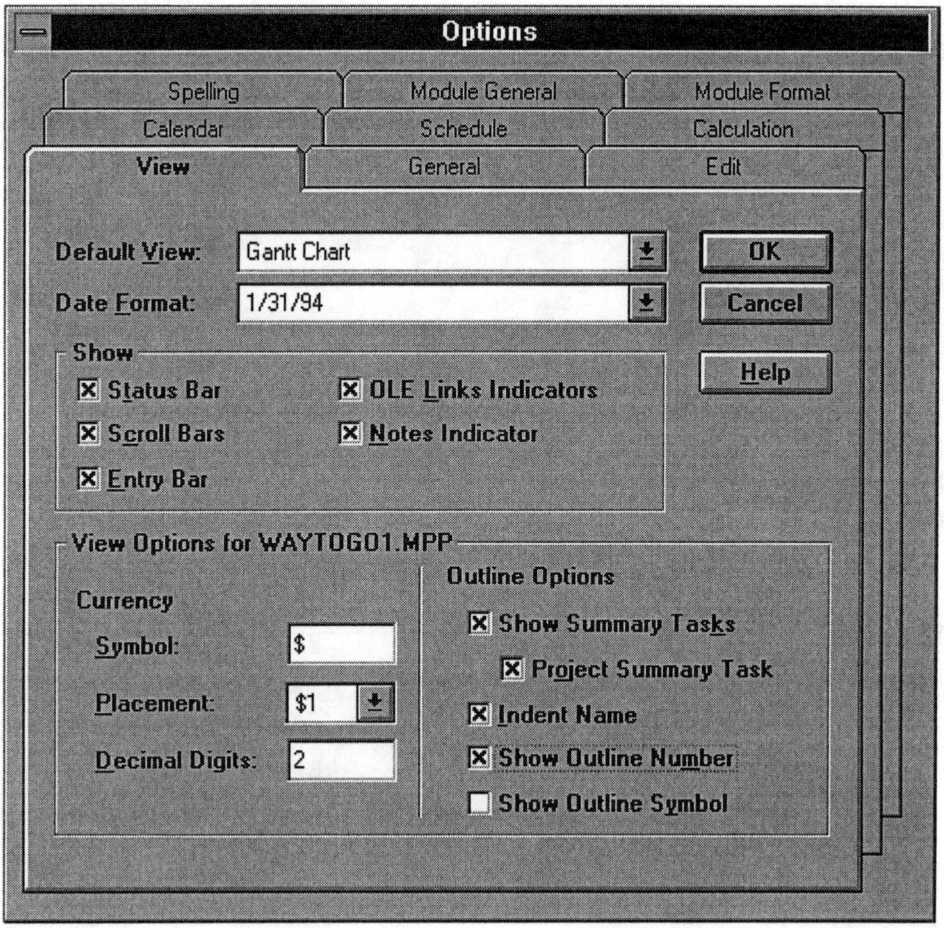

Scoping Out Your Project

Figure 3-6. Showing WBS Numbers

Customizing WBS Numbers

In many organizations, the WBS or outline numbers will need to be customized to conform to standard project numbering systems and/or accounting systems. You can overwrite the default WBS number field, and enter your own codes by using the task details form.

The Complete Planning Guide for Microsoft® Project

Fast Lane Tip #19

To enter customized WBS numbers

1. Click on **View**, or press **Alt/V**.

2. Choose **More Views**.

3. Select the **task details form**:

4. Once you have accessed the task details form, enter the customized codes in the WBS column.

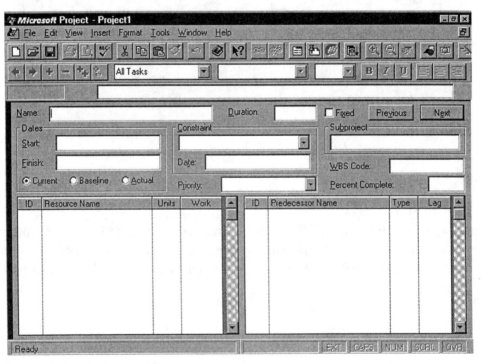

Figure 3-7. Task Details Form

To revert to the default WBS codes, select all of the new WBS codes under the WBS or outline column, and use the **Cut** icon or command. Standard numbers (1.1, 1.2, 1.3,...) will then be displayed.

Scoping Out Your Project

TIME ESTIMATING

Time estimating is one of the most formidable challenges in creating a project plan. It requires you to determine in advance exactly how long it will take to accomplish an activity or task. When combined for an entire project, time estimates and dependency relationships determine the estimated project duration.

After you have completed an outline of your project, you will need to estimate the duration for each of the lowest-level elements in the WBS. As part of this time-estimating process, attempt to identify the number of people and other resources needed to accomplish the activity or task within the estimated time. For example, if you are placing a layer of shingles on a 40' by 80' roof, it will take less time with two people than with one.

Be sure to consider skill level. A consulting engineer is likely to be more highly skilled than a junior level engineer, and consequently take less time to complete a task.

Entering Work Hours

By default, Microsoft Project accumulates work hours by adding duration hours. In an eight-hour day most professionals attend meetings, or work on other projects. This results in less than eight hours being spent on project tasks. Since many projects require precise tracking of the number of hours for billing purposes, you may wish to enter the actual work hours yourself. When you do this, you accumulate the actual work hours and their associated costs more precisely.

If you would like to customize Microsoft Project so that you can enter the actual number of work hours, do the following:

Fast Lane Tip #20

To enter actual work hours (as opposed to automatic calculation based on duration)

1. Click on **Tools**, or press **Alt/T**.
2. Choose **Options**, then the **Schedule** tab.
3. Remove the checkmark beside **Updating Task Status Updates Resource Status**.

Adding Duration

Now that the outline is complete, Jim asks if everyone has thought about how long it would take to accomplish their tasks, considering their overall workload. Most had written down time estimates for their work, and handed them to Chris to add to the project file. While she was working, the team discussed the remaining tasks and estimated their durations. Jim handed Chris the remaining durations, which she entered. To be safe, she immediately saved the file. Next she previewed and printed it, and gave everyone a copy to check before the next meeting, and asked them to identify predecessors and successors for all tasks.

An alternative to duration that is available in Microsoft Project is elapsed duration. With duration, the schedule is normally based on an eight-hour workday. With elapsed duration a twenty-four-hour day is used. If there is a reason that a task will consume a certain amount of time even though little or no work is actually done, you may want to use elapsed duration. This choice may be appropriate when you have distributed questionnaires and are waiting for them to be returned, or when waiting for paint to dry.

To indicate that you would like Microsoft® Project to use elapsed duration for a specific task, simply add an E to the duration increment. For example, use ed for elapsed days. The newly revised outline, complete with duration, appears in Figures 3-8, 3-9, and 3-10.

Scoping Out Your Project

ID	WBS	Task Name	Duration
	0	**Newsletter #1**	**64.21d**
1	1	**Define Budget Requirements**	**3.5d**
2	1.1	Start project	0d
3	1.2	Estimate production costs	20h
4	1.3	Obtain budget approvals	8h
5	2	**Schedule Production**	**1.75d**
6	2.1	Set production schedule	8h
7	2.2	List potential topics for article	6h
8	2.3	Submit topics to marketing committee	4h
9	2.4	Assign topics	4h
10	3	**Create Layout and Masthead Design**	**3.63d**
11	3.1	Brainstorming session of design ideas	4h
12	3.2	Create three preliminary designs	16h
13	3.3	Compare designs and select best design	2h
14	3.4	Develop final design	5h
15	3.5	Obtain approval	2h
16	4	**Write Newsletter Content**	**45.33d**
17	4.1	Select staff to write articles	8h
18	4.2	Recruit freelance writers	4w
19	4.3	Set deadlines	6h
20	4.4	Write articles	106.67h
21	4.5	Make revisions	32h
22	4.6	Approve final copy	8h

Figure 3-8. Outline with WBS Numbers and Duration Part I

The Complete Planning Guide for Microsoft® Project

ID	WBS	Task Name	Duration
25	5.1	Develop preliminary layout	6h
26	5.2	Edit copy to fit layout	8h
27	5.3	Revise layout	4h
28	5.4	Incorporate graphic elements	3h
29	5.5	Prepare and submit diskette t paste-up artist	2h
30	6	**Integrate Graphic Elements**	**1.75d**
31	6.1	**Choose or create graphics**	**1.5d**
32	6.1.1	Illustrations	12h
33	6.1.2	Photography	6h
34	6.1.3	Sidebars, quotes, excerpts	8h
35	6.2	Obtain and prepare photography	6h
36	6.3	Prepare and submit diskette t desktop publisher	2h
37	7	**Prepare Mechanicals**	**2.88d**
38	7.1	Download file and run out linotronic films	3h
39	7.2	Paste-up mechanicals	10h
40	7.3	Strip-in photos	8h
41	7.4	Submit mechanicals to printer	2h

Figure 3-9. Outline with WBS Numbers and Duration Part II

Note: task number 6.1 is bold because it summarizes three lower-level tasks.

Scoping Out Your Project

ID	WBS	Task Name	Duration
42	8	Print Newsletter	3.63
43	8.1	Do camera work	4
44	8.2	Obtain materials	3
45	8.3	Print color #1; dry	5
46	8.4	Print color #2; dry	5
47	8.5	Print black; dry	5
48	8.6	Collate and bind	5
49	8.7	Deliver to mailroom	2
50	8.8	Send samples to Project Manager	2
51	9	Distribute Newsletter	8.25
52	9.1	Schedule mailing and order envelopes	4
53	9.2	Prepare and send mailing labels to mailroom	8
54	9.3	Attach labels, stuff envelopes, apply postage	16
55	9.4	Mail newsletter	4
56	9.5	Premier party	0

Figure 3-10. Outline with WBS Numbers and Duration Part III

The Complete Planning Guide for Microsoft® Project

TASK ANALYSIS

While she and the team work, Chris clicks the right mouse button while the cursor is located on a summary task under the task name column to see which functions are available. She sees:

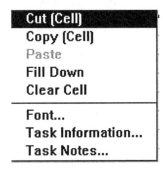

Figure 3-11. Right Mouse Button

She decides to choose **Task Information**, and sees:

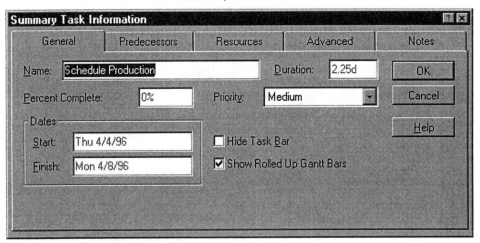

Figure 3-12. Summary Task Information Dialog Box

She cannot make any changes to the grayed data sections! This is because Microsoft® Project will not allow you to make certain changes to summary tasks, such as entering actual completion dates or duration. It does this for you automatically when you update the individual tasks that make up the summary task. If your cursor is on a summary task when you click on 🗒, you will notice that the title of the dialog box is Summary Task Information, as shown above.

82

The Task Analysis Worksheet

Before the meeting, Chris began to think about the type of information that the team would need about each task. Thinking back to previous projects, she decided that it would be a good idea to clarify completion criteria and a way to measure degrees of completion for certain tasks. She also knows that many tasks have associated risks that could delay the project.

She decides to create a worksheet that the team can use to record task-specific information. She creates a task analysis worksheet, and brings several copies to the meeting. During the meeting she will ask the other members of the team for their opinions on the worksheet and will make changes if necessary. See Figure 3-13.

The task analysis worksheet contains identifying information near the top and places to write completion criteria and how to measure it. In also includes a section at the bottom that can be used to identify risks that are related to the task, ratings for the risks, risk prevention tactics and a contingency plan.

See Chapter 7 to learn how to create a similar form in Microsoft® Project using the Dialog Editor.

Task Analysis Worksheet		
Task Name	WBS number	Responsible Team Member
Team Requirements:		
Other Resources:		
Predecessors:		
Successors:		
Completion Criteria:		
How measured:		
Duration:		

Risks:	Probability (1-10)	Severity (1-10)	Score
1.			
2.			
3.			
Ways to prevent:			
1.			
2.			
3.			
Contingency plan:			
1.			
2.			
3.			

Figure 3-13. Task Analysis Worksheet

Scoping Out Your Project

Identifying Information and Task Details

At the top of the task analysis worksheet, there are sections to identify the name of the task, WBS number, responsible person, team requirements, and predecessors and successors.

Completion Criteria

While developing time estimates, it is a good idea to define completion criteria. This job is made easier when the levels of work have been broken down sufficiently. All tasks on the newsletter project have been broken down to sufficient granularity to define completion criteria. Many have been broken down to two hours.

One way to approach completion criteria is to discuss expectations with those who will be responsible for successor tasks. When they would accept your work as being done? Is there an inspection it must pass? Editing completed? Temperature? Square feet? How will you know that the task is complete? In software development projects, measures commonly used are function points, feature points, and lines of code.

Once you have identified completion criteria, identify *degrees* of completion. If you have broken down your project work adequately, your job will be easier. How can you measure degrees of completion? Here are two examples from the newsletter project.

Completion Criteria Example 1

Task 3.2, Create three preliminary designs

Completion Criteria: All concepts have been translated into three tangible, presentable designs. Outputs will be produced as 650-dpi color laser-printed documents.

Degrees of completion will be measured by the number of completed designs. The three outputs will represent 33%, 33%, and 34% complete, respectively.

Figure 3-14. Completion Example #1

> Completion Criteria Example 2
>
> Task 9.2, Prepare and send mailing labels to mailroom
>
> Completion Criteria: All newsletter recipients are entered into the database, and all mailing labels have been printed and forwarded to the mailroom.
>
> Degrees of completion will be measured by determining the number addresses that have been entered into the database, the number of labels printed, and actual delivery to the mailroom as follows:
>
> 1000 addresses entered into the database = 90%
>
> 1000 labels printed = 5%
>
> Labels received by the mailroom = 5%

Figure 3-15. Completion Example #2

While gaining clarity about the work that needs to be done and how to measure it, certain assumptions and risks will be identified. These are discussed in the next section.

Risk Assessment

In every project there are many things that could go wrong (Murphy's Law). A *risk* is the threat that an undesirable ocurrance could jeopardize or delay the project. Risk management is an ongoing responsibility of every project leader and project manager.

Fast Lane Tip #21

To manage risks

1. Identify risks—for the project as a whole and for each task, what are your assumptions? Are you assuming an uninterrupted flow of materials? Funding by a specific date? Hidden in these assumptions are project risks.

2. Assess each risk—see the task analysis worksheet. Note that just because there is a number assigned, this does not suggest precision, only a comparison among the many risks. **High**, **Medium**, and **Low** may work just as well.

> 3. Prevent the risked event—take reasonable precautions to prevent the event from materializing.
> 4. Develop a contingency or backup plan.

Identify and analyze risks for the project as a whole and for each project task. Ask yourself these questions:

What are we assuming about the future of the project?

Are we assuming that funding will be available? Population growth? Decline?

Can anything go wrong that would delay or cancel the project?

Is there an event that could halt or cancel the project? Is there a market window within which the new product must be delivered? Could the company's assets suddenly be appropriated or nationalized?

What is the risk of losing any of the necessary resources?

Normally the "stars" will be lost first to another organization or project.

What are the risks associated with each task?

Failed tests? Late delivery of materials?

List all of the risks, as well as their probability and severity. Once that is done, develop contingency plans. Record the risk data. You may want to use a form like the task analysis worksheet, or design a form using Microsoft Project fields. If you have files from previous projects that are similar to this one in any way, there could be a few lessons learned about risks. Two of the risks identified in the newsletter project are shown below.

> **Risk Example 1**
>
> Task 6.1, Choose or create graphics
>
> There could be difficulty and a resulting delay in selecting from graphics that already exist, and reaching consensus on the choice.
>
> Probability rating—5
>
> Severity rating—8
>
> Risk rating = 40
>
> To prevent or reduce the probability of a delay, provide two choices for each graphic from existing graphics; as a backup plan, create two new graphics.

Figure 3-16. Risk Example #1

> **Risk Example 2**
>
> There is a risk that the printer could fail.
>
> Probability rating—2
>
> Severity rating—10
>
> Risk rating = 20
>
> To prevent or reduce the probability of a delay, test the equipment two days before delivery. As a backup plan, line up an outside vendor and attempt to gain assurance that the job could be printed on schedule.

Figure 3-17. Risk Example #2

Add-on software tools exist that will enhance Microsoft Project by helping you to quantify risk. Several are listed at the end of this chapter.

Now that the team has finished estimating duration and has completed task analysis worksheets for the project, and because it is lunch time, the group agrees to call it a meeting.

Chris asks if they can meet on the following Monday from 1:00-5:00 to attempt to complete the project schedule. All but Jim can make it, but he promises to work on predecessors and successors and to have them to her by Monday morning. They will all continue working on their respective tasks. Chris then thanks everyone for their input and adjourns the meeting promptly at 12:00.

Between now and the next meeting, Chris will be learning how to use Microsoft® Project to manage resources and fixed costs.

*COMPANION PRODUCTS RELATED TO THIS CHAPTER**

CHARTS NOW!, software tool used to create work breakdown structures, flow charts, precedence diagrams; Foundation Microsystems, Inc., (510) 814-1695.

GRANEDA Light, software tool used to create work breakdown structures, organizational breakdown structures and precedence diagrams; NETRONIC Software GmbH (int) 49-2408-1410.

MASTER.DG, software tool used to produce project structures, forms and diagrams; DiamondSoft, (206) 865-0678.

Risk +, software tool used to analyze cost and schedule risk; Program Management Solutions Inc. (805) 898-9571

WBS Chart, software tool used to create a work breakdown structure; Jim Spiller & Associates (707) 425-2484.

* Not all of these products are designed for Version 4.1.

4

Communication and Resources

In this chapter you will learn how to:

1. Create a communications plan
2. Develop a list of resources
3. Assign resources and costs
4. Estimate costs

INTRODUCTION

Communication between and among project stakeholders needs to be planned and cultivated throughout every project life cycle. Communication planning requires that the information needs of all stakeholders are understood, as well as the form, timing, and frequency of those information needs. Every stakeholder should understand their role in the project communication flow.

Managing project resources and costs and their timing requires detailed planning. This chapter will provide various communication options and choices for managing resources and costs. If costs will be accumulated for your project, you will need to estimate the amounts and timing of those costs. For many projects, this process and the data generated also aid in the preparation of Requests for Quotations (RFQs) or Requests for Proposal (RFPs), and the bidding process.

THE COMMUNICATION PLAN

For most projects, integrating the various resources and managing people are the most challenging and time-consuming aspects of managing the work. When the project begins, the customer, management, and other stakeholders will normally indicate the type of information they will need, and the frequency of those needs. If not, you will need to pursue and record their information needs.

During the project, the project leader or manager will need to be kept aware of the status of project tasks. Communication between and among all project stakeholders must be facilitated. You will need to establish a method for maintaining a dialogue with every member of the team, and every other stakeholder. In most cases, project team members will also need to be in touch with one another at many points in the project life cycle. Team members will need to be updated.

If you happen to be the project leader or manager, managing communication and resources means finding a variety of choices to make this as painless as possible for everyone. To reduce the number of unpleasant surprises, Chris and the newsletter team decide to develop a communication plan for the project. A *communication plan* is a plan to facilitate ongoing communications between and among all stakeholders. A communication plan should contain all or most of the following elements.

Communication and Resources

> **Fast Lane Tip# 22**
>
> To develop a communication plan consider these elements:
>
> - A list of stakeholders and their information needs
> - A schedule and system for gathering and updating the project status
> - A schedule for all project-related meetings
> - A list of all team members and other stakeholders (phone number, fax number, and e-mail address are normally included.)
> - A system for reporting results

Stakeholders and Information Needs

Chris makes a list of stakeholders for the project and their information needs. The newsletter team has the following stakeholders.

Table 4-1. Stakeholder information

Stakeholder	Information or Report	Frequency
Win Chen, Director of Communications	Milestone report: baseline vs. actuals for costs and schedule	bi-weekly
Sheila Roe, Director of Marketing	Schedule status Article topics	monthly as chosen
The project team	Status	weekly

Gathering Information and Updating Project Status

You will want to gather status information at regular intervals to be able to update the Microsoft® Project schedule. Try to make this as easy as possible for team members by providing options. Here are several:

93

- Personal visit—team members who work in the same area can drop by, or perhaps leave a note to advise you of completion dates, percent complete, costs, and other data.

- Telephone and voicemail—team members simply call in the status of their tasks.

- Electronic mail—team members communicate electronically.

- Status reports—inter-company mail or public mail system such as the US Mail or a private shipping company.

- Status meetings—the project team or a part of the team meet to present their status to the team and other appropriate stakeholders. For projects in which team members are geographically separated, this may be accomplished with teleconferencing, videoconferencing, or by using groupware such as Lotus Notes®.

- Other meetings—depending on the nature of your project, a wide variety of meetings may be necessary. A few types of meetings to consider are:
    - Kick-off meetings
    - Project planning meetings
    - Design review meetings
    - Prototype evaluation meetings
    - Production planning meetings
    - Milestone review meetings
    - Phase transition meetings
    - Owner's meetings
    - Safety meetings
    - Layout review meetings
    - Post-project review meeting

If the members of your team use Microsoft Mail or another electronic mail system that is MAPI/VIM compliant, you can send and receive status information electronically. Use the Answer Wizard in Version 4.1, and ask a question such as "How do I send electronic mail". You will see a list of related topics to choose from.

Version 4.0 of Microsoft® Project provides the following cue cards for E-mail users.

- Sending a Task Assignment Request

Communication and Resources

- Accepting or Declining a New Task Assignment
- Sending and Replying to an Update Message
- Sending and Responding to a Status Request Message
- Sending a Project Note to Resources Working on Your Project
- Sending a Project File
- Routing a Project File
- Viewing and Forwarding a Routed Project File

To display any of these cue cards in Version 4.0, click on **Help** or press **ALT/H**, then choose **Search for Help on**, and begin to type one of the titles. When the desired topic is displayed, click on the **Show Topics** button; select the cue card and choose the **Go To** button to display the desired cue card.

Chris is the only user of Microsoft Project on the team, and one of three members of the team that use electronic mail. This means that she can communicate with some of the team electronically, but will have to devise a strategy other than elecronic mail to gather status updates from other team members.

Chris develops a list of stakeholders, their phone numbers, and e-mail addresses which she will distribute at the next meeting. She will call it the project directory.

Table 4-2. Project directory

Project Directory			
Name	**Job Title**	**E-mail Address**	**Phone Number**
Forrest Boles	Graphic Designer		542-3212
Jack Boucher	Mgr., Printing	jboucher	542-2121
Win Chen	Dir. Of Comm.	Wchen	542-2100
Cynthia Kraft	Paste-up Artist		542-4563
Jim Mulligan	Writer/Editor		542-6663
Jane Parker	Desktop Publisher	jparker	542-4455
Sheila Roe	Dir. Of Mktg.	Sroe	542-6200
Chris Tomathy	Project Leader	ctomathy	542-7282

After talking with colleagues and some of the members of the newsletter team, Chris feels that it is important for the team to set up a routine of weekly status meetings so that team members can actually see the newsletter evolve. It will not be necessary for every team member to participate in every meeting. She feels that these meetings will only require about an hour each week. She will add the topic to the agenda of the next planning meeting to get the team's opinion.

Reports will be discussed in Chapter 7.

Vacations

In between meetings, Chris gets a call from Jim Mulligan. Jim would like to schedule a vacation during the last full week in April. This is an easy one. Chris recalls that to change a resource calendar she needs to go to the Tools menu and the Change Working Time submenu. She follows these steps:

Fast Lane Tip #23

To change hours or days for a particular resource

1. Click on **Tools**, or press **Alt/T**.
2. Choose **Change Working Time**. You will see the dialog box shown below.
3. Click on the down arrow ![arrow] beside **For:** near the top.
4. Click on the resource whose days or hours must be changed.
5. To change working hours, click and drag across the days of the week to select the entire work week and the entire month.
6. Change the hours in the **Working Time** section to the desired hours.
7. To change certain dates to nonworking dates, click on the date, or; click and drag for consecutive days
8. Click on **Nonworking** or press **Alt/N** to change days from working to nonworking.
9. Click on **OK**, or press **Enter**.

Communication and Resources

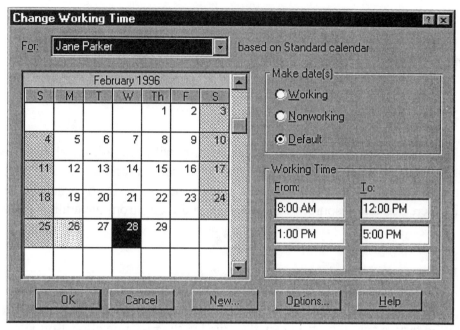

Figure 4-1. Change Working Time Dialog Box

THE RESOURCE MANAGEMENT TOOLBAR

The resource management toolbar provides a method to quickly enter or change resource information. To display the resource management toolbar, do the following:

Fast Lane Tip #24

To display the resource management toolbar

1. Click on **View** or press **Alt/V**.

2. Choose **Toolbars**. You will see the Toolbar dialog box.

3. Select **Resource Information.**

4. Click on **Show**, or press **Alt/S**. The resource management toolbar will be displayed, as shown in Figure 4-2.

Resource Management Toolbar Icons

Figure 4-2. Version 4.0 Resource Management Toolbar

Version 4.1 includes two additional icons for use with E-mail, as shown below in Figure 4-3. Before accessing the address book, (the icon/button on the left), or resource details (the one on the right), you will need to respond to a series of prompts. Resource pools can be created and resources can be assigned directly from the address book.

Figure 4-3. Version 4.1 additional Resource Management Icons

The resource management toolbar provides quick access to the resource allocation view, and the task entry view. You can also display the resource allocation view for the selected overallocated resource, and add, assign, or remove resources, display task assignments for a specific resource, level resources, and create pivot tables in Microsoft Excel®. Each icon is explained briefly in the following sections.

The Resource Allocation View

Resource Allocation View button—displays a combination view. This view consists of the resource usage view at the top, and a Gantt chart at the bottom, as shown below in Figure 4-4.

Using the keyboard, you can display this view by pressing **Alt/V**, then choosing **More Views**, then using the up or down arrow keys to choose resource allocation or another selection.

To switch between the top and bottom views, click on the alternate view, or press the **F6** function key.

To close one pane in the combination view, click and drag the split bar, or press **Shift/F6**, then use the up or down arrow key to close the view, then press **Enter**.

Communication and Resources

ID	Resource Name	Work	Mar 31, '96							Apr 7, '96						
			S	M	T	W	T	F	S	S	M	T	W	T	F	S
1	Chris Tomathy	10.8		1.6	1.6	1.6	2.4	1.6								
2	Jim Mulligan	200					8	8			8	8	8	8	8	
3	Jane Parker	6.75					1									
4	Forrest Boles	15.25					1	2			2	####				
5	Cynthia Kraft	16.5					2									
6	Jack Boucher	0.4					0.4									
7	Mailroom	16														
8	Marketing Committee	10.2					0.2				1	1				
9	Printing Department	29														

	Task Name		Mar 31, '96							Apr 7, '96					
			S	M	T	W	T	F	S	S	M	T	W	T	F
3	Estimate production costs							Chris Tomathy[0.2]							
4	Obtain budget approvals							Chris Tomathy[0.2]							
6	Set production schedule							Chris Tomathy[0.2],Jim Mulligan							
22	Approve final copy														

Figure 4-4. Resource Allocation View

The resource allocation view can be used to examine the schedule for a resource or group of resources. With this view, you can see specific dates on which resources are assigned, and also see the Gantt bars for the corresponding time period. By default, the Gantt chart displays the names of resources assigned to a task. If your Gantt chart does not display the names of resources, you can go to the Gantt Chart Wizard under the Format menu and choose to display this information.

The Task Entry View

 Task Entry View button—displays a combination view. This view of the project displays the entry table at the top of the screen and the task form at the bottom for the selected task as shown in Figure 4-5.

Using the keyboard, you can display this view by pressing **Alt/V**, then choosing **More Views**, then using the up or down arrow keys to make a selection.

To switch between the top and bottom views, press the **F6** function key.

To close one pane in the combination view, click and drag the split bar, or press **Shift/F6**, then use the up or down arrow key to close the view, then press **Enter**.

ID	WBS	Task Name	Duration	Start	Finish	Predecessors	Resource Names
7	2.2	List potentialtopics for articles	3	4/5/9	4/5/9	6	Jim Mulligan

The Complete Planning Guide for Microsoft® Project

![Task Entry View screenshot showing Name: Select staff to write articles, Duration: 4h, Start: 4/5/96, Finish: 4/8/96, Percent Complete: 0%, and a resource row for Jim Mulligan]

Figure 4-5. Task Entry View

The task entry view is useful for initially entering project details. You can enter a task name, its duration, and whether the duration is fixed. For example, if a task must be accomplished within a specified span of time, such as ten days, enter 10d beside **Duration**, and click on the check box beside **Fixed**.

Avoid entering start or finish dates. Microsoft Project interprets entered dates as constraints, which limit scheduling flexibility. If you have entered dates and thereby defined constraints, remove them as follows:

Fast Lane Tip #25

To view and remove constraints from a task view

1. Click on **View**, or press **Alt/V**.
2. Choose **Tables**, then **More Tables**.
3. Choose **Constraint Dates** from the list of tables. When you do, you will see a table that includes columns for constraint type and constraint date.
4. Make changes as necessary

100

Communication and Resources

Fast Lane Tip #26

To change one of the views in a combination view

1. Select the view that you would like to replace.
2. Click on **View**, or press **Alt/V**.
3. Choose **More Views**.
4. Choose the view you would like to use.
5. Choose **Apply**. The new view will appear.

GoTo Overallocation button—displays the resource allocation view as shown in Figure 4-5. Overallocated resources are shown in red on a color monitor and bold on a monochrome monitor. The hours of overallocation are shown in red on a color monitor and bold on a monochrome monitor beneath the dates of conflict.

Resource Assignment button,—also part of the standard toolbar, this button shows the Resource Assignment dialog box. This dialog box allows you to add, assign or remove a resource.

Using Resource button—displays the Using Resource dialog box shown below, which enables you to see a filtered list of tasks that use a specific resource or resource group.

Figure 4-6. Using Resource Dialog Box.

When you see the Using Resource dialog box, you can use the down arrow to select a resource, or you can type in the name of the resource. After selecting a resource, click

The Complete Planning Guide for Microsoft® Project

on **OK** or press **Enter** to see the tasks currently assigned to a specific resource. For example, the following table shows all of the tasks assigned to Jim Mulligan.

Table 4-3. Tasks assigned to Jim Mulligan

ID	WBS	Task Name	Duration	Start	Finish	Predecessors	Resource Names
6	2.1	Set production schedule	4	4/4/9	4/4/9	4	Chris Tomathy[0.2],Jim
7	2.2	List potential topics for articles	3	4/5/9	4/5/9	6	Jim Mulligan
8	2.3	Submit topics to marketing committee	2	4/5/9	4/5/9	7	Jim Mulligan,Marketing
9	2.4	Assign topics	2	4/5/9	4/5/9	8	Jim Mulligan
11	3.1	Brainstorming session of design ideas	4	4/4/9	4/4/9	4	Jim Mulligan,Jane Parker[0.25],Forrest
17	4.1	Select staff to write articles	4	4/5/9	4/8/9	9	Jim Mulligan
18	4.2	Recruit freelance writers	2	4/8/9	4/29/9	17	Jim Mulligan
19	4.3	Set deadlines	3	4/29/9	4/29/9	17,18	Jim Mulligan
20	4.4	Write articles	80	4/29/9	5/13/9	19	Jim Mulligan
21	4.5	Make revisions	16	5/13/9	5/15/9	20	Jim Mulligan
23	4.7	Submit diskette to desktop publisher	2	5/16/9	5/16/9	22	Jim Mulligan

Leveling Cue Cards button—can be used to access a cue card or procedure card that instructs you about how to resolve a resource overallocation. It also provides a list of other resource-related cards at the bottom.

Task Assignment Table—creates pivot tables in Microsoft® Excel. To do this it runs the Create Pivot Tables macro if you choose **Yes** at the prompt shown below.

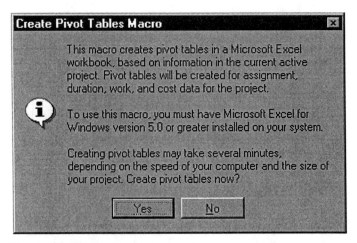

Figure 4-7. Create Pivot TablesMacro Screen

Communication and Resources

Click on **Yes** or press **Alt/Y** to create pivot tables in Microsoft Excel. When you indicate yes, there will be a delay as the tables are generated. You will then see the new table, as shown in Figure 4-8 below.

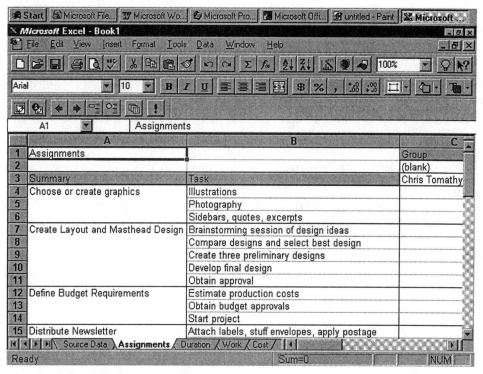

Figure 4-8. Pivot Tables from Microsoft Excel

After running the Create Pivot Tables macro, the Excel window shown above displays a book with five pivot tables. At the bottom of the window are tabs that can be used to display information about source, assignments, duration, work, and cost for all project tasks. These tables provide the calculating flexibility that is available in Microsoft Excel. Use the toolbar that is displayed to make modifications in tabular data.

The cost table is particularly useful for estimating costs and recording actual costs.

RESOURCES AND COSTS

If you have sufficient resources to accomplish every project task, your chances of being successful in managing the project are greatly improved. To manage this process, identify requirements early, and then closely monitor and negotiate resource use throughout the project life cycle. By managing this process, you can often minimize sudden crises related to resource shortages.

With Microsoft® Project, you can plan and manage a project schedule without assigning any resources. Without resources, schedules are calculated using duration. For example, if you are managing a very small project, and you are the only resource, it is probably not necessary to assign yourself to all project tasks. An exception would occur if resources are being shared among several projects. See Chapter 6.

In most projects, resource and cost information is needed throughout the project life cycle. Begin by identifying team requirements, proceed to assigning specific resources and fixed costs, estimate all project costs, and establish and manage the project budget. In some cases the project manager ensures that there is sufficient cash flow to fund the project.

You will need resource information to track, monitor, take corrective action, and prepare reports. To do all of this, you will need to keep track of the names of all resource and cost items, rates, and the availability of resources that are required to perform the work on project activities and tasks.

Throughout the project life cycle, you will need manage resources to ensure that adequate resources are in place. This responsibility may be broken down as follows:

1. Identify resource needs and fixed costs for your project
2. Develop a resource pool
3. Assign those resources and fixed costs to tasks
4. Manage and reassign those resources as necessary

In Microsoft® Project people are generally considered to be resources, and may be assigned to tasks in many ways. Machines, equipment, tools, and materials are also classified as resources.

Identifying Resource Needs and Fixed Costs

Whether or not you are tracking costs on your project, you are consuming resource time and therefore dollars. Consider this: for every hour of time spent on the project, these costs accumulate:

- The employee's hourly rate or salary
- The overhead rate or burden rate

The overhead or burden rate consists of allocations for office or facility space, utilities, and benefits. This rate can accumulate at 100–500% of the hourly rate or salary in many organizations! For this reason many organizations have integrated project budgeting

Communication and Resources

and cost accumulation with the internal accounting system and spreadsheet software tools.

To assist you in identifying and accumulating costs, Microsoft Project classifies all costs as cost per time period, cost per use, or fixed costs. Each is described below.

- **Cost per time period**—this includes hourly rates and other rates that can be assigned to a period of time. This category may be the most difficult to control. If an hourly resource is estimated to accomplish a task in forty hours, and actually consumes eighty hours, you may be 100% over budget for that task! If some of these hours are overtime hours, you may be *more* than 100% over budget for the task.

- **Cost per use**—a cost that is incurred at the same rate every time the resource is used. For example, some organizations may cross-charge departments for the use of a conference room on this basis.

- **Fixed cost**—a cost that remains the same regardless of the number of time units. A contract with a freelance writer to compose an article for Way To Go can be a fixed cost. A fixed-price contract is another type of fixed cost.

For some projects, resource management is likely to include the preparation of Requests for Quotations (RFQs) or Requests for Proposals (RFPs), followed by a formal bidding process. In most cases the bidding process occurs after a project has been approved.

Developing a Resource Pool

To assign people and other resources to your project, begin by developing a list of committed resources. As an alternative, you can also add resources one at a time as needed. Earlier, the newsletter team developed a list of the team requirements that can be used here. At this point, it is time for Chris to enter the resources into the WaytoGo1 file in Microsoft® Project. She enters the six resources that are known at this point, and also adds the mailroom, which will distribute the newsletter.

Fast Lane Tip #27

To create a list of resources and fixed costs

1. Click on **View**, or press **Alt/V**.
2. Choose **Resource Sheet**.

> 3. Enter data for resources and fixed costs.

Enter the names of people, and classes of resources such as technical writers, engineers, or electricians. List equipment, machines, assembly lines, or flow lines that are needed for the project. Table 4-4 displays the completed resource list for the newsletter project. Notice that the rate for the mailroom is $0.00. This is because their costs are allocated to all cost centers on a monthly basis, and are not calculated on a project-by-project basis.

Table 4-4. Resource sheet

ID	Resource Name	Initials	Group	Max. Units	Std. Rate	Ovt. Rate	Cost/Use	Accrue At	Base Calendar	Code
1	Chris Tomathy	C		0.	$27.50/	$0.00/	$0.0	Prorated	Standard	
2	Jim Mulligan	J		0.	$25.00/	$0.00/	$0.0	Prorated	Standard	
3	Jane Parker	J		0.2	$20.00/	$30.00/	$0.0	Prorated	Standard	
4	Forrest Boles	F		0.2	$23.00/	$0.00/	$0.0	Prorated	Standard	
5	Cynthia Kraft	C		0.	$14.00/	$21.00/	$0.0	Prorated	Standard	
6	Jack Boucher	J		0.	$17.00/	$0.00/	$0.0	Prorated	Standard	
7	Mailroom	M			$0.00/	$0.00/	$0.0	Prorated	Standard	
8	Marketing Committee	M			$0.00/	$0.00/	$0.0	Prorated	Standard	
9	Printing Department	P			$0.00/	$0.00/	$0.0	Prorated	Standard	

At this point, enter the names of the resources that will work on your project. Be inclusive. Though the employees of the mailroom will not work on the development of the newsletter, the mailroom will be counted on to distribute the newsletter.

You can be add, delete, or edit the column headings, just as you can with column headings in the Gantt view. Double-click on a column heading and choose from the fields displayed. Notice that all fields are related to resource management.

Fast Lane Tip #28

To replace or customize a column heading in the resource sheet

1. Double-click on the column heading.
2. Use the scroll button or down arrow key to choose and replace the current field and heading with a new field.
3. If desired, type in a customized heading.

4. Choose the desired **alignment** and **width**.
5. Click on **OK**, or press **Enter**.

The columns on the standard resource sheet include the following:

- **ID Number**—assigns a number to each resource.

- **Resource Name**—for most projects you will need a full name. However, for small projects, many teams choose to use only a first name. The resource name can also be used to show a group of resources, such as programmers or carpenters. If you use Resource Name in this way, increase the number of units to represent the number of interchangeable resources.

- **Initials**—of the resource. Microsoft Project automatically enters the first initial; if you would like two or three initials you will need to enter them.

- **Group**—can be used to indicate the type of resource, such as technical writers, marketing specialists, or electricians. For example, if you have four programmers working on the project, list "Programmers" under Resource Name and increase the number of units to four. Group can also identify the department or unit responsible, such as development engineering or finance. When you use it in this way, you can quickly prepare views and reports filtered to show one or more groups and related project data.

- **Max Units**—indicates the availability of the resource and the highest number of resources in a group. On the newsletter project, notice that most resources are only available for part of their time to work on this project. Chris is only available for 20% of her time, as represented by the .2 shown under Max Units. A group of resources such as manufacturing engineers, could have a larger number, such as 15 available for the project. When scheduling, Microsoft Project assumes that these types of resources are interchangeable.

- **Std. Rate**—used to accumulate standard hourly, weekly, or other standard rates. To change the default rate:

Fast Lane Tip #29

To change standard default rates for resources

1. Click on **Tools**, or press **Alt/T**.

2. Choose **Options**.
3. Under the **General** tab, near the bottom enter the new standard rate.
4. Choose **Set as Default**, and click on **OK** or press **Enter**.

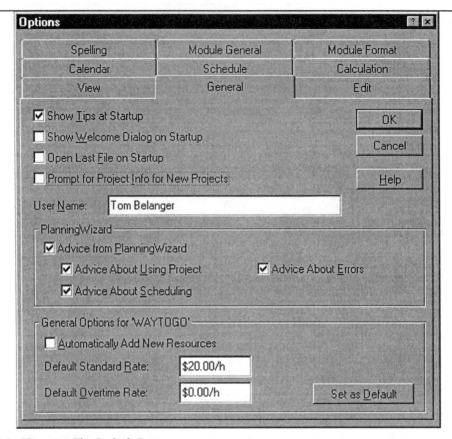

Figure 4-9. Changing The Default Rate

- **Ovt. Rate**—used to accumulate overtime hours worked for non-exempt hourly workers. This rate is normally one and one-half times the standard rate.

- **Cost/Use**—used to record a cost per use, a type of one-time cost such as a minimum setup charge for a printer regardless of the amount printed.

- **Accrue At**—costs can be accrued, or allocated to tasks in three ways:
  - At the *Start* of a task.
  - At the *End*, when a task is completed.
  - *Prorated*, according to percentage complete. This is the default setting.

Communication and Resources

- **Fixed Costs**—fixed amount, as used with fixed-price contracts. An example is if you requested bids for printing the newsletter, and contracted with the chosen vendor for a fixed-price contract. (When entering fixed costs on the resource sheet, enter "0" in the unit column.)

Fixed costs can be assigned to either a task, as described in the Fast Lane Tip #29 or to a resource. You assign a fixed resource cost in Version 4.1 by asking the Answer Wizard; in Version 4.0 see the cue card.

As an alternative or as a matter of preference, you may want to consider using the resource form to enter new resources at the beginning of a project. You can also use it to add a single resource once the project begins. The resource form can also be used to insert charts from Microsoft® Excel.

The resource form for Chris is shown below.

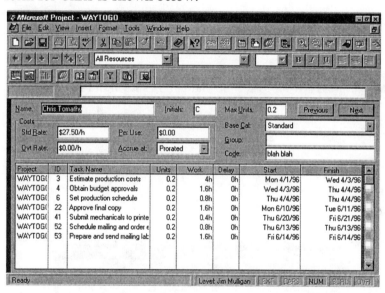

Figure 4-10. Resource Form

To access the resource form, choose **View**, then **More Views**, and select **Resource Form** from the list.

Assigning Resources and Fixed Costs

Once you have a pool of resources, you can assign them to specific tasks by clicking on the resource assignment button, and using the resource assignment dialog box. You may also assign resources one at a time on a task-by-task basis. If you assign resources in this way, you will need to assign rates and other data later. Once it is created, you can share the resource pool with other projects. See Chapter 6.

The Complete Planning Guide for Microsoft® Project

After you assign resources to a project, the resources and their tasks will be scheduled according to availability. For example, if a resource is available to work on the project for twenty percent of his time (.2), and the task is estimated to consume 10 hours of duration, the duration for the task will change to 50 hours. Microsoft® Project can also compare assignments to resource availability, and can alert you when resources are overcommitted. It does this by displaying a message on the status bar at the bottom of the page that instructs you to "Level (resource name)".

Fast Lane Tip #30

To assign a resource or fixed cost to a task

1. Select the task.

2. Click on , or press **Alt/F8** to see the dialog box shown in Figure 4-11.

3. Click on the resource that you would like to assign, or use the down arrow key to move to the appropriate resource or group.

4. Click on **Assign**, or press **Alt/A**.

5. Click on **Close**.

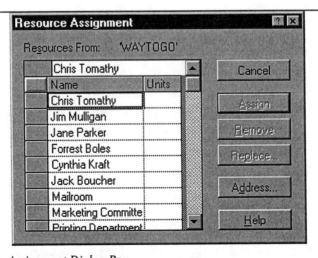

Figure 4-11. Resource Assignment Dialog Box

While you are assigning resources and costs, you can leave the Resource Assignment dialog box on the screen. Use the mouse to move to the next task, assigning resources to each task.

The printing department at HUPI cross-charges for printing jobs on a fixed-cost basis. They have agreed to print one thousand copies of the newsletter for $5,700. To assign a fixed-cost amount, do the following.

Fast Lane Tip #31

To enter a fixed cost from the Gantt chart

1. Click on **View**, or press **Alt/V**.
2. Choose **Table**, then **Cost**.
3. Select the task to be assigned the cost.
4. Under the **Fixed Cost** column, enter the fixed-cost amount.
5. Press **Enter** or the down arrow.

Managing and Reassigning Resources

With all known resources defined in the resource pool, you will then need to manage the use of resources throughout the project. In most cases, you will need to add new resources and make changes to resource assignments. In other situations, it may help to reduce a resource's hours, remove a resource from certain tasks, assign additional resources, or reduce the scope of the project by eliminating certain tasks.

You will also need to update the status of tasks and their impact on costs as the project unfolds. This will be discussed in Chapter 6.

If some of the members of your team work in different departments, you will need to gain commitments for their time. You may also need to arrange to have backup resources from those departments. When identifying and assessing risks, you may also want to list the loss of a key resource as a risk. If a certain resource has a highly specialized skill set, consider providing training for others to develop these skills, or identify an external source for a contract worker.

The Complete Planning Guide for Microsoft® Project

Changing Resource Data

You may need to change resource-related information for many reasons. You may need to:

- Increase the rate for a resource to reflect a raise
- Change the calendar being used to schedule the resource
- Change the accrual method for accumulating costs for a specific resource
- Change assignments

You have seen the resource sheet and resource usage sheet earlier in this chapter when you initially entered resource data. Those same worksheets can be used for this purpose, or you may prefer to use the Resource Information dialog box.

There are two versions of the Resource Information dialog box. The resource version can be reached by double-clicking on a particular resource name while in a resource view, or by clicking on the right mouse button and selecting **Resource Information**. When you do this, the resource version appears, as shown below. This Version contains cost information.

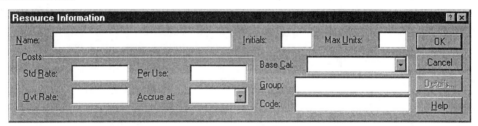

Figure 4-12. Resource Information Dialog Box,-Resource Version.

Using this form you can enter or change the following data:

- Name of the resource
- Initials
- Max Units
- Costs
- Base Calendar
- Group—a user-entered field that can be used to organize resources by department or group. This can help when a customized report is needed that shows details on a group-by-group basis.

112

Communication and Resources

- Code—a user-entered field that can be assigned any alphanumeric code. This field can be set up to identify cost categories that are compatible with the organization's accounting system. For example, you may classify costs into categories for direct and indirect labor, materials, and overhead.

The task version of the resource information form can be reached from a task view by double-clicking on the resource name, or by clicking on the right mouse button and then choosing **Resource Information**. When you see the Task Information dialog box, click on the **Resources** tab if it is not displayed. You will see the task Version of the Resource Information dialog box, shown in Figure 4-13.

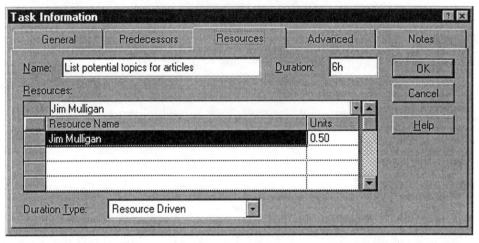

Figure 4-13. Resource Information Dialog Box,-Task Version

This version of the Resource Information dialog box contains the following information:

- Name (of the task)
- Duration
- Resources (availability)—shown as .50 for Jim. This means that he is available for 50% of his time to work on this project.
- Duration type—indicates whether the schedule for the task is dependent on the availability of the resources, or is of fixed duration. The default setting is resource-driven.

RESOURCE LEVELING

Every project and program has limited resources. There are only so many people, assembly lines, and printers. For these and other reasons, the planning and management

The Complete Planning Guide for Microsoft® Project

of resources on any but the smallest projects should be automated. To ensure that the newsletter is published and distributed on time, within budget, technical, and quality limits, Chris must examine all resource assignments and eliminate overallocations wherever possible. She can do this in several ways:

- Reassign one or more resources
- Delay or lengthen noncritical tasks (those with no slack)
- Ask Microsoft® Project to level resources

Each of these choices is explained below.

Reassigning Resources

Microsoft® Project has tables and views that will help you to manage the level of resource usage. You can reassign resources in many ways. Here are a few:

1. While in virtually any view, select a task for which you would like to add or remove a resource, or change the availability. Click on  , and make the desired change.

2. While in a view or table that has a Resource Name column, enter or delete the resource as needed.

3. Double-click on a resource to see the Resource Information dialog box. Click on a resource then click on the box to the left of the resource name and hold down the cursor. Drag the resource button to a task to assign the resource to that task.

Delaying or Lengthening NonCritical Tasks

You can reschedule the use of a resource on a task by adding a delay. You may want to do this when someone is not available or is not needed when a particular task begins. A delay can be added by using the task form.

Fast Lane Tip #32

To delay the start of work by a resource on the task form

1. Click on **Format**, or press **Alt/F**.

> 2. Choose **Details**, then **Resource Schedule**.
> 3. In the **Delay** field, enter a number of hours, days or other time increment to represent the amount of delay before the person begins work on the task.

You can also delay the start of a task by adding a lag to the predecessor-successor relationship. This will be discussed in Chapter 5.

You may also split the work of a resource. If, for example, a particular resource is scheduled to work on a task at the beginning, but then will not work on the task again until four weeks later, you may want to build a delay into the task. This will help to ensure that the schedule and costs for this task reflect the actual work time for this resource.

To split the work of a resource while in the Gantt chart, click on **View** then **More Views**, then **Task Form**. Next, click on **Format**, then **Details**, and choose the **Resource Schedule** display. You will see the task form with fields for work and delay. Assign the resource to two or more periods of work by entering the amount of the desired delay before the second assignment.

For example, if a resource is needed for eight hours on the first and last days of a ten day task, do the following: Enter the resource name once; enter Units as 1; enter work as 8h; and enter 0h beneath delay. Then, enter the resource name again; enter Units as 1; enter work as 8h; and enter 72h beneath delay.

Instructing Microsoft Project to Level Resources

You can level resources automatically. By using the Resource Leveling dialog box shown in Figure 4-14, you can resolve resource overallocation problems by delaying the start of a task until the necessary resources are available. However, leveling may result in gaps between assignments for some resources. Use the resource allocation view (Figure 4-4) or resource graph to check these gaps, and to reschedule as necessary. The resource graph will be explained in the next section.

When you are ready to level a resource or resource group, choose **Level Now**. Microsoft Project will stop at each overallocation to notify you that it will level the resource assignment by using slack time to delay the task.

> Note: Before attempting to level resources, all predecessor-successor relationships must be identified.

To level resources, click on **Tools**, or press **Alt/T**, then choose **Resource Leveling**. The resource leveling dialog box will appear.

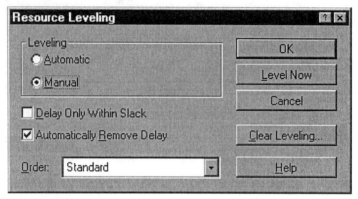

Figure 4-14. Resource Leveling Dialog Box

As a rule, leave the default setting on **Manual** resource leveling. This will prevent automatic leveling, which can result in undesirable rescheduling. In this way, you can maintain control by choosing when to level resources. Unless your project has much scheduling flexibility with room for significant delays, place a check in the checkbox beside **Delay Only Within Slack**. This will prevent a schedule delay that goes beyond the project goal date.

> Note: If you have chosen to schedule your project from the finish date, do not use leveling. No slack exists, because all tasks have been scheduled for as late a date as possible; therefore no tasks can be delayed.

If certain tasks are constrained, by being marked "must start on" or must finish on" specific dates, this limits the leveling capability of Microsoft Project.

Use priority, under the General tab, to indicate an order of preference. In the Task Information dialog box, you can also use the Priority section to increase or decrease the priority level, or to mark tasks as "Do not level" to block leveling for a particular task. You can also assign nine levels of priority, from lowest to highest.

Resource Graph

The resource graph displays a histogram that represents the assignments for a resource or resource group. With the resource histogram, you can quickly see if and when a resource is overallocated. The histogram can also be used to see assignment levels when you see a message to level a resource in the status bar at the bottom of your screen; for example, "Level Chris Tomathy" in the status bar.

Communication and Resources

To display the resource graph, click on **View** or press **Alt/V**, then choose **Resource Graph**. The resource graph presents a graphic view of assignments for a selected time period. See Figure 4-15. Notice that Jim is overassigned on in April and May. On one day he is overallocated by only two hours, but on the next day, he is overallocated by twelve hours! More of a challenge than anyone would like. Adjustments in the schedule will need to be made.

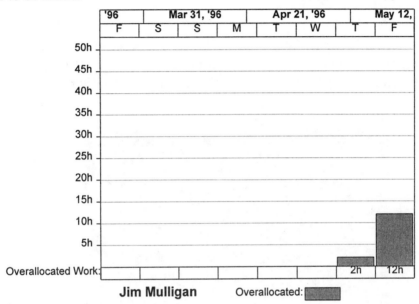

Figure 4-15. Resource Graph

When the resource graph is shown on your screen, you can use the horizontal scroll bar to move forward or backward in time. This will enable you to see the peaks and valleys in the scheduling of any resource or class of resource. Once you detect overcommitted resources, you can adjust your schedule and resource assignments one-by-one to reduce or eliminate overcommitment, or you can ask Microsoft Project to level resources for you, as described above.

Fast Lane Tip #33

To locate a resource overallocation

1. Click on **View**, or press **Alt/V**, then choose **Resource Graph**. You will see the resource graph.

The Complete Planning Guide for Microsoft® Project

2. Click on **View**, or press **Alt/V**. Then choose **Zoom**. You will see the Zoom dialog box, shown below.

3. Choose **Entire Project**.

4. Click on **OK** or press **Enter**. The histograms will display overallocations in red, or in bold on a monochrome monitor.

If you have the resource management toolbar displayed, you can also use the **Go To Overallocation** button to locate resource overallocations for specific resources.

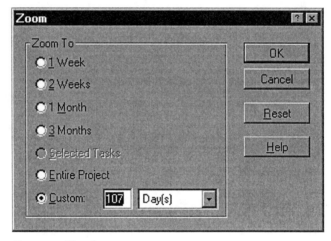

Figure 4-16. Zoom on Resource Graph

Replacing a Resource

In most projects, people come and go. You will need to add resources, remove resources, and replace resources. All of these functions can be performed using the Resource Assignment dialog box. Earlier you assigned resources; now you are likely to remove and replace one or more resources.

To remove a resource from a task, click on ![icon], or press **Alt/I** and choose **Resource Assignment**. You will see the Resource Assignment dialog box, shown below.

Communication and Resources

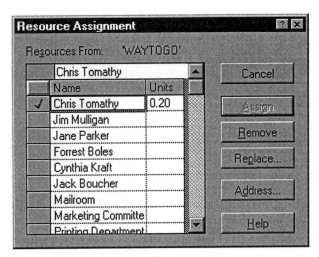

Figure 4-17. Removing and Replacing a Resource Assignment

To remove a resource, select the resource and choose **Remove**.

To replace a resource, select the resource to be replaced, then choose **Replace**. Select the new resource to be assigned, and choose **OK**.

THE PROJECT FUNDING AND BUDGET

Most projects, including the newsletter project, require funding approval. In new product development, a proposal that includes a business plan is typically included with program and project documentation. In most cases, a project budget must be prepared and approved before a project can begin in earnest.

By entering standard rates and other costs on the resource sheet, and then assigning resources to tasks, you have enabled Microsoft Project to accumulate project costs. This ability to accumulate costs will help you in developing a cost estimate and budget for your project, and in tracking costs as the project unfolds. As discussed earlier, the pivot tables created by Microsoft Project in Microsoft Excel can be used to create a wide variety of graphs and reports.

If you use Microsoft® Excel, you can export additional tables from Microsoft Project to Excel and perform various calculations and updates. You can also import the transformed data back into Microsoft Project. See Chapter 8.

On most projects, costs need to be estimated and monitored closely. Microsoft Project provides a variety of tables, views, and reports to help with this project management responsibility. The cost table will be discussed here; reports will be discussed in Chapter 7.

Fast Lane Tip #34

To see cost estimates (and actual costs and variances after the project begins)

1. Click on **View**, or press **Alt/V**.
2. Choose **Cost**. You will see the standard cost table shown in Table 4-5.

Table 4-5. Cost table

ID	Task Name	Fixed Cost	Total Cost	Baseline	Variance	Actual	Remaining
	Way To Go Newsletter #1	$0.00	$12,386.30	$11,936.55	$449.75	$5,873.80	$6,512.50
1	Define Budget Requirement	$0.0	$266.0	$266.0	$0.0	$266.0	$0.0
2	Start project	$0.0	$0.0	$0.0	$0.0	$0.0	$0.0
3	Estimate production costs	$0.0	$190.0	$190.0	$0.0	$190.0	$0.0
4	Obtain budget approvals	$0.0	$76.0	$76.0	$0.0	$76.0	$0.0
5	Schedule Production	$0.0	$1,138.0	$313.0	$825.0	$838.0	$300.0
6	Set production schedule	$0.0	$213.0	$138.0	$75.0	$213.0	$0.0
7	List potential topics for art	$0.0	$700.0	$75.0	$625.0	$400.0	$300.0
8	Submit topics to marketin	$0.0	$200.0	$50.0	$150.0	$200.0	$0.0
9	Assign topics	$0.0	$25.0	$50.0	($25.00)	$25.0	$0.0
10	Create Layout and Masthead	$0.0	$384.8	$310.0	$74.7	$384.8	$0.0
11	Brainstorming session of	$0.0	$177.8	$177.8	$0.0	$177.8	$0.0
12	Create three preliminary	$0.0	$92.0	$92.0	$0.0	$92.0	$0.0
13	Compare designs and sel	$0.0	$23.0	$11.5	$11.5	$23.0	$0.0
14	Develop final design	$0.0	$92.0	$28.7	$63.2	$92.0	$0.0
15	Obtain approval	$0.0	$0.0	$0.0	$0.0	$0.0	$0.0
16	Write Newsletter Content	$0.0	$4,201.0	$4,701.0	($500.00)	$4,201.0	$0.0
17	Select staff to write article	$0.0	$37.5	$100.0	($62.50)	$37.5	$0.0
18	Recruit freelance writers	$0.0	$1,500.0	$2,000.0	($500.00)	$1,500.0	$0.0
19	Set deadlines	$0.0	$75.0	$75.0	$0.0	$75.0	$0.0
20	Write articles	$0.0	$2,062.5	$2,000.0	$62.5	$2,062.5	$0.0
21	Make revisions	$0.0	$400.0	$400.0	$0.0	$400.0	$0.0
22	Approve final copy	$0.0	$76.0	$76.0	$0.0	$76.0	$0.0
23	Submit diskette to deskto	$0.0	$50.0	$50.0	$0.0	$50.0	$0.0
24	Edit and Revise Layout and	$0.0	$165.0	$115.0	$50.0	$115.0	$50.0

The cost table contains columns for Fixed Cost, Total Cost, Baseline, Variance, Actual, and Remaining Costs. Only fixed costs are isolated. Cost per time period and cost per use are accumulated under Total Cost together with fixed costs.

Total Cost reflects the expected project cost based on the current schedule. Baseline indicates the project budget after the baseline is saved. Variance is the difference between the actual costs to date and the baseline costs to date. Remaining costs are the costs that are expected to be incurred for the remainder of the project.

COMPANION PRODUCTS RELATED TO THIS CHAPTER*

CC: Mail, electronic mail for updating project status; Lotus Development Corporation 1-800-346-1305.

C/S Glue, software tool to integrate cost and schedule analysis; Program Management Solutions (805) 898-9571.

I/CSCS, software tool to analyze and measure project cost performance; Lucas Management Systems (714) 851-1999.

Lotus Notes®, software tool for team discussion, Lotus Development Corporation 1-800-346-1305.

Microsoft® Mail, electronic mail for updating project status; Microsoft Corporation 1-800-426-9400

PlanView, software tool for managing work and resources; PLANVIEW Inc. (512) 346-8600.

Project ToolBox, software tool for resource scheduling; adRem Technologies, (201) 740-0337.

TeamLinks, software tool for team communications; Digital Equipment Corporation 1-800-DIGITAL.

TEAMPROJECT, software tool for team discussion; Strategy Software Corporation 1-800-541-TEAM.

TeamTalk, software tool for team discussion; Trax Softworks, Inc. 1-800-367-8729.

TimeKeeper Windows, software tool to manage time and expenses; WSG (212) 675-2500.

TimeSheet Professional, software tool for time management and resource management for workgroups; TIMESLIPS Corporation (214) 248-9293.

WorkGroup Billing, software tool for time recording, invoicing and receivables, WorkGroup Solutions (206) 726-9377.

*Not all of these tools are designed for Version 4.1.

5

Scheduling The Project

In this chapter you will learn how to:

1. Schedule a project

2. Indicate predecessors and successors

3. Establish lead and lag relationships

4. Reduce project duration

5. Save the project baseline

INTRODUCTION

In this chapter you will examine a variety of views and charts that can be used to plan, schedule, and manage projects of every size. You will analyze the sequence of project work, and look for opportunities to do work concurrently.

You will also finalize your schedule by adding the information necessary to create a project calendar, Gantt chart, and a task network, referred to as a PERT Chart in Microsoft® Project. In addition, you will also seek opportunities to reduce project duration. When all planning is complete you will save the project baseline.

PROJECT SCHEDULING

A *project schedule* is a timetable for the accomplishment of project work. It requires detailed information about what is to be done, often in the form of requirements and specifications. It also requires the commitment of resources to the schedule. In virtually all projects, rescheduling should be done at regular intervals.

A project schedule is needed to manage both tasks and resources. To begin scheduling, a detailed breakdown of the project, usually in the form of a work breakdown structure, is needed. When project scheduling is attempted without breaking the work down to a sufficient level of detail, it is likely to bear little resemblance to what will actually occur.

Accuracy in project scheduling also requires the commitment and coordination of people and other resources. A project schedule is needed to manage the resources. When resources are routinely committed and then suddenly removed, few projects can succeed. Attempt to assign people to as few projects as possible. Although most of us must juggle several projects at once, it is difficult to maintain concentration and momentum when being asked to do this on a daily basis.

If your project is like most projects, more tasks will need to be added as the project unfolds, changing the schedule accordingly. This is a part of working in a project environment. There are at least five factors that increase this probability:

- Degree of "newness" represented by the project

- Size of the project

- Extent to which collaboration among the team is important
- Amount of experience that the team has working together
- Permanence of the project scope

Each factor is described in the following sections.

Newness

To some extent every project is unique. What this means to scheduling is that if the project is very similar to a previous project, there is a higher likelihood that all of the work will be identified while planning. On the other hand, if half of the project involves doing something that the team hasn't done before, you can be assured that the project will take some unexpected twists and turns. This occurs in advanced engineering projects and other "breakthrough" projects.

Size

A small project with fifty or fewer tasks is less likely to increase its scope than a project with hundreds or thousands of tasks.

Collaboration

Teams that require much ongoing interaction, such as system development teams, may discover possibilities for new "bells and whistles" that can be added. They may suggest changes in the functions of the software that will improve efficiency. When the customer or client approves the system changes, the original project scope expands.

Team Experience

In marketing departments, marketeers may work together frequently on projects. The teams in this environment may have developed their own "verbal shorthand" over many projects, months, or years. They understand one another, and take less time to communicate in most cases. This also happens in finance, engineering, and manufacturing. When team members have little or no experience working together, misunderstandings occur more often, resulting in project delays.

Permanence

In certain complex projects, such as software development and system development, it may not be possible to define the scope for the entire project at the outset. A project that includes installing off-the-shelf software, new software, customized programming, installation, and integration may evolve incrementally. In this type of project environment, scope changes are expected, and defined in a life cycle model such as the rapid application development (RAD) and evolutionary life cycles. See the Bibliography for readings on life cycle models.

Microsoft Project provides several views that assist in scheduling a project and managing tasks. Three will be discussed here:

- The calendar view—displays a common calendar view that can display a five-day or seven-day work week. It displays bars in which the name of the task is shown if the duration is long enough.

- The Gantt chart—displays tasks and other columns of data on the left side of the window, and task bars representing each task's duration on the right.

- The PERT chart—displays a task network that shows a box or node for each task. The tasks can be easily moved to any location.

Each of these will be explained in the following sections.

THE CALENDAR VIEW

The calendar view provides a familiar and useful format for examining project work. For small projects, such as the newsletter project, it may be possible to display all project work using this view. For larger projects, it can be useful when filtered to show the work of certain resources or for limited categories of project work such as critical tasks. It looks like an ordinary calendar, and includes project tasks and the related information that you choose.

To display the calendar view, click on **View** or press **Alt/V**, then choose **Calendar**. You will see a view that is similar to the window shown below.

Scheduling The Project

Figure 5-1. Calendar View with Seven-Day Week

To advance one week at a time, click on the arrows located on the vertical scroll bar at the right of the calendar. To move backward or forward one month, click on  , located in the top right corner of the calendar.

To display weekly dates in the leftmost column as shown in the display, click on **Format** or press **Alt/O**, then choose **Timescale Beside Weekly Titles** choose a date format such as **12/1/96**, and press **OK**.

The appearance of the calendar can be changed to display either seven-day weeks or five-day weeks.

Fast Lane Tip #35

To change the calendar display from seven days to five days

1. Click on **Format,** or press **Alt/O**.
2. Choose **Timescale**. You will see the box shown in Figure 5-2.
3. Choose the **Week Headings** tab.
4. Beneath **Display** click on **5 days**, or use the **Tab** key to move to 7 days, then type the number **5**.
5. Click on **OK**, or use the **Tab** key to move to **OK**, and press **Enter**.

127

The Complete Planning Guide for Microsoft® Project

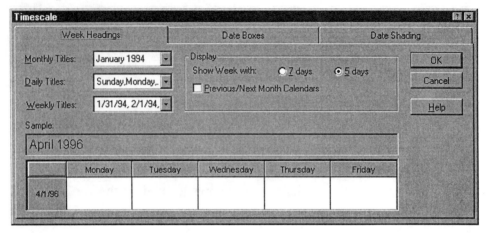

Figure 5-2. Calendar Timescale Dialog Box

After you have changed the calendar display to show five-day weeks, it will appear as shown below in Figure 5-3. Notice that there is now more room to display tasks from left to right. Place the cursor between the date columns and drag left or right to decrease or increase the width of the display.

To increase or decrease the height of calendar rows, place the cursor beneath the task bars on the line just above the bar that displays dates. When you see the ↕ symbol, drag upward or downward to increase or decrease cell height.

Figure 5-3. Calendar View with Five-Day Week.

Fast Lane Tip #36

To display all tasks scheduled for a particular date using a mouse

Scheduling The Project

Double-click the shaded area at the top of a date box beside the date. This will display a list of all tasks scheduled for a particular date, their duration, start and finish dates. See Figure 5-4.

Name	Duration	Start	Finish
✓ Newsletter #1	64.21d	Mon 4/1/96	Fri 6/28/96
✓ Assign topics	4h	Fri 4/5/96	Mon 4/8/96
✓ List potential topics for articles	6h	Fri 4/5/96	Mon 4/8/96
✓ Select staff to write articles	8h	Mon 4/8/96	Tue 4/9/96
✓ Create three preliminary designs	16h	Fri 4/5/96	Mon 4/8/96

Tasks occurring on: April 8, 1996
Double-click a task to see task details.

Figure 5-4. Calendar View Daily Tasks List

Creating a Task

You can create a task while in the calendar view. To create a task using a mouse:

Fast Lane Tip #37

To create a task in the calendar view using a mouse

1. Place the cursor beneath the date on which you would like the task to begin.

2. Click and drag the cursor to the right, far enough so that it represents the duration of the task. You will create a task bar. As you drag, you will see a box that displays the scheduled start and scheduled finish dates for the task.

3. Double-click on the task bar to open the Task Information dialog box.

4. Enter the task name, predecessors, priority, and other information as desired.

5. Click on **OK**, or press **Enter**.

> Reminder: You can move between sections of a dialog box by using the Tab key. Use the arrow keys to scroll among choices.

Editing Task Information

You can make many changes to task information, such as adding or removing predecessor-successor relationships, or changing the task priority, resources, or constraints, and much more. Table 5-1 displays information about making various edits.

Table 5-1. Changes to the calendar view

To change task details	Double-click on a task bar to make changes to the Task Information dialog box.
To change formats for placement of text in boxes, month and day titles, patterns and colors for date boxes	Double-click on the month and year located at the top left of the calendar view, or press **Alt/O**, then choose **Timescale** (see Figure 5-2). When you see the Timescale dialog box, experiment with choices, and make changes as necessary.

To change the appearance of gridlines	Click on **Format**, or press **Alt/O**, then choose **Gridlines**. When you see the Gridlines dialog box (shown in Figure 5-5), experiment with choices, and make changes as necessary.

Scheduling The Project

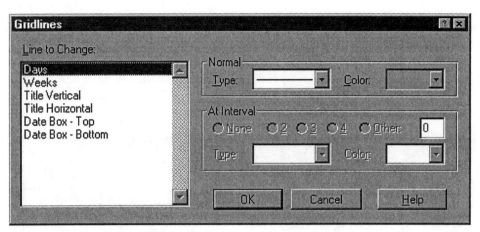

Figure 5-5. Calendar Gridlines Dialog Box

| To change the appearance of text | Click on **Format**, or press **Alt/O**, then choose **Text Styles**. When you see the Text Styles dialog box (shown in Figure 5-6), experiment with choices, and make changes as necessary. |

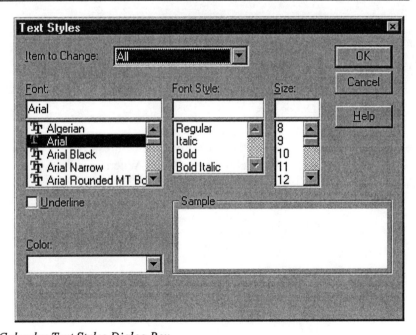

Figure 5-6. Calendar Text Styles Dialog Box

131

The Complete Planning Guide for Microsoft® Project

To change the appearance of bars	Click on **Format**, or press **Alt/O**, then choose **Bar Styles**. When you see the Bar Styles dialog box (shown in Figure 5-7), experiment with choices, and make changes as necessary.

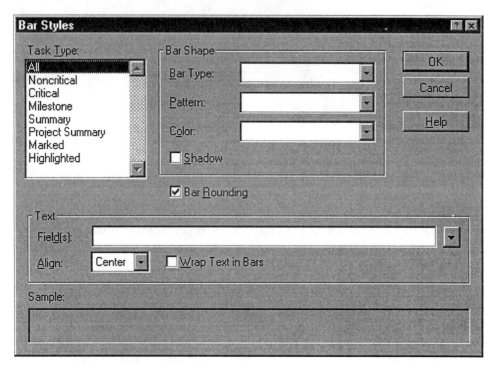

Figure 5-7. Calendar Bar Styles Dialog Box

To change the calendar layout	Click on **Format**, or press **Alt/O**, then choose **Layout**. When you see the Layout dialog box (shown in Figure 5-8), experiment with choices, and make changes as necessary.

Scheduling The Project

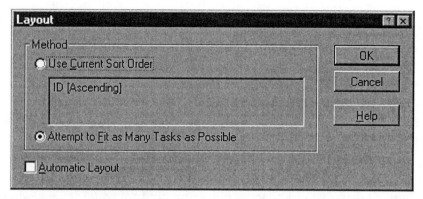

Figure 5-8. Calendar Layout Dialog Box

Fast Lane Tip #38

To change and format data in the calendar view with a mouse

1. Click on any date in the calendar, or use the arrow keys to move to a particular date.
2. Click either the left or the right mouse button to see a list of choices that include:

- Task List
- Go To
- Timescale
- Gridlines
- Text Styles
- Bar Styles
- Zoom
- Layout
- Layout Now
- Split

Most functions can be performed in many ways. However, you will increase your overall efficiency if you can become adept at using a mouse as well as the keyboard.

THE GANTT CHART

The Gantt chart, also known as a bar chart, was invented by Henry Gantt during World War I. It was given his name posthumously. The Gantt chart provides a quickly understood picture of an entire project, and is best used to plan and manage a project when it is paired with a task network, referred to as a PERT chart in Microsoft® Project. In its basic form, it displays tasks, and a corresponding schedule is represented by bars. The Gantt chart is the default view.

What a Gantt chart or bar chart does not do well for a large project is show predecessor-successor relationships, commonly known as *dependency relationships*, or simply *task relationships*. This is especially true on projects with hundreds or thousands of activities and tasks. Since many pages are required to show all activities and tasks on a large project, it may be impossible to see exactly which lines connect specific predecessors or successors.

An excerpt from a reengineering project is shown below. Figure 5-9 displays a basic Gantt chart. At the left of this Gantt chart are two columns of data: the first shows the ID number for tasks and the second shows the task name. The ID number is the number that Microsoft Project uses to identify predecessors and successors.

The Gantt bar section is located to the right of the table columns. To the right of each task name is its corresponding bar. The length of each individual task bar is determined by the task's duration. To show the horizontal bars on the Gantt chart when they are not displayed, click on the divider bar (it divides the Gantt table on the left from the bars on the right) and drag it to the left as far as needed.

On this particular Gantt chart, lines display dependency relationships, and the names of responsible team members are shown beside the task bars in the Gantt bar section. Only two columns of data are displayed on the table side: ID number and Task Name.

Scheduling The Project

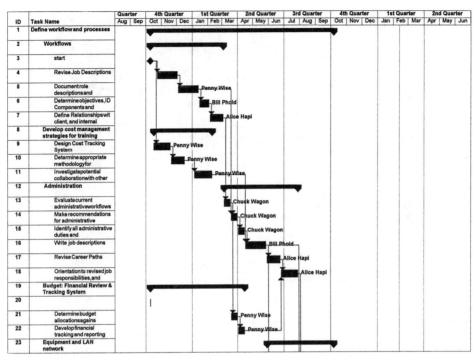

Figure 5-9. Reengineering Gantt Chart

Notice that summary tasks are indicated by a long bar with downward-pointing arrows at each end. These are default settings. The length of the bar for summary tasks reflects the duration of all subtasks as well as predecessor-successor relationships.

Editing the Gantt Chart

Changes can be made to the information and graphics in several ways. Each section below displays a method for making various changes in the appearance of the Gantt chart by using the menu bar, submenus and dialog boxes.

To change font, font style, size and color, and to add underline.	Click on **Format** or press **Alt/O**, then choose **Font**. When you see the Font dialog box (shown in Figure 5-10), experiment with choices, and make changes as necessary.

The Complete Planning Guide for Microsoft® Project

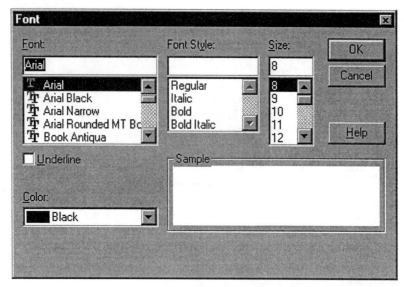

Figure 5-10. Gantt Font Dialog Box

To change the appearance of Gantt bars	Click on **Format**, or press **Alt/O**, then choose **Bar**. When you see the Format Bar dialog box (shown in Figure 5-11), experiment with choices, and make changes as necessary.

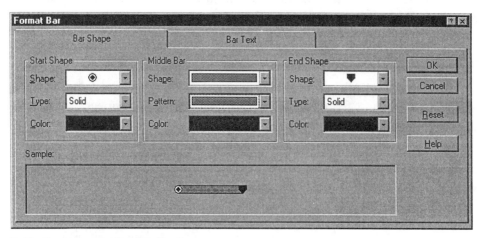

Figure 5-11. Gantt Format Bar Dialog Box

Scheduling The Project

To change the timescale used to display Gantt bars	Double-click the timescale, or press **Alt/O**, then choose **Timescale**. When you see the Timescale dialog box (shown in Figure 5-12), experiment with choices, and make changes as necessary.

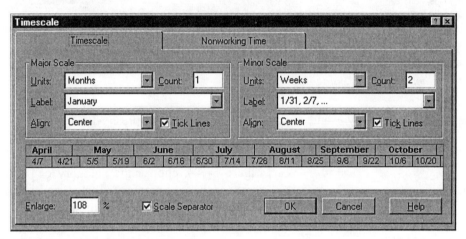

Figure 5-12. Gantt Timescale Dialog Box

To add, remove or make changes to gridlines	Click on **Format**, or press **Alt/O**, then choose **Gridlines**. When you see the Gridlines dialog box (shown in Figure 5-13), experiment with choices, and make changes as necessary.

The Complete Planning Guide for Microsoft® Project

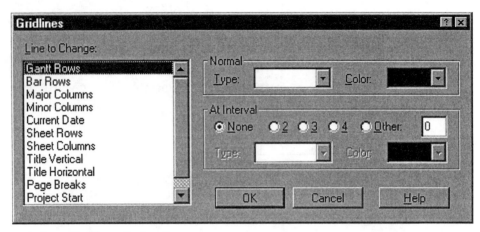

Figure 5-13. Gantt Gridlines Dialog Box

To change Font, font style and size, and to add underline to a category of tasks.	Click on **Format**, or press **Alt/O**, then choose **Text Styles**. When you see the Text Styles dialog box (shown in Figure 5-14), choose the category of tasks such as Summary Tasks, and change the appearance as desired.

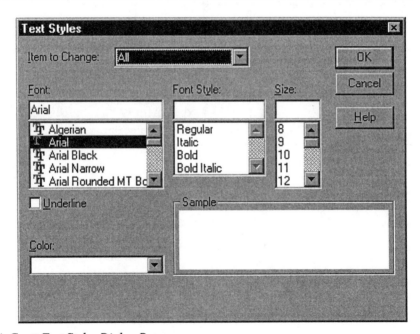

Figure 5-14. Gantt Text Styles Dialog Box

Scheduling The Project

To change the appearance of bars for a category of tasks	Click on **Format**, or press **Alt/O**, then choose **Bar Styles**. When you see the Bar Styles dialog box (shown in Figure 5-16), choose the category of tasks such as Summary Tasks, and change the appearance as desired.

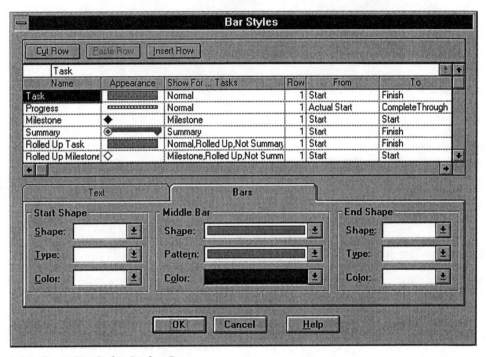

Figure 5-15. Gantt Bar Styles Dialog Box

To select or remove a line connecting predecessors and successors	Click on **Format**, or press **Alt/O**, then choose **Layout**. When you see the Layout dialog box (shown in Figure 5-16), experiment with the choices. Choose whether or not to display these lines, and the style of the links.

The Complete Planning Guide for Microsoft® Project

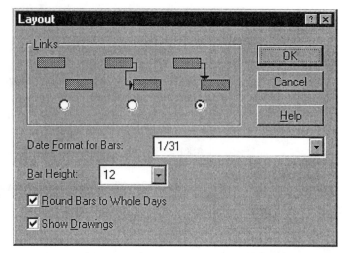

Figure 5-16. Gantt Bar Layout Dialog Box

Fast Lane Tip #39

To change the format of the Gantt bar section

1. With your cursor in an open area, click on the right mouse button.
2. Use either the left or right mouse button to choose from the following options:

- Gridlines
- Text Styles
- Layout
- Non-Working Time
- Gantt Chart Wizard
- Split (to display the task form at the bottom of the page)

Scheduling The Project

How to Use the Gantt Chart Wizard

The Gantt Chart Wizard provides a fast way to format the Gantt chart. With a series of questions and choices, you can choose whether or not to change the appearance of task bars, display resource names, and make several other choices.

For example, if you want to show the bars on the Gantt chart, the Gantt Chart Wizard will ask you three questions about:

- Which tasks to display
- Color scheme
- Whether or not you would like to use arrows to indicate predecessor-successor relationships

To use the wizard, click the **Gantt Chart Wizard** button/icon located at the right end of the standard toolbar. You will be prompted with a series of questions.

The Planning Wizard

In addition to the Gantt Chart Wizard, Microsoft Project also has an intelligent Planning Wizard working for you behind the scenes. (The Planning Wizard showed up in Chapter 1 when Chris saved her file, and asked her if she wanted to save the baseline.) The Planning Wizard can help you in many ways.

If the wizard notices that you are doing a repetitive task, such as entering 100% complete for three consecutive tasks, it will suggest that you select them all at once and then click on 100%!

If you have indicated that a task has another task as both its predecessor and successor, the Planning Wizard will alert you and caution you about the consequences of taking that action. If you create a loop among several tasks, the Planning Wizard will alert you.

> Caution: If you create a loop in your schedule, many scheduling functions such as schedule calculation, are immediately disabled.

Regardless of your skill level, it is probably a good idea to leave Planning Wizard functions operating. Advice about scheduling and errors may prevent you from making errors that could have disastrous results, such as creating dependency loops. The one exception, which was noted earlier is the Save Baseline appearance by the Planning Wizard.

You can make choices about the Planning Wizard functions by going to the **Tools** menu and choosing **Options** then the **General** tab.

TYPES OF PREDECESSOR-SUCCESSOR TASK RELATIONSHIPS

All of the tasks in every project should be connected to at least one predecessor and at least one successor. A *predecessor* is a task that immediately precedes one or more other tasks. A *successor* is a task that immediately succeeds one or more other tasks.

Fast Lane Tip #40

To establish predecessor-successor relationships in the Gantt bar section

Click and drag the cursor from a predecessor to a successor. This establishes a link only if the link icon is displayed while you drag the cursor.

The vast majority of dependency relationships are *finish-to-start* relationships. This means that an activity or task cannot start until its predecessor is finished.

Less common dependency relationships include:

Start-to-start—when one task begins, another can also begin. Under the Predecessor column, enter the ID number (located in the first column on the left), and then **ss**. For example, 44ss (upper and lower case both work) indicates that when ID number 44 starts, this task can also start.

Finish-to-finish—when one task ends, another can also end. Under the Predecessor column, enter the ID number of the predecessor and an **ff**. For example, 35ff means that the milestone where your cursor is located cannot finish until its predecessor is finished.

Lead time (or overlap)—a task can begin after a certain amount of time has elapsed, or after a certain percent complete. For example, if you enter **44ss+10d** it means that this milestone can begin ten days after its predecessor begins.

Lag time (or gap)—a task cannot begin until after a certain amount of time has passed after its predecessor is a certain percent complete. For example, if you enter **48fs+28d**, the successor cannot begin until 28 days have elapsed since the predecessor was complete.

Fast Lane Tip #41

To change task duration on the Gantt bar using the mouse

1. Place the cursor on the right border of a task bar until you see a small vertical line with an arrow pointing to the right.
2. Drag the image to the left to increase duration or right to decrease duration. While you drag, the amount of duration is displayed in a small rectangle.

An excerpt of the Gantt chart from the newsletter project is shown below in Figure 5-17. This chart was printed after predecessor-successor relationships were defined, and it displays the WBS number and responsible person. Notice that the symbols used on the bars have been customized by using the Bar Styles dialog box, and display the amount of free slack with a thin line. The line represents the amount of free slack. Free slack begins with the early finish date and ends with the late finish date. If the task slips beyond the late finish date, it may become part of the critical path.

The Complete Planning Guide for Microsoft® Project

ID	WBS	WBS	Task Name	Resp	Predec	Succes	3/3	4/7 April 5/12	6/16	7/21 July 8/25	9/29 October 11/3	12/8
		0	Newsletter #1									
1	1	1	Define Budget Requirements									
2	1.1	1.1	Start project			3						
3	1.2	1.2	Estimate production costs	Chris Tomathy[0.2	2	4						
4	1.3	1.3	Obtain budget approvals	Chris Tomathy[0.2	3	6,11,52FS+50d						
5	2	2	Schedule Production									
6	2.1	2.1	Set production schedule	Chris Tomathy[0.2	4	7						
7	2.2	2.2	List potential topics for articles	Jim Mulligan[0.5	6	8FS-1d						
8	2.3	2.3	Submit topics to marketing committee	Jim Mulligan[0.5	7FS-1d	9						
9	2.4	2.4	Assign topics	Jim Mulligan[0.5	8	17						
10	3	3	Create Layout and Masthead Design									
11	3.1	3.1	Brainstorming session of design ideas	Jim Mulligan,Jan	4	12						
12	3.2	3.2	Create three preliminary designs	Forrest Boles[0.25]	11	13						
13	3.3	3.3	Compare designs and select best design	Forrest Boles[0.25]	12	14						
14	3.4	3.4	Develop final design	Forrest Boles[0.25]	13	15						
15	3.5	3.5	Obtain approval	Marketing Committee	14	19						
16	4	4	Write Newsletter Content									
17	4.1	4.1	Select staff to write articles	Jim Mulligan[0.5	9	19,18						
18	4.2	4.2	Recruit freelance writers	Jim Mulligan[0.5	17	19						
19	4.3	4.3	Set deadlines	Jim Mulligan[0.5	17,18,15	20						
20	4.4	4.4	Write articles	Jim Mulligan[0.7	19	21						
21	4.5	4.5	Make revisions	Jim Mulligan[0.5	20	22						
22	4.6	4.6	Approve final copy	Chris Tomathy[0.2	21	23						

Figure 5-17. Gantt Chart Excerpt From The Newsletter Project

Fast Lane Tip #42

To display free slack beside task bars

1. Click on **Format**, or press **Alt/O**.

2. Choose **Bar Styles**. You will see the Bar Styles dialog box.

3. Using the cursor or the tab key and down arrow, move to the first empty space beneath the Name column. Type **Free Slack** and press the right arrow key. You will see a large bar beneath the **appearance** column.

4. Using the cursor or **Tab** key, move to the **Shape** section near the bottom under the Bars tab.

5. Use the cursor or press the **A** key to see the bar and line choices, and choose the last

Scheduling The Project

option, using the cursor or down arrow key a thin line (or another choice).

6. Select the **Show For...** Tasks column, and move to the entry bar near the top of the dialog box. Use the scrolling arrow to select **Noncritical**.

7. Move to the **From** column and use the entry bar and scroll arrow to select **Early Finish**.

8. Move to the **To** column and use the entry bar and scroll arrow to select **Late Finish**.

9. Choose **OK**. Your Gantt chart will display free slack to the right of each task that has free slack, as shown above.

Additional Gantt charts are shown in Chapter 7.

THE PERT CHART

The task network used in Microsoft® Project is referred to as a *PERT chart*. It is also referred to as a *network diagram, precedence diagram, arrow diagram, CPM chart* and other names in various project management circles. PERT is an acronym for Program Evaluation and Review Technique, which was developed in 1958 through a collaboration of the United States Navy, Booz-Allen Hamilton, and Lockheed Corporation. It is a task network that uses a box, sometimes known as a node to display a task and related details, such as ID number, WBS number, duration, and start and finish dates. Figure 5-18 displays an excerpt of the PERT task network from the newsletter project.

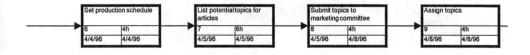

Figure 5-18. PERT Task Network Excerpt

For large projects, many program and project managers have found the task network an indispensable tool for both planning and managing their projects. A task network displays the flow of all project work, beginning at the left, proceeding through several paths, and ending at the right. A *path* is a sequence of tasks that are connected by predecessor-successor relationships. The *critical path* is the path with the longest duration. It is the result of a calculation by Microsoft Project that adds the durations of every path in the task network, and identifies the longest path.

All tasks on the critical path need to be managed closely. This is because if any task on the critical path is delayed or takes longer than planned, the entire project will be delayed unless an alternative strategy can be found. Tasks that are not located on the critical path are known as *noncritical tasks*, and do have some amount of slack.

Two types of slack are identified for each task: free slack and total slack. *Free slack* is the amount of time that a task can be delayed without delaying a successor task.

Total slack the amount of time that a task can be delayed without delaying the project. No task on the critical path has any free slack or total slack. These are the default settings.

All or part of the critical path may change during the course of most projects. If, for example, a noncritical task is suddenly delayed beyond available total slack, that task and certain successors are likely to become part of the critical path.

The Fourth Team Meeting

Before the fourth team meeting, Chris made several phone calls to enter the necessary resource information. She was able to enter rates for each resource, as well as his or her availability for the project. This will add much precision to the schedule. During the meeting, the team will finalize the schedule.

Scheduling The Project

When the team meets, they will actually build a task network for the project, and then enter the information into the Microsoft® Project file. The team will also need to decide about how they should meet to update one another. Should they all plan for one hour each week? It doesn't seem necessary for everyone to be at every meeting. The team will need to discuss this.

Creating the Task Network with Stickies

At this meeting, Chris will facilitate the development of a task network for the team. After the task network is complete, she will enter the predecessors and successors into the WAYTOGO1 file and create a PERT task network.

Resources needed:

- "Stickies" for every project task. Each should indicate the task name and WBS number. In addition, create a sticky note for the Start of the project, and one for the Finish.

  > Note: "stickies", or sticky notes are small, adhesive-backed notes. The recommended size is 3" by 3".

- Markers with wide tips, such as those used to write on transparencies. The names of tasks will be easier for team members to read from a distance of 6-10 feet as the task network is being developed.

- A wall on which you can place stickies. You can also tape or pin large sheets of paper, such as flip chart paper, on a wall.

- A PC, workstation, or terminal loaded with Microsoft® Project, and a person who is skilled in using the tool.

    1. Place a START stickie/node at the far left of your working area, in the vertical center.

    2. Beside the START node, to its right, in a vertical column, place every task that can begin immediately. **Be sure to consider resource limitations**. For example, if you have only four team members, it is usually impossible to begin ten tasks.

    3. For each task/stickie, ask: "When this task is complete, or partially complete, which tasks can begin?" Place these nodes to the immediate right of their predecessors. Recall that:

- Lead time indicates that a successor activity can begin after its predecessor has reached a certain point, such as a number of days or a percent complete.

- A lag, or delay, indicates that a successor can begin once a period of time has elapsed after completion of its predecessor.

4. Using a pencil, draw arrows to connect activities and to convey predecessor-successor relationships. The larger the project, the more likely it is that you will need to make revisions later.

5. Working from left to right, complete the task network.

6. After all tasks have been connected, use arrows to connect the last tasks to the "Finish" node.

7. When complete, enter all predecessor-successor information into Microsoft® Project. It will calculate the project duration, end date, critical path, start and finish dates for all activities, as well as the amount and location of slack time. The critical path is normally drawn in red or with a darker line.

8. Use the PERT view to rearrange tasks as necessary. You can do this by simply clicking and dragging any task. See the Modifying the PERT Task Network section.

Establishing Predecessor-Successor Relationships

While the team is working on the board, Chris establishes the dependency relationships in Microsoft Project. You can create predecessor-successor relationships in many ways, for example, in the Gantt chart and on the task sheet as shown below.

Fast Lane Tip #43

To establish a predecessor-successor relationship in a Gantt chart or task sheet

1. Select a predecessor and one or more successor tasks. With the keyboard you can do this by holding down the **shift key** while using the up arrow or down arrow to select other adjacent tasks.

   To select a nonadjacent task, click on that task while pressing the **Ctrl** key.

Scheduling The Project

2. Click on ▭, or press **Alt/E**, then choose **Link Tasks**. The tasks will be linked in a predecessor-successor relationship.

Modifying The PERT Task Network

While working in the PERT task network, you can make many changes to its appearance. You can change the location of each task in the task network, change box styles and the information contained in each node, add and remove tasks, change dependency relationships, change text styles, change arrow styles, insert objects, and see an alternate layout for the entire task network.

Before changing the location of tasks in the network, you may save yourself some time by trying the Layout Now command. To do this, click on **Format**, or press **Alt/O**, then choose **Layout Now**. Inspect the new layout to see if all paths and dependency relationships convey the real flow of the project. To change the location of any task in the network, click on and drag the task to its new location.

Fast Lane Tip #44

To change a dependency relationship in the PERT chart to reflect lead or lag time

1. Double-click on the line connecting a predecessor and successor. The Task Dependency dialog box appears.
2. Beside **Type:** , choose the type of task dependency relationship, such as start to start.
3. Beside **Lag**: , enter a duration or percent complete.
4. Click on **OK**.

149

The Complete Planning Guide for Microsoft® Project

You can also reflect lead or lag time from the Gantt chart by using the steps shown below.

1. Click on **View**, or press **Alt/V**.

2. Choose **More Views**.

3. Choose the **task details form** or the **task form**.

4. To add lag time: Beneath the Lag column, enter a number such as **2d** (two days) or 2ed (two elapsed days) to reflect a delay, or lag of two days after the predecessor is complete.

5. To add lead time: Beneath the Lag column, enter a number such as **-1d**, -25 % or 25e % to tell Microsoft Project to give the predecessor one day or 25% lead time before starting.

6. Choose **OK**. The lead or lag time will be reflected in the schedule.

A task box/node from the newsletter project is shown below.

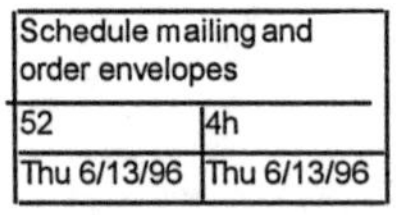

Schedule mailing and order envelopes	
52	4h
Thu 6/13/96	Thu 6/13/96

Figure 5-19. Task Node

This node displays the default settings in each of the five fields. To change the information contained in each box on the PERT chart, select the node, click on **Format**, or press **Alt/O**, then choose **Box Styles**. If necessary, click on the **Boxes** tab or press the right arrow key. You can also display the Box Styles dialog box by clicking the secondary mouse button and then choosing **Box Styles**.

Scheduling The Project

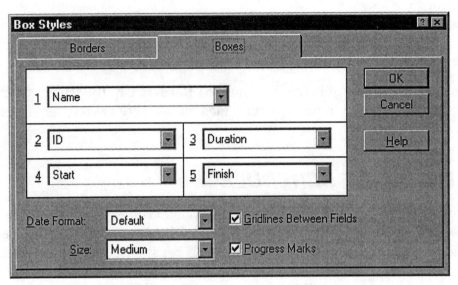

Figure 5-20. Box Styles for the PERT Task Network

When you see the contents of the Boxes tab, use the cursor or Tab key to move to one or more of the fields that you would like to change. Use the scrolling arrow to choose a different field of information. You can choose from more than one hundred fields of information, including user-entered fields. Possible changes can include replacing the following and many other items:

- Replacing the ID number with a WBS number
- Replacing duration with slack
- Replacing the start date with slack

You may want to create more than one PERT task network for different audiences, just as you will with Gantt charts. See Chapter 8 to add additional PERT charts to the View submenu.

The Boxes tab also provides choices about the date format and the size of each box. Use the scrolling arrow to change the date format if desired. If you would like to see a view of the task network that shows only the ID number in each node, make that choice by using the scrolling arrow beside Size. Use a Gantt chart or table with the ID number displayed to quickly identify tasks.

Gridlines Between Fields— inserts lines between the fields of information displayed as shown in Figure 5-19.

Progress Marks—lets Microsoft Project "cross off" tasks on the node as they are partially or wholly completed, as indicated by an X across the node. Remove the check from the checkbox if you would not like to see completed tasks crossed off.

You can change the type of border by using the **Borders** tab. By default, tasks on the critical path are displayed in red on a color monitor. Non-critical tasks are displayed in black.

FINALIZING THE SCHEDULE

After you have entered all scheduling information, you will need to finalize the schedule in preparation for setting the baseline. First, check to see if there is a suggestion such as "Level (resource)" on the status bar at the bottom of the screen. This suggestion indicates that the schedule for that resource is overallocated.

When resource overallocations are identified, you will normally need to have discussions with the person who is overcommitted, and/or his or her manager, gain agreement on a schedule change, and make the change to the schedule. In many cases, you can use Microsoft Project's resource leveling function to level resources, and then confirm the changes with the resource or the manager of the resource.

When a resource is overallocated, there may be a serious scheduling problem. It may be that a resource was "double-booked" at some point during the project. In each instance of overallocation of resources, try to investigate immediately.

Resolving Resource Overallocations

After scheduling is complete on the newsletter project, Chris notices that the message "Level Jim Mulligan" has appeared on the status bar at the bottom of the window. She decides to investigate; she chooses the **Resource Usage View** from the **View** menu, and sees the following:

ID	Resource Name	Work	F	S	S	M	T	W	T	F	S
						Apr 7, '96					
1	Chris Tomathy	10.8									
2	Jim Mulligan	200	7			7h	4	4	4h	4	
3	Jane Parker	6.75				1h					
4	Forrest Boles	15.25				1.5	2	2	1.25		
5	Cynthia Kraft	16.5				2h					
6	Jack Boucher	0.4				0.4					
7	Mailroom	16									
8	Marketing Committee	10.2	0.2						2h		
9	Printing Department	29									

Figure 5-21. Resource Usage View

Scheduling The Project

In looking at the hours assigned, she sees that Jim is assigned for seven hours on Friday, April 5, and on Monday, April 8. All numbers indicate the total hours assigned on that date. Since both of these dates have 7h displayed in red, some part of the number represents an overallocation.

To see the exact amount of overallocation that is involved, Chris next goes to the **Resource Graph**, also on the **View** submenu. There she sees histograms for overallocations and beneath each bar a number of hours representing overallocations. There she sees that Jim is overallocated by three hours on both days. (This is because Jim is assigned to the newsletter project for half of his time, or four hours per day.)

She scrolls to the right and sees that Jim has an open week beginning on April 20, is overallocated on several days in May, and has several open weeks in June. She wants to resolve as many of his overallocations as possible. She has several options to deal with the scheduling conflict; she can:

- Increase Jim's availability by increasing his Max Units on the resource form or other view or form that contains Max Units.

- Use the Resource Leveling function to delay and reschedule Jim's work.

- Get some help for Jim on those dates.

- Ask Jim if he is able to work three extra hours on both April 5 and April 8, or commit to finishing those tasks on schedule.

- Change the sequence of work for Jim's tasks.

She decides to try to play "what if" by choosing the **Resource Leveling** function under the **Tools** menu. She will do this by first using the resource leveling function, then opting to **Revert** to the schedule that existed before using leveling if the changes made by Microsoft Project are unsatisfactory.

When the Resource Leveling dialog box appears, as shown in Figure 5-22, she removes the checkmark beside **Delay Only Within Slack**. She does this to see if she can level Jim's assignments without missing the project goal date. She then chooses **Level Now**. After several prompts, Jim's hours are leveled by delaying his work, and the project can still be completed on time. She saves the changes by clicking on **OK**. She plans to provide an updated schedule at next week's status meeting and to clear up any conflicts at the meeting. She will be sure to talk with Jim if he is not at the meeting.

The Complete Planning Guide for Microsoft® Project

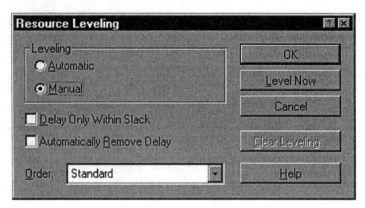

Figure 5-22. Resource Leveling for Jim Mulligan

Next, Chris plans to print a copy of both a Gantt chart and a PERT task network. With the PERT task network, she will re-examine the flow of project work. She will use the Gantt chart to see the timing of tasks in relation to the calendar and the corresponding resource assignments.

Reducing Duration

- Though the newsletter project appears to be on schedule, in most projects you will want to find ways to reduce the project duration. Many reductions in duration can be found by closely examining the tasks with the longest duration. See "Sorting and Filtering" in Chapter 7. Reducing duration is almost always possible by using one or more of the following options.

- Reduce the project scope by excluding certain tasks.

- Reduce the functionality of the product.

- Eliminate certain "bells and whistles."

- Look for opportunities for more concurrent work.

- Make the "finish" task the successor for certain tasks.

- Eliminate end-of-phase work stoppages.

- Use rapid prototyping and iterative prototyping.

- Add resources to a task.

- Schedule overtime.

Scheduling The Project

- Schedule another shift.
- Move resources from noncritical tasks to critical tasks.
- Outsource or subcontract part of the project.

You may discover additional methods for reducing duration.

When Planning Is Complete, Set The Baseline

Detailed planning is essential to project tracking and control. When the project plan is complete, it becomes the basis for comparison to actual results. For this reason, the initial schedule and resource requirements are called the *baseline*. After the baseline is established, actual duration, costs, technical requirements, and quality metrics can be compared to the baseline.

For projects with frequent changes or those that span many months or several years, you can also establish five additional "interim" baselines. On many projects, such as those that will include the development and installation of a software solution, this is a more realistic approach since the requirements may change several times between project kickoff and final customer acceptance of the solution.

The baseline should not be changed without appropriate approvals. In many projects, it is essential that the original baseline and interim baselines be approved and supported by the customer, client, sponsor, and other key stakeholders.

After you have made all necessary changes to resource assignments, schedule, and milestones for a new project, you can "set" the project baseline. This means that you are putting a "stake in the ground" for the project, and are therefore establishing a basis with which to compare the actual schedule and costs.

Fast Lane Tip #45

To save the project baseline

1. Click on **Tools**, or press **Alt/T**.
2. Choose **Tracking**.

The Complete Planning Guide for Microsoft® Project

> 3. Choose **Save Baseline**. You will see the Save Baseline dialog box shown in Figure 5-23.
>
> 4. Click on **OK**.

Use these same steps to save interim baselines.

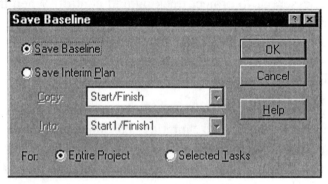

Figure 5-23. Save Baseline Dialog Box

If the project scope changes measurably for whatever reason, and you need to reset the baseline, you would use the **Save Interim Plan** choice at this point. You can set up to five interim plans, including all or just selected parts of the project.

Microsoft Project provides a variety of tables, views and reports that you can use to compare baseline with actual progress. These will be discussed in Chapter 7.

COMPANION PRODUCTS RELATED TO THIS CHAPTER*

GRANEDA Light, software tool to create precedence diagrams, work breakdown structures and organizational breakdown structures; NETRONIC Software GmbH (int) 49-2408-1410.

Milestones, Etc. software tool to create Gantt charts and schedules; Kidasa Software (512) 328-0168.

Project Partner, software tool to create bar charts and task network charts, histograms, S-curves and spreadsheets; GTW Corporation (206) 874-8884.

TimeKeeper Windows, software tool to manage project execution, deadlines, and resources, WSG (212) 675-2500.

TimeSheet Professional, software tool to record actual time, expenses, and notes against projects; TIMESLIPS Corporation (214) 248-9293.

* Not all of these tools are designed for Version 4.1.

6

Managing a Great Many Projects

In this chapter you will learn how to:

1. Use toolbars and tables for project tracking
2. Create a master project and subprojects
3. Consolidate several projects
4. Create a project template
5. Establish links between projects

INTRODUCTION

In many project environments, team members customarily juggle the needs and requirements of several projects at the same time. Learning to manage several projects begins with learning to manage a single project successfully. Equipped with the techniques that are used to manage a single project, you will be able to streamline the management of many projects when you add new Microsoft® Project functions.

In this chapter, you will examine several techniques that will help you to manage one project and several projects. You will see examples of various tables that can be used to give you information about project status. You will learn to use tracking functions, share resources and customized elements among several projects, create subprojects, consolidate projects and save several projects as a workspace.

MANAGING ONE PROJECT

You can massively improve the management of a project by planning in sufficient detail. After you have planned your project in detail, begin project work, implement the communication plan, and maintain a flow of information among stakeholders. As discussed in Chapter 4, establish a system for monitoring cost, schedule, technical and quality information.

How can you tell if you are successful in managing one project? If you have established a schedule, budget, quality metrics, and technical requirements and specifications, your success can be measured by conformance to these plans. In addition, many teams explicitly define the criteria for success.

Central to managing a project in many organizations is the management of the bidding process and then the management of one or more contracts. This effort is enhanced substantially when you have planned your project in detail, and have included completion criteria and a method to measure percent complete.

An ongoing responsibility of many project leaders and managers is to provide the necessary support for the team, including partners and suppliers. This often includes training, and may mean regular negotiations and last-minute changes in assignments. It often means ensuring that team members have the materials, equipment, space, and time to do project work.

Controlling scope creep and the boundaries of a project is another ongoing responsibility. One of the better-known villains in the world of projects is *scope creep*. What this means is that if the scope of a project is not carefully defined and controlled, it will expand. However, even when the scope is clearly defined at the outset, there are many other reasons why new tasks may suddenly need to be added, or other changes made, as shown below:

- Exclusions or "Not-to-be done" items are not clarified
- Team members leave the project
- Communication gaps, caused by geographical separation of team members
- Communication gaps, caused by language and cultural differences
- Materials are delayed or defective
- Equipment breaks down, and workarounds must be developed
- Resource schedules are not honored
- Completion criteria has not been defined, resulting in unnecessary or incomplete work
- A method has not been established to measure degrees of completion
- Requirements change

Controlling project scope and maintaining sufficient project resources are key responsibilities in managing all projects. If you address each of the above items and take the precautions suggested, you will be successful in eliminating most scope creep.

Fast Lane Tip #46

To update percent complete on Gantt chart bars

1. Drag the cursor on the left of the bar until you see a percent sign cursor.
2. Drag to the right or left until you see the desired percent complete, and release the button.

You can also update percent complete by double-clicking on a node while in the PERT task network, then entering the desired percent; or, by clicking on the information button while in either the Gantt chart or Pert chart and entering the percent complete.

The Tracking Toolbar

To manage a single, bounded project or multiple projects, consider displaying the tracking toolbar. The tracking toolbar, shown in Figure 6-1, provides several icons that can be used to update project status. Each will be discussed.

Figure 6-1. Tracking Toolbar

The function of each icon is explained below.

 Project Statistics button—displays statistics on the project schedule, cost, and work, as displayed in Figure 6-2. Using the keyboard, press **Alt/F**, then choose **Project Info** (Version 4.1) or **Summary Info** (Version 4.0), then choose the **Statistics** button.

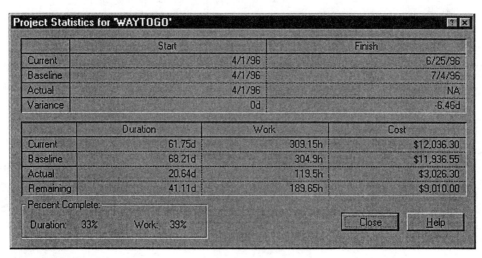

Figure 6-2. Project Statistics Box

Managing a Great Many Projects

Update as Scheduled button—updates selected task(s) to reflect on-schedule accomplishment and percent complete as calculated by the percent of planned duration up to the current date. Using the keyboard, press **Alt/T**, then choose **Tracking** and **Update Project** to see the dialog box shown below.

If the effective date of the update is not the current date, enter the correct date beside **Update Work As Complete Through:** All Actual fields are updated.

If you are using a system in which tasks are either 0% or 100% complete, check the lower percent complete calculation.

At the bottom of the box, ensure that you choose either **Entire Project** or **Selected Tasks**, as appropriate.

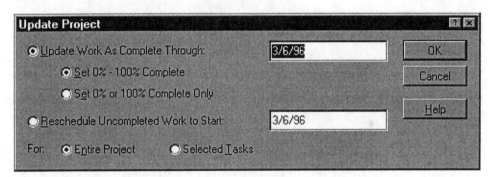

Figure 6-3. Update Project Dialog box

Reschedule Work button—schedules the selected tasks or entire project to continue from the current date or another date. Press **Alt/T**, then choose **Tracking** and **Update Project** to see the same dialog box as shown in Figure 6-3.

Change the date beside **Update Work As Complete Through:** as necessary.

Beside **Reschedule Uncompleted Work to Start:** enter the date to resume work.

163

Update Tasks button can be used to update a selected task while in the Gantt chart, PERT task network or task sheet. With the keyboard, press **Alt/T**, then choose **Tracking** and **Update Tasks** to see the dialog box shown in Figure 6-4.

Update the actual start and finish dates, actual and remaining duration, percent complete, and task notes.

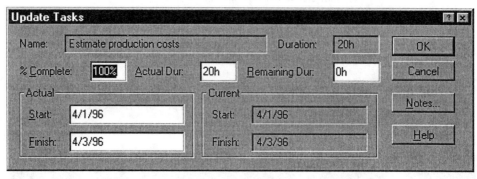

Figure 6-4. Update Tasks Dialog Box

 Update Task Range button—activates a macro that steps you through all tasks in a date range that you define, one-by-one, enabling you to update each task. To do this with the keyboard, choose a table that contains the fields that you would like to update, such as the tracking table or cost table, (discussed later in this chapter).

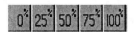 **Update Percent Complete** buttons—for selected tasks to indicate a degree of completion. With the keyboard, select a table that includes percent complete such as the tracking table.

 Update Resources—enables you to update the actual work and schedule dates for all resources or for one resource. Use this button and timesheet to increase the precision of work hours calculation and cost calculation.

Open the Resource Update Options dialog box shown in Figure 6-5, and choose either **All**

Managing a Great Many Projects

Resources or **One Resource**, then enter a date range. Choose **OK**, and you will see the Visual Basic timesheet shown in Figure 6-6. On the timesheet, make changes as necessary and choose **OK**.

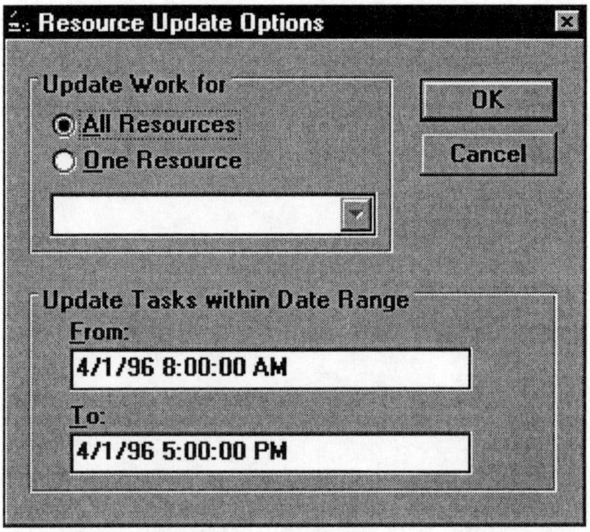

Figure 6-5. Resource Update Options Dialog Box

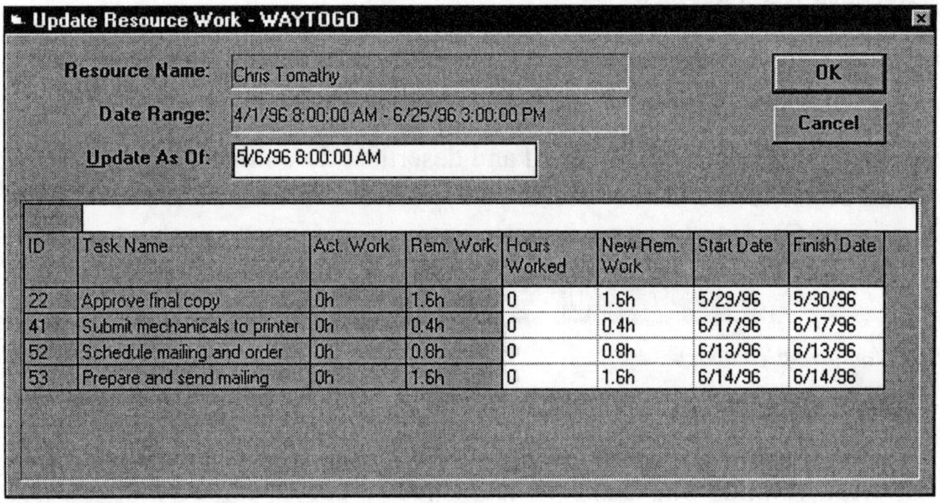

Figure 6-6. Update Resource Work Timesheet

If you would like to manually update the actual hours worked, hours remaining, and schedule dates, use the timesheet as described above. If you would like to let

The Complete Planning Guide for Microsoft® Project

Microsoft® Project calculate work hours and schedule based on duration, do the following:

Fast Lane Tip #47

To enable Microsoft Project to calculate work hours and schedule based on duration

1. Click on **Tools**, or press **Alt/T**.
2. Choose **Options**, then the **Schedule** tab.
3. At the bottom, place a check beside **Updating Task Status Updates Resource Status**. Duration will determine work hours.

 Workgroup toolbar button—enables you to display a toolbar with workgroup functions, as shown in the next section.

The Workgroup Toolbar

The workgroup toolbar provides many useful functions for using electronic mail, Schedule +, and a database to manage one or more projects.

Several of the buttons that are displayed and described do not have corresponding menu items. If you prefer to use the keyboard, you may need to customize one or more menu items. Please see Chapter 8 to learn how to customize a menu.

Figure 6-7. Workgroup Toolbar

 Add Routing Slip button—enables you to add or edit a routing slip. Using the keyboard, press **Alt/F**, then choose **Add Routing Slip** or **Edit Routing Slip**. Projects that already have a routing slip will show the Edit Routing Slip command.

Managing a Great Many Projects

 Send Mail button—gives the command to send electronic mail. Using the keyboard, press **Alt/F**, then choose **Send**.

 Update Read Only button—shows the most recent Version of a read-only project file. You may need to customize your file menu to display this choice. See "Changing the Menu" in Chapter 8.

 Toggle Updates button—provides a choice between Read only and Read and Write. You may need to customize your file menu to display this choice. See "Changing the Menu" in Chapter 8.

 Consolidate Projects button—enables you to consolidate project files. Using the keyboard, press **Alt/T**, then **Multiple Projects**, then **Consolidate Projects**. See "Consolidating Projects" later in this chapter.

 Open From Database button—opens a database file from MS Access® or other database. Using the keyboard, press **Alt/T**, then **Multiple Projects** and **Open Database**.

 Save to Database button—saves a file to MS Access or another database. Using the keyboard, press **Alt/T**, then **Multiple Projects** and **Save To Database**.

 TeamAssign button—notifies a resource of an assignment by electronic mail. Using the keyboard, press **Alt/T**, then **Workgroup** and **TeamAssign**.

 TeamUpdate button—notifies team members of changes in schedule or assignments via electronic mail. Using the keyboard, press **Alt/T**, then **Workgroup** and **TeamUpdate**.

 TeamStatus button—requests updated information through electronic mail from the resources assigned to tasks. Using the keyboard, press **Alt/T**, then **Workgroup** and **TeamStatus**.

 Set Reminders button—enables you to use MS Schedule +® to set reminders before the start or finish of selected tasks. Using the keyboard, press **Alt/T**, then **Workgroup** and **Set Reminders**.

The Tracking Table

When project data is tracked, issues and problems often surface early enough for you to take corrective action. Several tables provide valuable information to assist in this effort. In addition to current status, tables can also point to symptoms of larger problems, and can provide information that will improve the management of future projects.

At this point, Chris has gathered and updated information about the first issue of Way To Go. She updated the file on May 1. Now she needs to analyze the data, negotiate with team members and others, and make the adjustments necessary to keep the project on track. To do this, she will take several "snapshots" of the project by printing several standard tables. All of these tables can be customized by adding or deleting columns, or by changing their titles.

Several tables and views have been designed to track projects and to monitor project progress. In this section you will see several tables and an interpretation of the data displayed. Reports will be explained in Chapter 7. Tables discussed in the following sections include:

- Tracking table
- Variance table
- Cost table (task version and resource version)
- Work table (task version)

To display the tracking table, click on **View**, or press **Alt/V**, then choose **Table** and **Tracking**.

The tracking table, shown below, displays Remaining Duration and:

- Actual start
- Actual finish
- Percent complete
- Actual duration
- Actual cost
- Actual work

Table 6-1. Tracking table excerpt

ID	Task Name	Act. Start	Act. Finish	% Comp.	Act. Dur.	Rem. Dur.	Act. Cost	Act. Work
	Newsletter #1	4/1/9	N	33	20.64	41.11	$3,026.3	119.5
1	Define Budget Requirements	4/1/9	4/4/9	100	3.5	0	$266.0	5.6
2	Start project	4/1/9	4/1/9	100	0	0	$0.0	0
3	Estimate production	4/1/9	4/3/9	100	20	0	$190.0	4
4	Obtain budget approvals	4/3/9	4/4/9	100	8	0	$76.0	1.6
5	**Schedule Production**	4/4/9	4/17/9	100	8.75	0	$838.0	33
6	Set production schedule	4/4/9	4/8/9	100	14	0	$213.0	7.8
7	List potential topics for	4/8/9	4/12/9	100	4	0	$400.0	16
8	Submit topics to marketing	4/15/9	4/16/9	100	2	0	$200.0	8.2
9	Assign topics	4/17/9	4/17/9	100	2	0	$25.0	1
10	**Create Layout and Masthead Design**	4/17/9	4/24/9	100	5.25	0	$384.8	19.4
11	Brainstorming session of	4/17/9	4/17/9	100	4	0	$177.8	8.4
12	Create three preliminary	4/17/9	4/19/9	100	16	0	$92.0	4
13	Compare designs and	4/19/9	4/22/9	100	4	0	$23.0	1
14	Develop final design	4/22/9	4/24/9	100	16	0	$92.0	4
15	Obtain approval	4/24/9	4/24/9	100	2	0	$0.0	2
16	**Write Newsletter Content**	4/17/9	N	22	7.82	27.06	$1,537.5	61.5
17	Select staff to write articles	4/17/9	4/18/9	100	3	0	$37.5	1.5
18	Recruit freelance	4/18/9	NA	50	1.5	1.5	$1,500.0	60
19	Set deadlines	NA	NA	0	0	6	$0.0	0
20	Write articles	NA	NA	0	0	110	$0.0	0
21	Make revisions	NA	NA	0	0	32	$0.0	0
22	Approve final copy	NA	NA	0	0	8	$0.0	0

The tracking table provides data about actual data at a particular point in time. Because Chris created a summary task for the project, she can quickly see the summary figures at the top. It appears that the project is about 33% complete, has spent $3,026.30, has consumed 119.5 work hours, and has slightly more than 41 days of remaining duration.

The Variance Table

The variance table displays schedule variances. To see the variance table, click on **View**, or press **Alt/V**, then choose **Table** and **Variance**. It contains the following fields of data:

- Task ID

The Complete Planning Guide for Microsoft® Project

- Task Name
- Start (actual start date)
- Finish (currently scheduled finish)
- Baseline start (start date in the saved baseline)
- Baseline finish (finish date in the saved baseline)
- Start variance (difference between baseline start and actual start)
- Finish variance (difference between the baseline finish date and the currently scheduled finish date)

Table 6-2. Variance table excerpt

ID	Task Name	Start	Finish	Baseline Start	Baseline Finish	Start Var.	Finish Var.
	Newsletter #1	4/1/9	6/25/9	4/1/9	7/4/9	0d	-6.46
1	Define Budget Re	4/1/9	4/4/9	4/1/9	4/4/9	0	0
2	Start project	4/1/9	4/1/9	4/1/9	4/1/9	0	0
3	Estimate prod	4/1/9	4/3/9	4/1/9	4/3/9	0	0
4	Obtain budget	4/3/9	4/4/9	4/3/9	4/4/9	0	0
5	Schedule Produc	4/4/9	4/17/9	4/4/9	4/9/9	0	6
6	Set productio	4/4/9	4/8/9	4/4/9	4/5/9	0	0.75
7	List potential t	4/8/9	4/12/9	4/5/9	4/8/9	0.75	4
8	Submit topics	4/15/9	4/16/9	4/8/9	4/8/9	4.75	6.25
9	Assign topics	4/17/9	4/17/9	4/8/9	4/9/9	6.25	6
10	Create Layout an	4/17/9	4/24/9	4/9/9	4/12/9	6	7.63
11	Brainstorming	4/17/9	4/17/9	4/9/9	4/9/9	6	6
12	Create three p	4/17/9	4/19/9	4/9/9	4/11/9	6	6
13	Compare desi	4/19/9	4/22/9	4/11/9	4/11/9	6	6.25
14	Develop final	4/22/9	4/24/9	4/12/9	4/12/9	6.25	7.63
15	Obtain approv	4/24/9	4/24/9	4/12/9	4/12/9	7.63	7.63
16	Write Newsletter	4/17/9	6/5/9	4/9/9	6/12/9	6	-4.46
17	Select staff to	4/17/9	4/18/9	4/9/9	4/10/9	6	5.38
18	Recruit freela	4/18/9	5/16/9	4/10/9	5/15/9	5.38	0.38
19	Set deadlines	5/16/9	5/16/9	5/15/9	5/16/9	0.38	0.38
20	Write articles	5/16/9	6/5/9	5/16/9	6/4/9	0.38	0.79

Notice that in the Finish Variance column there is a -6.46 days. This is actually very positive information. It indicates that the project is currently scheduled to finish nearly six and one-half days ahead of schedule. This is very good news in most cases. When this happens, be sure that those responsible for successor tasks are informed as soon as possible.

Looking down the Start Variance column, notice that Assign topics finished 6.25 days after the baseline finish date. There were some difficulties in finding a contractor to write a certain article.

Also notice that when a predecessor is delayed, it is likely to delay several successor tasks.

The Cost Table

Two versions of the cost table exist: one that is accessed from a resource view, and another that is accessed from a task view. Both tables provide information about actual costs, remaining costs, and the variance from the baseline. The task version of the cost table displays the Task Name column at the left beside the ID column.

The Task Version of the Cost Table

The task version of the cost table displays the following columns:

- ID number—identifies line items. When a task is added or deleted, every ID number that follows that line item changes. For example, if you were to delete the task represented by ID #4, every ID number from 4 upward will change.

- Task Name—names of objectives and tasks

- Fixed Cost—a category of cost that will not change with the addition of resources, duration, or work.

- Total Cost (estimate)—the accumulation of estimates for fixed cost, cost per time period, and cost per use.

- Baseline—planned cost or budget.

- Variance—the difference between baseline cost and total cost.

- Actual—costs that have been incurred or spent.

- Remaining—estimated cost to complete the task.

To see the cost table from either the resource or task perspective, click on **View**, or press **Alt/V**, then choose **Table** and **Cost**.

The Complete Planning Guide for Microsoft® Project

Table 6-3. Task version of the cost table (excerpt)

ID	Task Name	Fixed Cost	Total Cost	Baseline	Variance	Actual	Remaining
1	Define Budget Require	$0.0	$266.0	$266.0	$0.0	$266.0	$0.0
2	Start project	$0.0	$0.0	$0.0	$0.0	$0.0	$0.0
3	Estimate production	$0.0	$190.0	$190.0	$0.0	$190.0	$0.0
4	Obtain budget appro	$0.0	$76.0	$76.0	$0.0	$76.0	$0.0
5	**Schedule Production**	$0.0	$838.0	$313.0	$525.0	$838.0	$0.0
6	Set production sche	$0.0	$213.0	$138.0	$75.0	$213.0	$0.0
7	List potential topics f	$0.0	$400.0	$75.0	$325.0	$400.0	$0.0
8	Submit topics to mar	$0.0	$200.0	$50.0	$150.0	$200.0	$0.0
9	Assign topics	$0.0	$25.0	$50.0	($25.00)	$25.0	$0.0
10	**Create Layout and Mast**	$0.0	$384.8	$310.0	$74.7	$384.8	$0.0
11	Brainstorming sessi	$0.0	$177.8	$177.8	$0.0	$177.8	$0.0
12	Create three prelimi	$0.0	$92.0	$92.0	$0.0	$92.0	$0.0
13	Compare designs an	$0.0	$23.0	$11.5	$11.5	$23.0	$0.0
14	Develop final design	$0.0	$92.0	$28.7	$63.2	$92.0	$0.0
15	Obtain approval	$0.0	$0.0	$0.0	$0.0	$0.0	$0.0
16	**Write Newsletter Conte**	$0.0	$4,201.0	$4,701.0	($500.00)	$1,537.5	$2,663.5
17	Select staff to write a	$0.0	$37.5	$100.0	($62.50)	$37.5	$0.0
18	Recruit freelance wri	$0.0	$1,500.0	$2,000.0	($500.00)	$1,500.0	$0.0
19	Set deadlines	$0.0	$75.0	$75.0	$0.0	$0.0	$75.0
20	Write articles	$0.0	$2,062.5	$2,000.0	$62.5	$0.0	$2,062.5
21	Make revisions	$0.0	$400.0	$400.0	$0.0	$0.0	$400.0
22	Approve final copy	$0.0	$76.0	$76.0	$0.0	$0.0	$76.0
23	Submit diskette to d	$0.0	$50.0	$50.0	$0.0	$0.0	$50.0
24	**Edit and Revise Layout**	$0.0	$115.0	$115.0	$0.0	$0.0	$115.0
25	Develop preliminary	$0.0	$30.0	$30.0	$0.0	$0.0	$30.0

One approach to analyzing the cost table is to look first at the Variance column and examine the variances for each task. What caused the variance? Is it something that can happen again later in the project?

Actual costs for the Schedule Production objective were $838, while the baseline was only $313—more than double! This objective contains the largest variance, $525. Looking at the tasks shown under Schedule Production, only Assign topics took less time than was estimated. The task list potential topics… took much longer than expected, because there were several unplanned meetings required with stakeholders outside the project team. The meetings were required because there were disagreements about several proposed topics that resulted in examining and refining the guidelines for topic inclusion. In addition, several new topics were proposed by the marketing committee after the final topics were submitted, delaying the task: submit topics to marketing committee. Now that these issues have, for the most part, clarified newsletter content issues, most similar disagreements will be avoided in future issues.

The Resource Version of the Cost Table

The resource Version of the cost table displays data related to each resource assigned to the project. To see this version, first display a resource view, then choose **View**, **Table** and **Cost**. The table displays the following columns:

- ID number—the number assigned to each resource as he or she is added to the pool

- Resource Name—the unique name of the person, group, equipment, or fixed-cost category

- Cost—actual cost plus remaining cost; can exceed the baseline cost

- Baseline Cost—planned cost that is part of a saved baseline

- Variance—the difference between baseline cost and actual cost

- Actual Cost—costs that have been incurred

- Remaining—estimated cost to complete a task

Table 6-4. Resource version of the cost table

ID	Resource Name	Cost	Baseline Cost	Variance	Actual Cost	Remaining
1	Chris Tomathy	$513.0	$513.0	$0.0	$304.0	$209.0
2	Jim Mulligan	$5,025.0	$5,000.0	$25.0	$2,437.5	$2,587.5
3	Jane Parker	$135.0	$135.0	$0.0	$20.0	$115.0
4	Forrest Boles	$425.5	$350.7	$74.7	$230.0	$195.5
5	Cynthia Kraft	$231.0	$231.0	$0.0	$28.0	$203.0
6	Jack Boucher	$6.8	$6.8	$0.0	$6.8	$0.0
7	Mailroom	$0.0	$0.0	$0.0	$0.0	$0.0
8	Marketing Committee	$0.0	$0.0	$0.0	$0.0	$0.0
9	Printing Department	$0.0	$0.0	$0.0	$0.0	$0.0

To analyze the costs related to each resource, look first at the Variance column. The largest variance is $74.75 for Forrest Boles. Currently, the cost (actual + remaining) of completing his work is $425.50, and the baseline cost is $350.75. Since his work is only partially complete, the cost and the variance could potentially increase further. Chris should probably talk to Forrest to find out if she can remove obstacles or provide support in any way for his remaining tasks.

The Work Table

Two versions of the work table are available: the task version and the resource version.

The Task Version of the Work Table

The task version of the work table provides work data as it relates to each project task. It also makes it possible to forecast the number of hours of work required to finish the project. To see the task version from a task view such as the Gantt chart, click on **View**, or press **Alt/V**, then choose **Table** and **Work**. The table displays the following columns.

- ID—the task identifier.

- Task Name—identifies line items. When a task is added or deleted, every ID number that follows that line item changes. For example, if you were to delete the task represented by ID #4, every ID number from 4 upward would change.

- Work—hours of work associated with completing the task.

- Baseline—the time estimate for the task as saved in the baseline.

- Variance—the difference between the baseline hours and the actual hours.

- Actual—the actual number of hours worked.

- Remaining—the difference between the Work column and the Actual column

- % W. Comp.—the percent of the work that is complete.

Managing a Great Many Projects

Table 6-5. Task version of the work table (excerpt)

ID	Task Name	Work	Baseline	Variance	Actual	Remaining	% W. Comp.
1	Define Budget Requirement	5.6	5.6h	0	5.6	0h	100
2	Start project	0h	0h	0	0h	0h	0%
3	Estimate production cost	4h	4h	0	4h	0h	100%
4	Obtain budget approvals	1.6	1.6h	0	1.6	0h	100%
5	Schedule Production	33h	12h	21	33	0h	100
6	Set production schedule	7.8	4.8h	3	7.8	0h	100%
7	List potential topics for a	16	3h	13	16	0h	100%
8	Submit topics to marketi	8.2	2.2h	6	8.2	0h	100%
9	Assign topics	1h	2h	-1	1h	0h	100%
10	Create Layout and Masthea	19.4	16.15	3.25	19.4	0h	100
11	Brainstorming session of	8.4	8.4h	0	8.4	0h	100%
12	Create three preliminary	4h	4h	0	4h	0h	100%
13	Compare designs and s	1h	0.5h	0.5	1h	0h	100%
14	Develop final design	4h	1.25	2.75	4h	0h	100%
15	Obtain approval	2h	2h	0	2h	0h	100%
16	Write Newsletter Content	174.6	194.6	-20	61.5	113.1	35
17	Select staff to write articl	1.5	4h	-2.5	1.5	0h	100%

One way to analyze the data displayed in the table is to examine the Variance column. If you look first at the objectives, which are summary tasks, you again see that tasks that make up Schedule Production were 21 hours more than planned. This resulted in the delaying of several project tasks and twenty-one hours of unplanned labor cost. As discussed earlier in this section, this was because there were issues regarding newsletter topics that resulted in additional discussion before topics could be assigned.

The Resource Version of the Work Table

To access the resource Version of the work table while in a resource view, click on **View** or press **Alt/V**, then choose **Table** and **Work**.

The resource Version has the following columns of data:

- ID—the number assigned to each resource as he or she is added to the pool.

- Resource Name—the unique name of the person, group, equipment, or fixed-cost category.

- % Complete—the percent of work assigned to the resource that has been completed.

- Work—the total number of hours estimated to complete all tasks assigned to the resource. For a resource with work remaining, this is an estimate; for completed tasks this is the accumulated total (see Jack Boucher).

- Overtime—the number of overtime hours.

- Baseline—the planned number of hours for all tasks assigned to this resource.

- Variance—the difference between work necessary to complete all tasks assigned to this resource and the baseline hours.

- Actual—actual hours worked on the project.

- Remaining—estimated number of hours of work that are remaining for this resource.

Table 6-6. Resource version of the work table

ID	Resource N	% Comp.	Work	Overtime	Baseline	Variance	Actual	Remaining
1	Chris Tomat	59	10.8	0	10.8	0	6.4	4.4
2	Jim Mulliga	49	201	0	200	1	97.5	103.5
3	Jane Parker	15	6.75	0	6.75	0	1	5.75
4	Forrest Bole	54	18.5	0	15.25	3.25	10	8.5
5	Cynthia Kraft	12	16.5	0	16.5	0	2	14.5
6	Jack Bouche	100	0.4	0	0.4	0	0.4	0
7	Mailroom	0	16	0	16	0	0	16
8	Marketing Co	22	10.2	0	10.2	0	2.2	8
9	Printing Dep	0	29	0	29	0	0	29

To analyze the resource version of the work table, examine the Variance column to identify the largest variances. At this point, after 10 hours of actual work (Actual column), Forrest has spent 3.25 hours more than expected on his tasks. Was the work not defined clearly? Should time estimates for future tasks be reexamined? Chris will need to collaborate with Forrest.

The six tables discussed in this section are intended to provide you with some basic tools for examining project data and for managing one or more projects. Each of the tables presented can be customized to conform with your information requirements, and in most cases local practices. In addition, there are many other tables that can be used. You will need to experiment with the various views and tables to prepare the variety of reports that are necessary to analyze progress on your projects. This is an integral part of task, resource, and communication management.

MANAGING MANY PROJECTS

Wouldn't it be nice if you only had one project to work on at any given time? Sure, but most organizations and individuals have many projects underway at any point in time.

Managing a Great Many Projects

With rapidly changing technology and a constant need to improve efficiency, it is likely that project leaders, managers, and team members must all juggle several projects, often every day. Fortunately, managing several projects simultaneously is a strength of Microsoft® Project. You can:

- View several open projects simply by choosing **Arrange All** from the **Window** menu

- Click on a task and drag one or more tasks to another open project

Many other features enable multiproject management. You can share resources, tables, views, calendars, forms, reports, toolbars, menu bars, filters, and modules, such as a database or pivot table. You can also break a large project into a master project and subprojects; break those subprojects into their own sub-projects, consolidate projects and create project templates. Each of these will be discussed in the following sections:

- Creating Project Templates

- Saving Several Projects as a Workspace

- Sharing Common Elements as Global Files

- Sharing Resources with Other Projects

- Creating Subprojects

- Linking Master Project and Zsubproject Dates

- Consolidating Projects

- Links Between Any Projects

Creating Project Templates

If your organization tends to plan and manage several similar projects, you can save much time and prevent duplication of effort by creating standard project templates. Standard project templates usually begin with an ordinary Microsoft® Project file that includes a WBS outline containing a basic structure that can be used on many similar projects.

For example, if you work in an information systems organization or another organization that compares and selects software tools, you may use a template similar to the one shown in Figure 6-8. Once you have standardized the structure and tasks, save the file as a template. Once it is saved as a template, it can be customized and used for all similar projects.

The Complete Planning Guide for Microsoft® Project

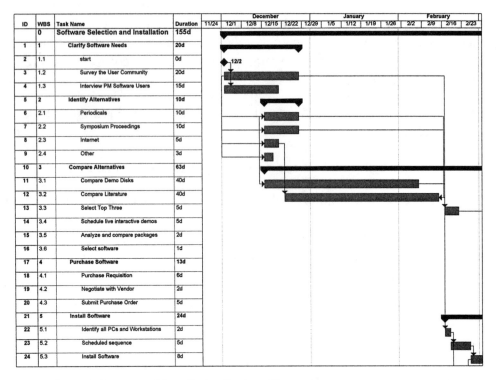

Figure 6-8. *Software Selection and Installation Project (Excerpt)*

Fast Lane Tip #48

To save a project file as a template

1. Modify the file so that it reflects common tasks.
2. Click on **File**, or press **Alt/F**.
3. Choose **Save As**.
4. At the bottom of the window, beside **Save File as Type:**, indicate **Template**.
5. Choose a folder or file and a name for the template.

Choose **Save** (Version 4.1) or **OK**. (Version 4.0)

Managing a Great Many Projects

Saving Several Projects as a Workspace

If you commonly work on several projects, you may want to consider saving them as a *workspace*. By doing this, you can open and close all of your projects at the same time. When considering this option, also consider the amount of memory you have on your computer. Large files may slow down many operations.

Fast Lane Tip #49

To save several files as a workspace

1. Open all of the files that you would like to include as part of the workspace.
2. Choose **File**, then **Save Workspace**.
3. When you see the box below, enter a name for the collection of files in the **File name** box, and choose **Save** (Version 4.1) or **OK** (Version 4.0).

Note: Although the box appears different in Version 4.0, the choices are the same.

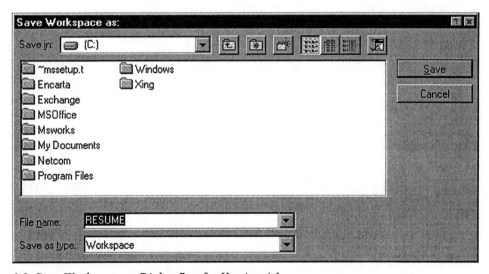

Figure 6-9. Save Workspace as Dialog Box for Version 4.1

Sharing Common Elements as Global Files

Once you have created a new table, or have made changes to other elements, such as calendars and views, in the current file, you may want those same elements available to yourself and others when working in other files. To do this, you will want to save the table to a global file so that it is available to all Microsoft® Project files. Global settings assist in managing several projects, whether on a standalone PC or in a networked environment.

By sharing elements such as calendars, tables, and reports, you can improve efficiency by preventing many other users from spending their time creating the same elements. It also helps in efforts to standardize project management practices and terminology in the organization.

The Organizer dialog box shown below enables you to share common:

- Views
- Calendars
- Forms
- Reports
- Toolbars
- Tables
- Modules
- Menu Bars
- Filters

Each of these options has its own tab as shown below.

Managing a Great Many Projects

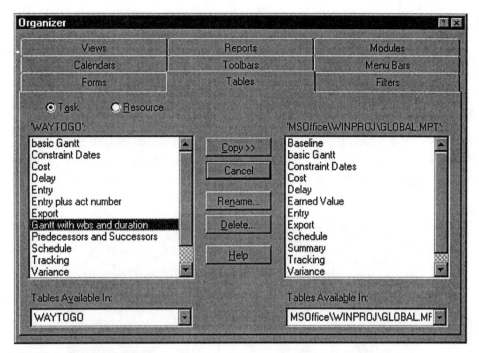

Figure 6-10. Organizer Dialog Box

Fast Lane Tip #50

To save a common element as a global file

1. Click on **View**, or press **Alt/V**, then **More Views**, then **Organizer**.

2. Choose from the tabs shown (for example, if you would like to copy a table, choose the Tables tab).

3. When the tab you want is displayed, choose either **Task** or **Resource** as appropriate for the element.

4. Use the (Tables) **Available In** box on the bottom left of the dialog box to display the file that contains the table or other element that you want to make available from other files.

5. Select the table or other element that you would like to copy to a global file from the list displayed on the left.

6. Use the (Tables) **Available In** box on the bottom right of the dialog box to show the global file.

7. Choose **Copy**. The name of the table or other element will then be displayed in the list of global files.

8. Choose **Close**, then **Close** again, and the file is available to other projects.

181

Sharing Resources with Other Projects

If you are managing several projects using Microsoft Project, you can share the same resources among all projects. This is an especially valuable feature when people in your organization typically work on several projects simultaneously. By sharing resources, you can quickly see the consequences of any overallocations, delays, or reassignments.

Two Versions of the Share Resources Dialog Box are available: one that appears if you are working on a project in the active window (shown below), and one that appears if a resource pool is open in the active window.

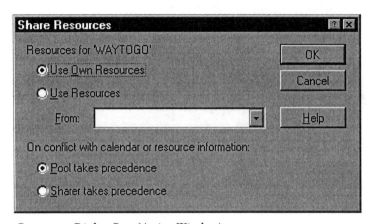

Figure 6-11. Share Resources Dialog Box (Active Window)

To display the dialog box shown above, click on **Tools**, or press **Alt/T**, then choose **Multiple Projects** and **Share Resources**.

This dialog box asks you two important questions:

1. *Should the project use its own resources or use resources from another project?*

2. *When a scheduling conflict occurs, does the sharer or the pool take precedence?.*

If you choose to use resources from another project, you can access a resource pool in a different file on your own PC or workstation, or from a network. If you choose **Sharer takes precedence**, and you are making resources from your pool available, any resource conflicts will result in your project getting the resource.

Managing a Great Many Projects

Fast Lane Tip #51

To share resources among several projects

1. Open the projects that contain the resources to be shared.

2. From a project without resources, click on **Tools**, or press **Alt/T**.

3. Choose **Multiple Projects**.

4. Choose **Share Resources**.

5. Choose **Use Resources From**.

6. Use the down arrow to see and select open projects.

7. Indicate whether the pool or sharer takes precedence in a conflict.

8. Choose **OK**.

Creating Subprojects

For some projects, it may be clear from the beginning that the number of activities and tasks will number in the hundreds or thousands. Working with a project of this size will consume more computer memory, and is likely to reduce the processing speed of your computer. Reports from projects of this size can sometimes be large enough to wallpaper a room! Because of the large number of activities and tasks, it will often make sense to divide a large project and create a master project and subprojects.

For new or "breakthrough" projects, the size and complexity of the effort may not become apparent until the project is underway. When the project expands to an extent where there is a noticeable decrease in processing speed, or you would like to segment a project for more efficient tracking and control, consider splitting the project into a number of subprojects.

Subprojects can be created in two ways. You can create a subproject from several tasks in an active project, or you can create a task to summarize an existing project and then identify the new subproject. There is a Fast Lane Tip to guide you in creating a subproject using both methods shown below.

The Complete Planning Guide for Microsoft® Project

Commonly used approaches for partitioning large projects into subprojects are to divide by:
- Project phase or objective
- Organization
- Organizational function
- Project manager or leader

Fast Lane Tip #52

To create a sub-project from several tasks in the active project

1. Select the tasks that you wish to use to form a subproject.

2. Cut the tasks.

3. Click on  ,or press **Alt/F**, then **N**.

4. Click on **Edit**, or press **Alt/E**, then choose **Paste**. The tasks that form the new project are created.

5. Save and name the new file. (See the next section to link project dates.)

After dividing a large project into subprojects, information about subprojects is summarized and is represented by one task in the master project.

Managing a Great Many Projects

Fast Lane Tip #53

To create a subproject by inserting an existing project

1. While in the Task Name column of a Gantt table, position the cursor on the task that follows the desired insertion point.
2. Press the **Insert** key. A space for a new task is created.
3. Type a task name that is descriptive of the subproject.
4. Click on [icon], press **Shift/F2**.
5. Choose the **Advanced** tab.
6. Use the **Browse** button to choose the project that you want to be a subproject from the **Subproject Filename** box.
7. Choose **OK**. The chosen project will be linked to the master project. (See the next section for information about linking dates.)

To open a subproject from the master project, double-click on the subproject task.

Linking Master Project and Subproject Dates

Master projects control the start dates of subprojects by default. In many projects this is desirable. In other projects, however, you may want to have the subproject dates reflected in the master project. To do this, ensure that the subproject has a summary task. To create a project summary task, choose **Tools**, then **Options**. Under the **View** tab, place a check in the checkbox beside **Project Summary Task**, and choose **OK**.

> **Fast Lane Tip #54**
>
>
>
> To enable the subproject to control its start date
>
> 1. Ensure that both the master project and the subproject have a table in the active view with the **Duration** column to the left of the **Start Date** column.
> 2. Select the duration and start (date) fields for the project summary task in the subproject.
> 3. Choose **Copy**.
> 4. Move to the master project and select the **duration** and **start** fields.
> 5. Choose **Edit**, then **Paste Special**, then **Paste Link**.
> 6. Save the file.

After you have linked the start dates and duration for a subproject and a master project, schedule changes in the subproject will automatically be reflected in the master project. If it is important for data to be updated in both directions, going to and from the master project and subproject, consider consolidating projects.

Consolidating Projects

If your department or organization commonly manages many projects at the same time, consolidating projects is probably a good idea. You can display all projects in a single window by consolidating them. When several projects have been consolidated, it appears as if all of the tasks make up one project. This enables you to print consolidated reports of all projects that make up a program, all of the current projects in a department, or all projects of a certain type. You name it.

In addition to the newsletter project, Chris is also working on a project to reengineer her department's work processes, and another project to choose desktop publishing software. For her it would be a good idea to consolidate the projects so that she can see resource assignments and other data for all three projects. After using the Help menu and user guide to read up on consolidating projects, she decides to consolidate the three projects.

She decides to attach and link the projects together so that changes made in the consolidated project window will be reflected in the source projects. Since all of the projects are relatively small, she decides not to hide subtasks.

Fast Lane Tip #55

To consolidate projects

1. Click on [icon] or press **Alt/T**, then **Multiple Projects**, then **Consolidate Projects**. The Consolidate Projects dialog box appears.

2. In the Consolidate Projects dialog box, place the cursor on the first line beneath **File Name**. Use the **Browse** button and the **Add Files** button to choose and add the project that you would like to appear first when the projects are merged, on the second line the second project, and so on, depending on the number and order of projects you want to consolidate. Use the up and down arrows to the right of the file names in the dialog box to change the position of a file.

3. Beside each project, choose whether or not the file can be accessed and edited by others, or if you want **Read Only** access.

4. Choose whether or not you want the files to be attached (linked) to the source files.

5. Choose whether or not to **Combine Resource Pools**.

6. Choose whether or not to **Hide Subtasks**.

7. Choose **OK**.

The Complete Planning Guide for Microsoft® Project

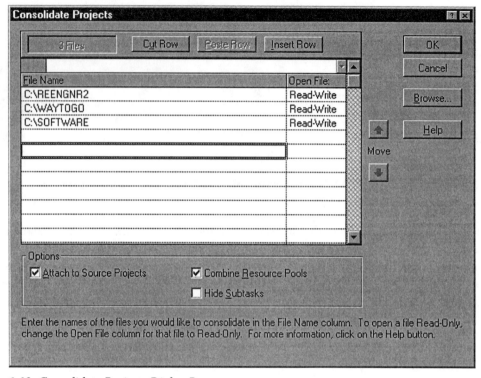

Figure 6-12. Consolidate Projects Dialog Box

Figure 6-12 displays the Consolidate Projects dialog box as Chris completed it. She chose to **Attach toSource Projects** and to **Combine Resource Pools**. Since her projects are small, she chose not to **Hide Subtasks**. These choices are discussed below.

Attaching to Source Projects

When you attach, or link, a consolidated project to a source project, most changes made in the consolidated project or source project are reflected in both. There are two exceptions:

- Format changes

- Projects opened as read-only

You can also consolidate several projects without this dynamic link. If your only purpose in consolidating is to prepare reports, you may not want to check the Attach to Source Projects checkbox. When you make this choice, the data is simply copied into the consolidated project.

Managing a Great Many Projects

Combining Resource Pools

One reason for consolidating projects is to combine and share resource pools. To do this, you also need to check the Attach to Source Projects checkbox, explained above. With a consolidated resource pool created, you can monitor all of the organization's people, equipment, fixed costs, and other costs, and their schedules.

Hiding Subtasks

When you choose Hide Subtasks, the consolidated project displays only the summary task for each consolidated project. Double-click on any summary task to see its subtasks.

Links Between Any Projects

You can create links to reduce the time needed to update related projects. For example, if a predecessor-successor relationship exists between two tasks in two different projects, you can link them. If, for example, you would like the finish of a predecessor in one project to determine the start date of a successor in another project, you can create a link between the two. This way the finish date of a task in a "source" project will automatically update the start date of its successor task in the "destination," or target, project.

This method applies whether or not there is a master-subproject relationship.

Fast Lane Tip #56

To link start and finish dates from tasks in different projects

1. Select and copy the **finish date** from the source task.
2. Select the **Start** field for the task in the target or destination task.
3. Choose **Edit** from the menu bar.
4. Choose **Paste Special** and **Text Data**.
5. Click on **OK**, or press **Enter**.

If the finish date of the task in the source project changes, the start date of the task in the target project will automatically change.

*COMPANION PRODUCTS RELATED TO THIS CHAPTER**

Distributed Project Management, software tool that works with Microsoft Project and Microsoft® Mail to provide multiproject timesheet capabilities; Information Management Services (802) 748-5013.

Multi-Project, software tool to extend a single-user system to an enterprise-wide solution with interproject links; Information Management Services (802) 748-5013.

Program Gateway, summarizes work from up to 500 project schedules into Lotus Notes; Lucas Management Systems, (714) 851-1999.

Project Gateway, software tool to coordinate Microsoft Project and Lotus Notes and create a wide-area project multiproject information system; Lucas Management Systems (714) 851-1999.

ProjectServer, software tool to update tasks in a multiproject environment and build an interactive bridge between Microsoft Project and open relational databases; MICRO Frame (800) 235-4142.

*Not all of these tools are designed for Version 4.1.

7

Do It Your Way Reports and Forms

In this chapter you will learn how to:

1. Define informational requirements for reporting
2. Choose standard and custom reports
3. Sort and filter
4. Print reports

INTRODUCTION

Part of the job of maintaining project control and keeping all project stakeholders informed is to prepare and distribute an appropriate set of reports. To do this, you need to devise a system for defining the information needs for each stakeholder audience, and then develop a means to provide that information at reasonable intervals.

This chapter includes descriptions of all the standard reports that are available. In addition, suggestions are made for using the data contained in the reports, and for creating standard and customized reports. Other topics include sorting and filtering data, using page setup, and printing reports.

DEFINING INFORMATION REQUIREMENTS

Attempt to identify all stakeholders and their information needs as early as possible in the project life cycle. Begin with customer or client requirements and project success criteria. Continue by defining the needs and reporting requirements of customers or clients, the organization's management, the project manager or leader, and the project team.

All project stakeholders have informational needs, some different from others. At one end of the spectrum is management, who typically require summary information such as total costs, milestone schedules, and summarized quality metrics. Management may need the information on a weekly, monthly, or other basis. At the other end of the spectrum are the project manager or leader and other members of the project team, who will normally need detailed status information—sometimes on a daily basis—to do their work.

Once you find out the information needs of all project stakeholders, you can choose from a wide variety of tables, views, and standard reports the View menu. By customizing, you can design hundreds of tables, reports, and charts in addition to these standard reports.

In many project environments, reports are used to disseminate information on project cost, schedule, resource, technical, and quality requirements. Some of these needs can be met by using standard reports; other needs must be met by customizing standard tables and reports. In general, reports display two types of information:

- Information that you enter, such as resource rates

Do It Your Way Reports and Forms

- Information calculated by Microsoft® Project, such as the calculation required to multiply resource rates by work hours

To see your choices of reports, click on **View**, or press **Alt/V**, then choose **Reports**. You will see the choices shown below:

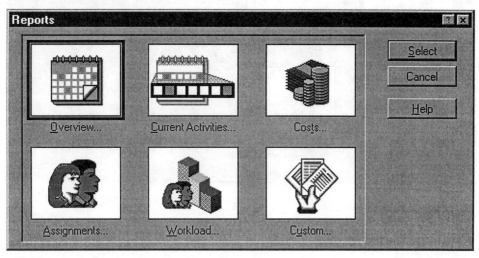

Figure 7-1. Report Categories

The following sections will describe and examine these reports, and suggest the best uses for each.

OVERVIEW REPORTS

Overview reports present various configurations of rolled-up project data. Once you define the reporting needs of your stakeholders, you will need to compare the available tables and reports and choose those that match their needs.

When you choose **Overview**, then **Select**, you will see the following choices of overview reports:

The Complete Planning Guide for Microsoft® Project

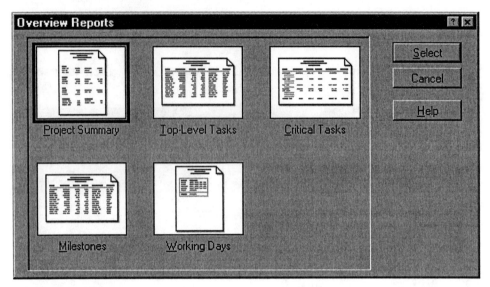

Figure 7-2. Overview Reports

Five standard overview reports are available:

- Project Summary
- Top-Level Tasks
- Critical Tasks
- Milestones
- Working Days

Each of these reports is described below.

Project Summary

The dark box that surrounds the Project Summary icon indicates that it has been selected. Use the mouse or arrow keys to move between reports. When you choose Select, the Project Summary report, calculated as of the current date, is displayed in print preview.

The Project Summary report provides the following information:

- Dates—Baseline Start, Actual Start, and Start Variance; Baseline Finish, Actual Finish, and Finish Variance

- Duration—(currently) Scheduled, Baseline and Duration Variance, Remaining and Actual Duration, and Percent Complete based on duration

- Work—(currently) Scheduled, Baseline and Work Variance, Remaining and Actual Work, and Percent Complete based on the number of work hours

- Costs—(currently) Scheduled, Baseline and Cost Variance, Remaining and Actual Costs

- Task Status—(number of) Tasks not yet started, (number of) Tasks in progress, (number of) Tasks Completed, and (number of) Total Tasks

- Resource Status—(number of) Resources, (number of) Overallocated Resources and (number of) Total Resources.

At the bottom of the project summary report are the notes that you entered into the Notes section of the Task Information dialog box for the project summary task. For example, you may have entered the project goal.

On one page, the project summary report provides a quick overview of key project information. It provides a glimpse of what the project has accomplished and cost up to the current date and a forecast of the remaining duration, work, and costs. You can add textual information to supplement, interpret, or explain the summary data as required.

Top-Level Tasks

The Top-Level Tasks report contains information for the project summary task and the next level of work in the outline, referred to as objectives in the newsletter project. It displays much of the same information as the Project Summary report, but for the top two levels of work.

The Top-Level Tasks Report also prints the notes from the project summary task beneath that task. It displays the following columns of data:

- ID—the task ID number

- Task Name—the names of each objective

- Duration—the currently scheduled duration

- Start—the actual start date

- Finish—the currently scheduled finish date

- % Complete—the percent complete based on duration

- Cost—total anticipated costs based on the current schedule

- Work—total number of work hours based on the current schedule

This report provides a way to identify the project components that require the most work and the highest cost. It also allows you to examine the expected finish dates for reassignment purposes. In some cases, you can use the data to update the organization budget and project budget, forecast spending, and measure performance.

Critical Tasks

The Critical Tasks report displays those tasks on the critical path that have not been completed, and the summary tasks to which they roll up. If you have redefined critical tasks to include tasks with a minimal amount of slack (not recommended), these tasks are also displayed.

The report also includes notes from the project summary task. The Critical Tasks report contains the following columns:

- ID—the task ID number

- Task Name—the names of each objective, task and subtask

- Successor Name—the task(s) that immediately follow the named task

- Type—the types of predecessor-successor relationship that exist, such as Finish-to-start (FS)

- Lag—the amount of lag time necessary before the successor can begin. (Lead time is indicated by a [-] minus sign)

- Duration—the currently scheduled duration

- Start—the scheduled start date

- Finish—the scheduled finish date

- Predecessors—tasks that must be accomplished in their entirety or in part before this task can begin

- Resource Name—the names of resources assigned and their availability, expressed in units. For example, someone who is assigned for 100% of her time to the tasks will be shown as [1]; 50% availability is shown as [.5]

This report provides details about the critical path. It can be used to analyze predecessor-successor relationships, assignments, and dates. As a result of seeing this report, you may want to adjust availability levels, or change some of the dependency relationships to adjust the schedule.

Milestones

The Milestones report displays milestones in a format that is very similar to the Critical Tasks report. Tasks listed include all of those tasks identified as milestones. It includes the following columns:

- ID—the task ID number

- Task Name—the names of each milestone

- Successor Name—the task(s) that immediately follow the named task

- Duration—the currently scheduled duration

- Start—the scheduled start date

- Finish—the scheduled finish date

- Predecessors—tasks that must be accomplished in their entirety or in part before this task can begin

- Resource Name—the names of resources assigned, if they are assigned at the level displayed

This report can be particularly useful for larger projects, and for projects with many milestones identified. It renders a quick glimpse of scheduled dates and predecessors.

Reminder: milestones may or may not have duration.

Working Days

The Working Days report displays the base calendar that is used to schedule tasks and resources. It displays working days and hours as well as nonworking days and hours.

CURRENT ACTIVITY REPORTS

Current activity reports include:

- Unstarted Tasks
- Tasks Starting Soon
- Tasks In Progress
- Completed Tasks
- Should Have Started Tasks
- Slipping Tasks

When you choose **Current Activities** from **Reports**, then **Select** you will see the six current activity reports that are available.

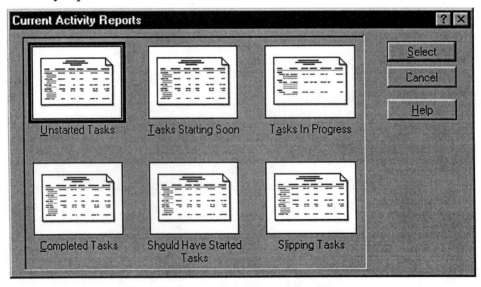

Figure 7-3. Current Activity Reports

Unstarted Tasks

The Unstarted Tasks report provides a filtered list of remaining tasks that must be accomplished to complete the project. This report presents highly detailed information about each task. For each task, the following data is displayed:

- ID—the task ID number

- ID—the resource ID number

- Task Name—the names of each milestone

- Resource Names—the names of resources assigned, if they are assigned at the level displayed

- Units—the availability of the resource: if a resource is available for 100% of her time the number [1] is displayed; if the resource is available for half of his time [5] is displayed

- Work—total number of work hours, based on the current schedule

- Duration—the currently scheduled duration

- Delay—a user-entered delay that indicates how long a resource is delayed before beginning work on a task. For example, if the delay is four hours (4h) it means that the resource is scheduled to begin working on the task four hours after it starts

- Start—the currently scheduled start date for the task

- Finish—the currently scheduled finish date for the task

- Predecessors—tasks that must be accomplished in their entirety or in part before this task can begin

This report provides many details about each unstarted task. Using this report, you can examine predecessors and delays as a strategy for reducing project duration.

Tasks Starting Soon

This report format is identical to the one used in the Unstarted Tasks report. The difference is that this report shows tasks that fall within a date range that you specify. Normally this list of tasks is shorter than a list of all unstarted tasks.

Tasks In Progress

The Tasks In Progress report format is identical to the Unstarted Tasks and Tasks Starting Soon report formats. This is likely to be a short list relative to project size, since it only includes tasks that are currently underway.

Completed Tasks

The Completed Tasks report renders a filtered list of all tasks that are complete as of the date of the report. It contains less detail than the previous Current Activity report

- ID—the task ID number

- Task Name—the names of each objective, task, and subtask

- Duration—the currently scheduled duration

- Start—the scheduled start date

- Finish—the scheduled finish date

- % Complete—100% complete is shown for all tasks, since they are complete

- Cost—the actual costs for completed tasks

- Work—total number of work hours required to complete each task

This report provides a way to see several project details on completed tasks. It can be used to compare work hours and their related costs. If you print it every week, you can see a growing list of completed tasks as the project unfolds.

Should Have Started Tasks

The Should Have Started Tasks report provides a filtered list of tasks that should have begun as of the date you specify. It includes the following data columns:

- ID—the task ID number

- Task Name—the names of each objective, task, and subtask

- Successor ID—the ID numbers of all successors

- Successor Name—the task(s) that immediately follow the tasks that should have started

- Type (of Predecessor)—finish-to-start, start-to-start, or other dependency relationship

- Lag—the delay between the finish of a predecessor and the start of its successor (Lead time is indicated by a [-] minus sign)

- Start—the scheduled start date

- Finish—the scheduled finish date

- Baseline Start

- Baseline Finish

- Start Variance—the difference between the (scheduled) start and the baseline start; variances expressed as a negative number indicate that the task is ahead of schedule

- Finish Variance—the difference between the (scheduled) finish and the baseline finish; variances expressed as a negative number indicate that the task is scheduled to finish ahead of schedule

This report can be used to compare the currently scheduled start and finish dates with the baseline start and finish dates for tasks that should have started.

Slipping Tasks

The Slipping Tasks report lists tasks that have started late, are scheduled to finish late, or which have a duration that is longer than the baseline. It displays the same columns of data shown on the Should Have Started Tasks report.

This report is valuable for quickly identifying tasks that may jeopardize the project schedule. If critical tasks are delayed, the project is likely to be delayed. During certain points in the project lifecycle, particularly when many successors are dependent upon one predecessor, print this report. It may provide an early enough warning for you to take effective corrective action.

Cost Reports

Cost reports provide an array of analysis tools focusing on project expenditures. Five standard cost reports are available:

- Weekly Cash Flow
- Budget
- Overbudget Tasks
- Overbudget Resources
- Earned Value

Each will be described below. When you choose Costs you will see the following choices:

Do It Your Way Reports and Forms

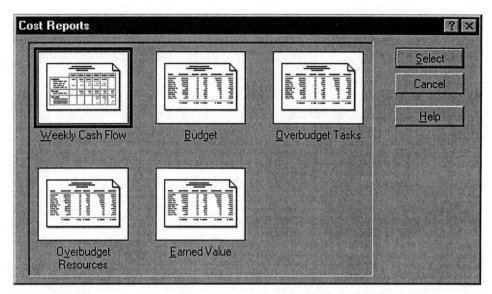

Figure 7-4. Cost Reports

After a project begins, and as activities and tasks are completed, you will want to record progress.

Weekly Cash Flow

The Weekly Cash Flow report displays a table that shows the timing of project costs. It includes the following data:

- Task Name—a list of all levels of project work

- Costs By Week—costs associated with each subtask. Costs are not accumulated to the summary task level.

Because this table shows the exact timing of all project costs, it is useful for preparing the project budget and department budget. You may want to export this table to a spreadsheet application for additional analysis.

Budget

The Budget report provides a task-by-task breakdown of all costs and variances from the baseline. The list is sorted by total cost, with the highest total cost shown first and the lowest total cost shown last. It includes the following data columns:

- ID—the task ID number

- Task Name—the names of each task that incurs costs

- Fixed Cost—a cost that does not change with an increase or decrease in hours or duration

- Total Cost—the accumulation of period costs, cost-per-use, and fixed costs

- Baseline—the planned costs as saved in the baseline

- Variance—the difference between total cost and baseline cost

- Actual—costs that were incurred

This report can be used to quickly see the variance from the baseline. You can compare the actual costs to date with the baseline cost, and identify the tasks that represent the largest variances. This information can be used to improve cost estimating on future projects.

Overbudget Tasks

The Overbudget Tasks report displays a filtered list of only those tasks that have exceeded baseline costs, and have a negative variance as of the date of the report. The list is sorted by variance in descending order.

The data columns are identical to those used in the Budget report.

The Overbudget Tasks report helps to focus attention on tasks that may have had inaccurate time estimates. It may also help to focus attention on requirements for tasks that are less familiar to the team.

Overbudget Resources

The Overbudget Resources report displays a filtered list of resources that have cost more than planned and saved as the baseline. It includes the following data columns:

- ID—the task ID number

- Task Name—the names of each task that incurs costs

- Cost—the total cost that is scheduled for the use of a particular resource

- Baseline Cost—the planned cost for a particular resource as saved in the baseline

- Variance—the difference between total cost and baseline cost

- Actual Cost—costs that were incurred

This report spotlights resources that have exceeded the baseline cost. It can be used to isolate project trouble spots, such as inaccurate time estimates, unclear requirements or completion criteria, or poor communication among team members working on the task. It may be a signal to provide training and development to certain resources, or to look outside of the organization for contractors with specialized skills.

Earned Value

The Earned Value report displays all project subtasks and several measures of performance. It includes the following data columns:

- Task Name—the names of each task that incurs costs; summary task data is not shown

- BCWS—Budgeted Cost of Work Scheduled; the baseline cost multiplied by the planned percent complete as of the current date

- BCWP—Earned Value or Budgeted Cost of Work Performed; the baseline cost multiplied by the percent complete as of the current date

- ACWP—Actual Cost of Work Perfomed; the actual cost of accomplishing a task

- SV—Schedule Variance; BCWP minus BCWS

- CV—Cost Variance; BCWP minus ACWP

- BAC—Budgeted at Completion; the planned budget for the task, which includes all cost categories

This report and similar reports are most commonly used to manage government contracts. It is used to identify and examine:

- Earned value for each task and the project as a whole

The Complete Planning Guide for Microsoft® Project

- Difference in cost between the original schedule and the current schedule

- Difference between the original cost and the currently forecasted cost

Use the report as a signal to explore the causes of variances. Variances can be caused by not planning in sufficient detail, a slowdown caused by a technical breakthrough or problem, inflation, work stoppage, or other reasons.

ASSIGNMENT REPORTS

Four reports are available to help in managing resources.

- Who Does What
- Who Does What When
- Weekly To-do List
- Overallocated Resources

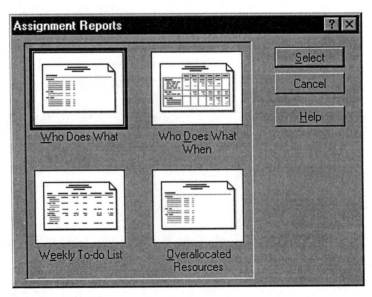

Figure 7-5. Assignment Reports

Who Does What

The Who Does What report shows each resource, the total work hours assigned, and that resource's assignments throughout the project. It shows the following data columns:

- ID—the ID number for the resource
- Resource Name—the name of the resource or resource group
- Work—the total work hours assigned to the resource during the project
- ID—the task ID number
- Task Name—the names of each task that incurs costs
- Units—the availability of the resource; if a resource is available for 100% of her time, the number [1] is displayed; if the resource is available for half of his time, [.5] is displayed
- Work—the number of work hours assigned to each listed task
- Delay—a user-entered delay that indicates how long a resource is delayed before beginning work on a task; for example, if the delay is four hours (4h), it means that the resource is scheduled to begin working on the task four hours after it starts
- Start—the currently scheduled start date for the task
- Finish—the currently scheduled finish date for the task

This report can be used as a reference by all managers who have assigned team members to the project. When prepared for consolidated projects, it can show all resource assignments to each project managed by a group, unit or department.

Who Does What When

The Who Does What When report, like the Who Does What report shows all tasks that are assigned to each resource. Beside each task the report displays a table of weekly calendar dates such as 4/1, 4/8, and so on to show the exact distribution of work hours, by task, during every week in the project schedule.

Weekly To-do List

The Weekly To Do List report shows all of the tasks assigned to a resource for every week that the resource has an assignment. For each week that the resource has an assignment, the report shows:

- ID—the task ID number

- Task Name—the names of each task to which the resource is assigned

- Duration—the currently scheduled duration

- Start—the currently scheduled start date for the task

- Finish—the currently scheduled finish date for the task

- Predecessors—tasks that must be accomplished in their entirety or in part before this task can begin

This report can be distributed to team members on a regular basis, for example, weekly. It can be used by each team members as a checklist and reminder of schedule dates. Team members can also quickly see the predecessors to their tasks. In many projects, those responsible for tasks may need to discuss scheduled handoff dates and assumptions with those responsible for predecessors and/or successors.

Overallocated Resources

The Overallocated Resources Report shows all work assignments, but only for each overallocated resource. It shows the following columns of data:

- ID—the task ID number

- ID—the resource ID number

- Resource Name—the name of the resource or resource group

- Task Name—the names of each task that incurs costs

- Work—the total number of hours that are assigned to the resource during the project

Do It Your Way Reports and Forms

- Units—the availability of the resource; if a resource is available for 100% of her time, the number [1] is displayed; if the resource is available for half of his time [.5] is displayed

- Work—the number of work hours assigned to each listed task

- Delay—a user-entered delay that indicates how long a resource is delayed before beginning work on a task; for example, if the delay is four hours (4h), it means that the resource is scheduled to begin working on the task four hours after it starts

- Start—the currently scheduled start date for the task

- Finish—the currently scheduled finish date for the task

This report can be used to manage resource assignments. Used with the resource graph, this report may be used to insert delays where slack exists, or to change the units or work to reduce or eliminate an overallocation.

WORKLOAD REPORTS

Workload reports provide detailed information about tasks and resources. There are two workload reports:

- Task Usage report

- Resource Usage report

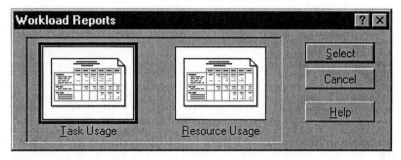

Figure 7-6. Workload Reports

Task Usage

The Task Usage report shows all levels of project work, the resources assigned to each task, the dates, and the work hours. It includes these columns:

- Task and Resource—the levels of project work; resources assigned to a task are shown beneath the task.

- Weekly —beneath a column heading that is dated and displayed in weekly time periods, the number of hours required to accomplish the tasks is shown. Beneath the number of work hours estimated for the task is a breakdown of those hours by resource.

This report can be used to analyze the timing of task accomplishment as it relates to resource usage. It may be used with the Budget report and/or with a table that includes a column for slack to analyze possible delays within slack and the cost ramifications.

Resource Usage

The Resource Usage report, like the Who Does What report, shows each resource name and all tasks assigned to the resource. It includes these columns:

- Resource and Task—the resource name, beneath which are all tasks assigned to that resource.

- Weekly—beneath a column heading that is dated and displayed in weekly time periods, the number of hours required to accomplish the tasks are shown. Beneath the number of work hours estimated for the resource is a breakdown of those hours by task.

This report can be used to analyze the timing of resource usage as it relates to task accomplishment. It may be used together with the resource usage sheet or resource graph.

CUSTOM REPORTS

Every standard report can be customized. You can also design your own reports by choosing **Task**, **Resource**, **Monthly Calendar** or **Crosstab** from the Define New Report dialog box shown in Figure 7-8. Custom reports enable you to configure or

Do It Your Way Reports and Forms

reconfigure the information contained in the standard reports so that reports to stakeholders meet their needs as precisely as possible.

Reports that can be customized are all shown in the Custom Reports dialog box shown below. Use the scroll bar to see additional choices. To access this box, choose **View**, then **Reports**, **Custom**, and **Select**.

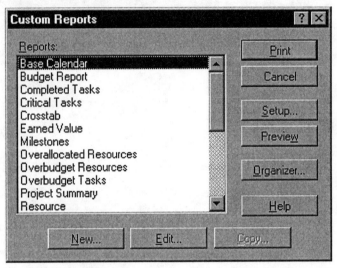

Figure 7-7. Custom Reports Dialog Box

If you choose New from this dialog box, you will see the Define New Report dialog box, shown in Figure 7-8.

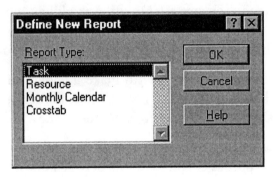

Figure 7-8. Define New Report Dialog Box

Task

When you choose **Task** from the four categories of reports, you will see a dialog box like the one shown in Figure 7-9, with three tabs:

211

- Definition
- Details
- Sort

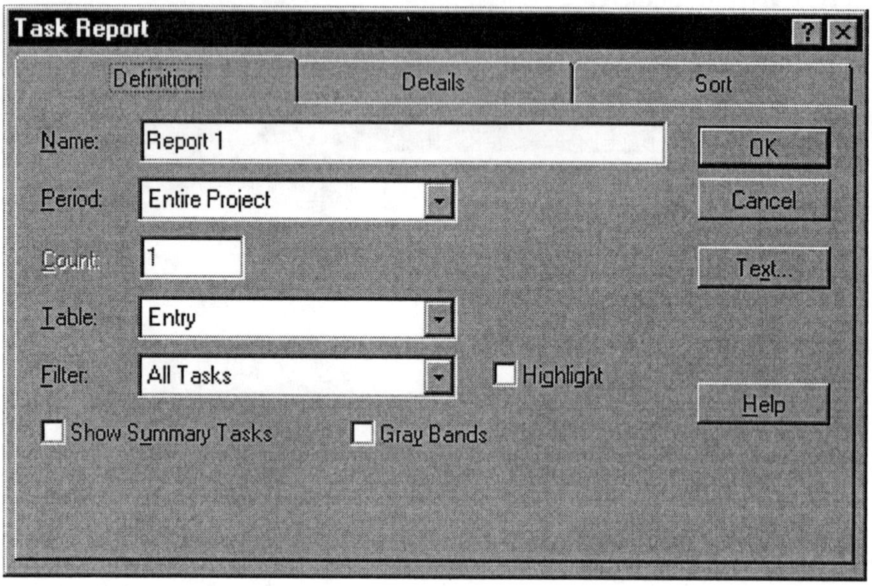

Figure 7-9. Task Report Dialog Box

The Definition tab for a task report can be used to name the report, change the time period covered by the report, choose a table, filter/highlight, choose whether or not to show summary tasks, and choose whether or not to show gray bands to partition the report with shaded horizontal bands. You may also change text formatting.

The Details tab for a task report asks you to make a choice about whether to display details such as notes, objects, predecessors, successors, borders around details, or totals. In addition, you are asked to choose whether or not to show resource schedules, costs and work.

The Sort tab for a task report asks you to define between one and three sorting criteria. By default, Microsoft® Project sorts by ID number and lists tasks in numerical order. See "Sorting and Filtering" later in this chapter.

As with all other tables and reports, you may want to experiment by choosing each possibility and using print preview to compare choices.

Do It Your Way Reports and Forms

Resource

When you choose **Resource** from the four categories of reports, you will see a dialog box like the one shown in Figure 7-10 with three tabs:

- Definition
- Details
- Sort

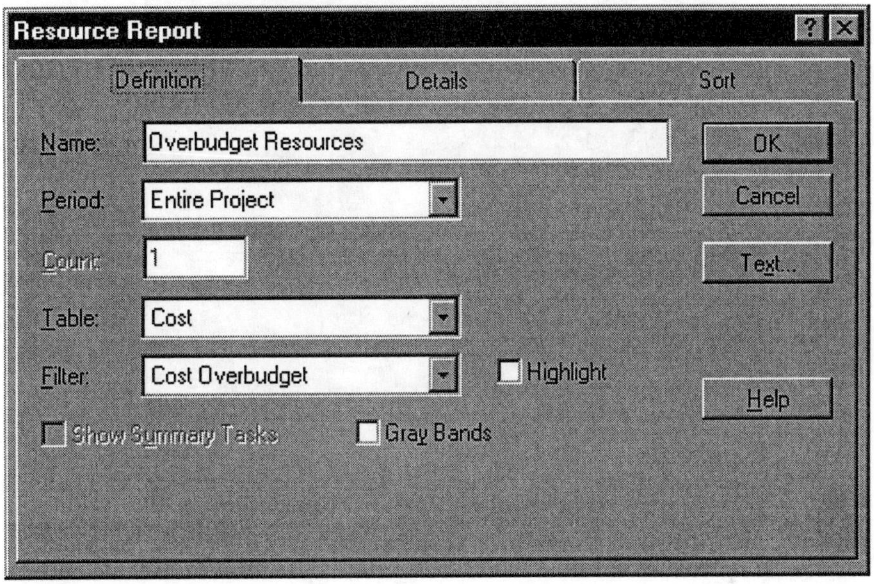

Figure 7-10. Resources Report Dialog Box

The Definition tab for a resource report can be used to name the project; choose a display period such as years, months, weeks or days; choose a standard table to use; and a filter to show all resources or certain resources.

The Details tab for a resource report enables you to make choices about resource-related notes, objects, and calendar, whether or not to display a border around details, and whether or not to show totals. In addition, for tasks shown, you can choose to show schedule cost or work hours related to resource use.

The Sort tab for a resource report provides choices about sorting order, using up to three sorting criteria. See "Sorting and Filtering" later in this chapter.

The Complete Planning Guide for Microsoft® Project

As with all other tables and reports, you may want to experiment by choosing each possibility and using print preview to compare choices.

Monthly

When you select **Base Calendar**, then **New** from the Custom Reports dialog box, and **Monthly Calendar** from the Define New Report dialog box, you will see the Monthly Calendar Report Definition dialog box, as shown below.

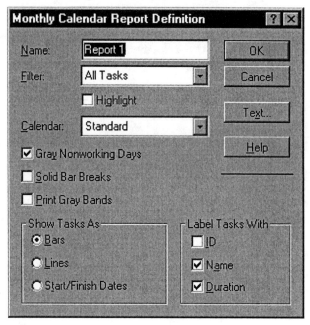

Figure 7-11. Monthly Calendar Report Definition Dialog Box

The Monthly Calendar Report Definition dialog box provides choices about the report name, and the task filter to apply, such as all tasks, critical tasks, or complete tasks; and whether to show the standard calendar or a resource-specific calendar.

The box also provides display choices about whether or not to show gray nonworking days, solid bar breaks, or horizontal gray bands. Additional choices enable you to show tasks as bars, lines, or start and finish dates, and to label tasks with an ID number, name, and/or duration.

As with all other tables and reports, you may want to experiment by choosing each possibility and using print preview to compare choices.

Crosstab

When you select **Crosstab**, then **New** from the Custom Reports dialog box, and **Crosstab** from the Define New Report dialog box, you will see the Crosstab Report dialog box shown below.

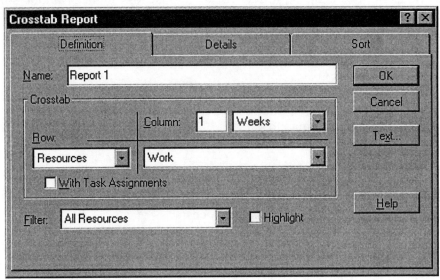

Figure 7-12. Crosstab Report Dialog Box

The Definition tab for the custom Crosstab report is used to name the report and make a choice about whether to show tasks with resource assignments or resources with their respective tasks. You also choose to show cost or work categories and time increments, such as weeks or months, to be displayed in columns. This tab also includes choices about whether or not the report is filtered, and if so, whether it should be a highlight filter.

The Details tab for the custom Crosstab report provides choices about whether or not to show summary tasks, row totals, column totals, and gridlines. You also use this tab to choose whether to show zero values, repeat the first column on every page, choose a date format, and make changes to text style and size.

The Sort tab for a Crosstab report provides choices about sorting order using up to three sorting criteria. See "Sorting and Filtering" later in this chapter.

As with all other tables and reports, you may want to experiment by choosing each possibility and using print preview to compare choices.

SORTING AND FILTERING

By using sorting and filtering, you can create concise reports that are arranged in an easy-to-read format. Most views, tables and reports, can be sorted and filtered. In the reports sections of this chapter you were able to access choices about sorting and filtering report data by using the report dialog boxes. You can also choose to sort or filter data that is displayed in views and tables.

Sorting

Sorting is a technique that is used to change the display order of tasks, resources, or other data. It is similar to sorting a database.

Sorting Tasks

To change the display order of tasks for a table or view, choose **Tools** from the menu bar, then **Sort**. You will see five standard choices:

- By start date—chronological sequence beginning with the earliest start date
- By finish date—chronological sequence beginning with the earliest finish date
- By priority—highest-priority tasks shown first; lowest-priority tasks shown last
- By cost—highest cost shown first, lowest cost shown last
- By ID—default setting; ID # 1 shown first, highest ID # shown last

In addition, if you would like to sort data by using other criteria, or if you would like to reverse the sort order by showing the task with the lowest cost first, for example, choose **Sort by**. You will see the Sort dialog box, shown below.

Do It Your Way Reports and Forms

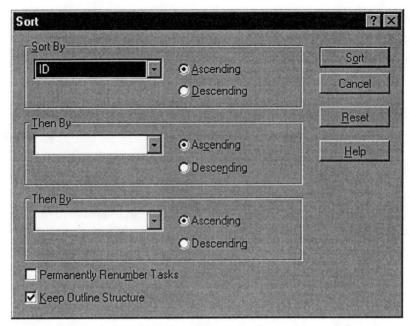

Figure 7-13. Sort Dialog Box

If, for example, you would like to arrange the tasks in a table to show critical tasks first, then (with the remaining tasks) by start date, do the following:

Fast Lane Tip #57

To sort tasks by critical path, then by start date

1. Click on **Tools**, or press **Alt/T**.
2. Choose **Sort**, then **Sort by**. You will see the Sort dialog box shown above.
3. Use the scrolling arrow beneath **Sort by** to choose **Critical**.
4. Use the mouse or **Tab** key to move to **Then by**. Use the scrolling arrow to choose **Start**.
5. Choose **Sort**. The tasks will be sorted to display critical tasks first, then the remaining tasks beginning with the earliest start date.

The Sort dialog box may provide additional choices. Permanently Renumber Tasks lets you permanently change both the ID number and the WBS number. Use this choice cautiously. Making a permanent change to either numbering system will tend to make comparisons over time more difficult, and complicate archiving systems.

Making the choice to Keep Outline Structure will move parent tasks with their sorted subtasks.

Sorting Resources

To sort resources from a resource view, choose **Tools**, then **Sort**. You will see three choices: By Cost, By Name, and By ID. You can choose from these choices, or choose **Sort by** to see the Sort dialog box for resources. You may want to choose from among the many additional choices, such as e-mail address or actual work.

Fast Lane Tip #58

To apply the same sort order again

Press Ctrl/Shift/F3.

Filtering

Filtering is a technique that is used to limit or highlight selected tasks, resources, or other displayed data. When you choose a filter, you choose to actually "filter in" only the data that you would like to see (or highlight), just as a coffee filter "filters in" only coffee while "filtering out" the grounds.

Filtering Tasks

To choose a filter while in a task view, choose **Tools** from the menu bar, and then choose **Filtered for**. You will see the following choices:

Do It Your Way Reports and Forms

- All Tasks—the default setting
- Completed tasks—all tasks that are complete
- Critical—tasks on the critical path
- Date Range—tasks that start or finish after a specified date
- Incomplete tasks—tasks that have begun
- Milestones—tasks identified as milestones
- Summary Tasks—tasks that have data summarized from subtasks
- Task Range—tasks between a range of ID numbers
- Using Resource—tasks with a certain resource assigned
- More Filters—displays additional filters

If you would like to see all tasks, but highlight the tasks that meet the criteria, choose More Filters, then select the filter to be used and choose highlight. The filter will be applied.

Filtering Resources

By applying a filter to resources, you can quickly see an abbreviated or highlighted list of resources. To choose a filter while in a resource view, choose **Tools**, then **Filtered For**. You will see the following choices:

- All Resources—the default setting
- Cost Overbudget—resources that have exceeded the dollar budget
- Group—a group of resources, such as programmers
- Overallocated Resources—resources with assignments exceeding availability
- Resource Range—resources within a range of ID numbers

- Work Overbudget—resources that have exceeded the planned number of hours

- More Filters—additional choices and a choice to use a highlighted filter

If you would like to see all resources, but highlight those that meet the criteria, choose **More Filters**, then select the filter to be used and choose **Highlight**. The filter will be applied.

Fast Lane Tip #59

To apply the same filter again

Press **Ctrl/F3**.

PRINT PREVIEW

It is usually a good idea to see what your table or report will look like before printing it, especially if there are many pages. To do this, click on 🔍 , or choose **File**, then **Print Preview**. You will see the first page of the report.

To see the number of pages required, and the layout of all pages, click on 🗔 . This allows you to see the number of pages in the report, and whether all desired columns are displayed. Use 🔍 examine specific parts of the view, table, or report.

Use the ◀▶▲▼ arrows near the top left portion of the screen to move between pages.

Do It Your Way Reports and Forms

PAGE SETUP

After you have used print preview to make choices about reports, you may want to use page setup to define page orientation, headers, footers, legends, page breaks, and other data.

If you will be printing a table or report, you can access the Page Setup dialog box from print preview, or from the Custom Reports dialog box by choosing **Setup**. The Page Setup dialog box is shown below.

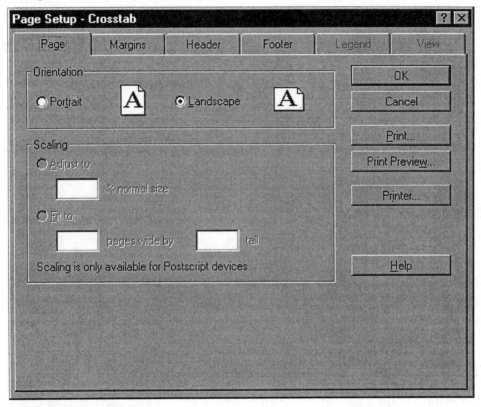

Figure 7-14. Page Setup Dialog Box

You can access the Page Setup dialog box from the print preview window, or from the menu bar.

221

> **Fast Lane Tip #60**
>
>
>
> To add headings for tables, views, and reports from the menu bar
>
> 1. Click on **File**, or press **Alt/F**.
> 2. Choose **Page Setup**. You will see the dialog box shown in Figure 7-14. (It will read "Page Setup" only.)
> 3. Choose the **Header** tab.
> 4. Choose **Left**, **Center**, or **Right Alignment**.
> 5. Use the mouse or Tab key to move to the appropriate space beneath the header, and type in the desired heading for the report, such as **Earned Value Report** (on line 1) and "October 31, 1997" (on line 2).
> 6. Choose **OK** when finished.

Choices about footers, margins, page orientation, legend, and view can also be made here if desired. For example, you can add page numbers, the project manager's name, and other information to the footer.

PRINTING

You can print a table, view, or report in several ways. If you are working in a table or view, and are sure you want to print "as is", click on , the report will print immediately. Another way is to press **Ctrl/P**, then press **Enter**. Often however, you will want to make some changes while in the Print dialog box. See Figure 7-15.

You can also print from the print preview window by choosing **Print**, then **OK**.

Do It Your Way Reports and Forms

Figure 7-15. Print Dialog Box

Choices about timescale, page range, page breaks, and print quality can be made using this dialog box.

Fast Lane Tip #61

To print all columns (even those not showing)

1. Click on **File**, or press **Alt/F**.
2. Choose **Page Setup**.
3. Choose **View**.

The Complete Planning Guide for Microsoft® Project

---

4. Choose **Print All Sheet Columns**.

5. Click on **OK**, or press **Enter**.

CREATING CUSTOM FORMS

As you gain experience with Microsoft® Project, you may find yourself shifting between the same tables and forms repeatedly to enter certain data. A solution may be to customize an existing form from the Custom Forms dialog box, or create a new form that has exactly the fields of data that you need. This is one of the many ways you can customize Microsoft Project to match your work style and take advantage of its available features.

You can create a new form with resource-related information (see Figure 7-16 below0, or with task-related information (see Figure 7-25 later in this chapter).

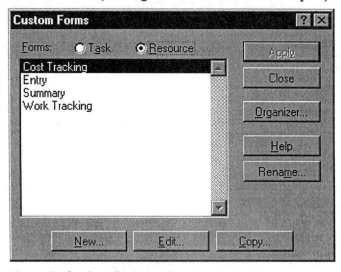

Figure 7-16. Custom Forms Dialog Box (Resources)

Use the Custom Forms dialog box to create a new form, beginning with a blank form, and edit an existing form by using either the Edit or Copy button, just as you do with tables.

The Dialog Editor

Microsoft® Project has a built-in Dialog Editor application that you use to create new forms and edit existing forms that are listed in the Custom Forms dialog box. When invoked, the Dialog Editor uses its own menu bar with three menus: File, Edit and Item.

The custom forms toolbar provides quick access to several standard forms that can be used to manage task and resource data. You can use them as they appear, or you can customize the form by adding or removing fields of data. Although the Dialog Editor is available in Versions 4.0 and 4.1, the toolbar is available only on Version 4.1.

Figure 7-17. Custom Forms Toolbar (Version 4.1 only)

Use these buttons as follows:

 Entry button—displays the Entry dialog box, which you use to enter basic task information about duration, start, or finish dates, and whether or not to roll up task information about the selected task.

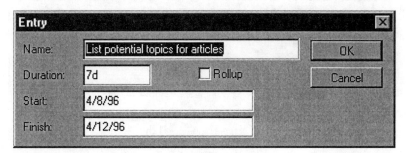

Figure 7-18. Entry Form Dialog Box

 Cost Tracking button—displays the cost tracking dialog box, which you use to enter cost, duration, percent complete, and work data for the selected task.

The Complete Planning Guide for Microsoft® Project

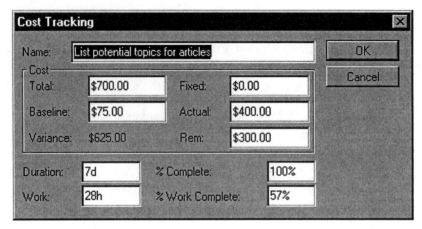

Figure 7-19. Cost Tracking Dialog Box

 Work Tracking button—displays the Work Tracking dialog box, which you use to enter data about work hours and other data for the selected task.

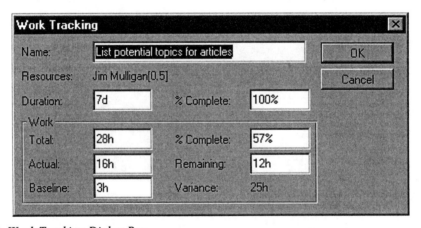

Figure 7-20. Work Tracking Dialog Box

 Task Earned Value button—displays the Earned Value dialog box, which you use to examine earned value variance data for the selected task.

Do It Your Way Reports and Forms

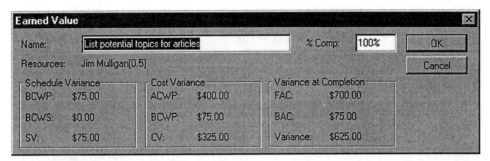

Figure 7-21. Earned Value Dialog Box

 Schedule Tracking button—displays the Schedule Tracking dialog box, which you use to analyze schedule data by comparing the baseline to scheduled dates and show variances.

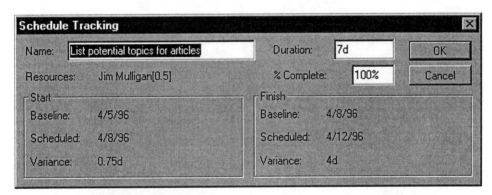

Figure 7-22. Schedule Tracking Dialog Box

 Task Relationships button—displays the Task Relationships dialog box, which you use to examine predecessors and successors to the selected task.

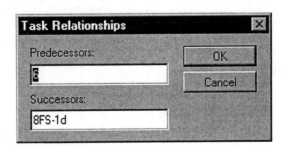

Figure 7-23. Task Relationships Dialog Box

The Complete Planning Guide for Microsoft® Project

 Tracking button—displays the Tracking dialog box, which you use to analyze task details, such as dates, remaining duration, and percent complete for the selected task.

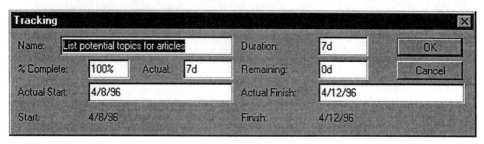

Figure 7-24. Tracking Dialog Box

 Custom Forms button—displays the Custom Forms dialog box, which you use to edit a form, or create a new custom form.

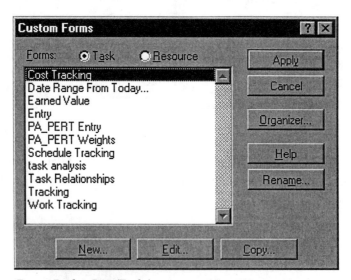

Figure 7-25. Custom Forms Dialog Box (Tasks)

Fast Lane Tip #62

To create a new custom form for task analysis

1. Create a draft of the form that you would like to create, using pen and paper or a word processor. Include a heading for each field and space for each field.

2. Click on **Tools**, or press **Alt/T**.

3. Choose **Customize**, then **Forms**. You will see the Custom Forms dialog box.

4. Choose **New**. The Define Custom Form dialog box will appear.

5. Type a name for the new form in the **Name** box. Click on **OK**, or press **Enter**. You will see the new blank form with the name you entered at the top.

6. Choose **Item**, then **Text** to add headings for each field of data that you would like included on the new form. The box will appear at the bottom of the form. You can drag each box to position it where you would like it to appear and size the heading. Use the **Backspace** key to remove the word **Text**, then enter the name that you would like to use as the heading for the field. Press **Enter** to see additional text fields.

7. Choose **Item**, then **Field** to select a field from the Microsoft® Project list. You will see a small dialog box that asks you to choose a field. Use the scrolling arrow to see and choose additional fields. Drag each field so that it appears beside or beneath the heading. Size each field by dragging. Choose **Show As Static Text** for fields that you want to remain unchanged. You will not be able to edit these fields from the form.

8. Choose **Save**.

9. Choose **Exit** (from the Dialog Editor). You can access the new form by choosing it from the Custom Forms dialog box list.

The dialog box shown in Figure 7-26 was created using the Dialog Editor.

The Complete Planning Guide for Microsoft® Project

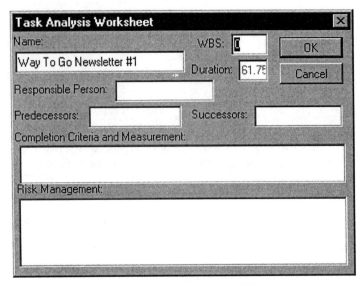

Figure 7-26. Task Analysis Worksheet Created with the Dialog Editor

COMPANION PRODUCTS RELATED TO THIS CHAPTER:

All products listed in previous chapters are capable of preparing reports.

8

Advanced Features

In this chapter you will learn how to:

1. Customize menus, toolbars, and toolbar buttons

2. Create and run macros

3. Import and export data

4. Link and embed data and objects

INTRODUCTION

There are two or more ways to perform most operations when using Microsoft® Project. While you are becoming familiar with the tool, you will use your time well if you can find ways to work that require fewer steps. For example, by using a mouse, you can often perform a function with one click that would require two or more steps using the keyboard.

There are many other ways to save steps and time while working. In this chapter, you will learn to make substitutions and changes to the toolbar and toolbar buttons, and create a new button. In addition, you will learn how the standard macros can improve efficiency, how to import and export, and how to link and embed objects.

CUSTOMIZING MENUS, TOOLBARS, AND TOOLBAR BUTTONS

You can do much to customize the appearance and features of Microsoft Project to meet the needs of your project environment, and your own personal preferences. You can add, remove, or customize:

- Menus and submenu commands
- Toolbars
- Toolbar buttons

Each will be explained in the following sections.

Changing the Menu

You may decide to make your work easier by adding a new menu item to the menu bar. For example, let's say that you would like to create a new Status Menu Bar item that pulls together all of the commands that are used to send and receive status information and electronic mail to and from stakeholders. The fast lane tip shown below shows how it is done.

To prepare yourself to use the fast lane tip, make a list of submenu commands that you want to include under the new menu item. In the fast lane tip below, a new Communication menu item will be created that combines several communication-related commands, as follows:

Advanced Features

- Communication—new menu bar item
- Open Mail—from the workgroup toolbar
- Post Mail—from the workgroup toolbar
- Send Mail—from the File Menu
- Add Routing Slip—from the File menu
- TeamAssign—from the Tools menu, Workgroup command
- TeamUpdate—from the Tools menu, Workgroup command
- TeamStatus—from the Tools menu, Workgroup command
- Set Reminder—from the Tools menu, Workgroup command
- Send Schedule Note—from the Tools menu, Workgroup command
- Update Read Only—from the Workgroup toolbar
- Toggle Updates—from the Workgroup toolbar

The fast lane tip for creating a new menu appears below.

Fast Lane Tip #63

To add a new menu to the menu bar

1. Click on **Tools**, or press **Alt/T**.
2. Choose **Customize**, then **Menu Bar**, and you will see the dialog box shown in Figure 8-1.
3. Select the menu that you would like to modify, and choose **Edit**. You will now see the Menu Bar Definition dialog box, shown in Figure 8-2. Enter a name for the new menu bar.
4. From top to bottom, the dialog box lists all menu items and their submenu commands.
5. Scroll down the list of menus and submenus, using the scroll bar or the up and down

arrows. Stop on the line beneath the insertion point where you would like to place the new menu and submenu commands.

6. Click on the **Insert Row** button once for the menu item and once for every additional submenu command that you would like to include. (If you decide you would like to add or remove items while you are working, use the **Insert Row** button or the **Cut Rows** button as necessary.)

7. Type in the name of the new item to appear on the menu bar (**Communication** in this example) and press **Enter**. Choose the left outlining arrow to define the item as the menu bar item and to make the title bold.

8. Type in the remaining submenu commands.

9. In the **Command/Macro** field, use the scrolling arrow beside the entry bar to choose the macro or command from the list of all Microsoft® Project commands.

10. When the menu is constructed as you would like it to appear, choose **OK**.

11. Choose **Apply** when you see the Menu Bars dialog box. The new menu will appear.

Figure 8-1. Menu Bars Dialog Box

In the example shown above, a Communication menu was created. Many of the commands, such as Send Mail, were taken from other menus. You can choose to leave them in two places or to cut them from their previous locations. To cut them, return to the Menu Bar Definition dialog box and use the **Cut Rows** button to remove them.

In the fast lane tip above you edited an existing menu bar. If you would like to return the menu to its original contents, choose the Edit button in the Menu Bars dialog box shown above, and then choose **Reset**. The Menu Bar and submenus will be returned to their original configuration.

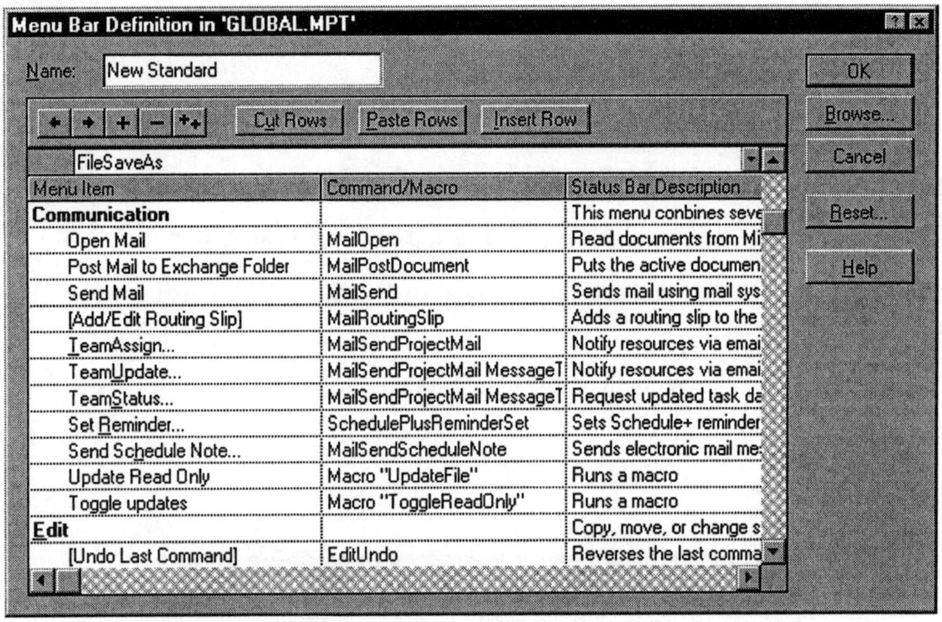

Figure 8-2. Menu Bar Definition Dialog Box with Communication Menu

Adding a New Task Network To The Menu

To meet the needs of different audiences, or simply to see the project from a variety of perspectives, you may need to display. more than one PERT task network. You can do this in a number of ways:

- Change the contents or size of boxes/nodes each time it is needed. See Chapter 5.

- Create a macro to format and create one or more task networks. See "Creating a Macro" later in this chapter.

- Add a new PERT task network to the View menu.

The fast lane tip shown below describes the steps necessary to add another task network to the menu bar.

The Complete Planning Guide for Microsoft® Project

Fast Lane Tip #64

To add a new PERT task network to the menu bar

1. Click on **View,** or press **Alt/V.**
2. Choose **More Views,** then **PERT Chart.**
3. Choose **Copy.** You will see the View Definition dialog box shown in Figure 8-3.
4. Enter a new name such as **Task Network with WBS,** to distinguish it from other task networks.
5. Choose **Apply.** You have created a new submenu command.

Figure 8-3. View Definition Dialog Box

Once you have created the new menu item, modify the information contained in each node/box, as shown below. In the example below, the ID number is replaced with the WBS number.

From the new PERT task network, change the contents of the boxes from ID to WBS. To do this:

Fast Lane Tip #65

To change box contents in the PERT task network

1. Click on **Format**, or press **Alt/O**.

2. Choose **Box Styles**, then select the **Boxes** tab. You will see the Box Styles dialog box shown in Figure 8-4.

3. Change the ID number field to **WBS** by clicking on the scrolling arrow beside **ID**, or using the down arrow key, then typing **W**, and choosing **WBS**. (Or change another field.)

4. Choose **OK**. You have changed the box contents in the newly created view.

Figure 8-4. Box Styles Dialog Box

Deleting Items from the Menu

As you learn more about Microsoft® Project, your work preferences are likely to change, and you may wish to remove items from the menu bar or a submenu. To do this, use the Menu Bar Definition dialog box and the **Cut Rows** button, as described earlier.

To remove a view from the menu, you will need to use the Organizer dialog box, as described below.

Fast Lane Tip #66

To remove a view from the View menu

1. Click on **View**, or press **Alt/V**.
2. Choose the **Organizer** button, then the **Views** tab.
3. Select the name of the view that you would like to remove from the views box on the right, and choose the **Delete** button. The view is deleted.
4. Choose **Yes** to confirm the deletion.
5. Choose **Close**.

Customizing Toolbars and Buttons

A skilled user of Microsoft Project is likely to use a large number of buttons on the working toolbar. They provide one-step access to many functions. If you are new to using a mouse, try to ease yourself into the using point-and-click features available with a mouse. Many functions can be performed only with a mouse. In addition, you can often save yourself steps by clicking on a button, and moving to different sections while in a dialog box.

There are many strategies for setting up the toolbar to meet your preferences. One strategy is to use a minimum number of toolbars, and display other toolbars only as needed. For example, go to the **View** menu, choose **Toolbars**, and then choose the **Formatting** toolbar to create a WBS outline. Once you have finished creating an outline for your project, you can then choose to **Hide** the formatting toolbar. This strategy will help to minimize the number of buttons in your toolbar section.

Another strategy to help you minimize the space committed to the toolbar is to customize the toolbar section by picking and choosing specific buttons from the wide assortment available. Begin with the standard toolbar. Since you are likely to need all

Advanced Features

or most of the functions performed by the Standard toolbar, choose to show it. One modification to consider is to remove either the  or the . Both display the Task Information dialog box.

Fast Lane Tip #67

To remove a toolbar button using the mouse

1. Hold down the **Shift** key.
2. While pointing to the button that you would like to remove, hold down the cursor and drag the button off the toolbar. It is immediately removed.

You can also remove and add new buttons, using the keyboard, from both the View menu and the Tools menu. The Tools menu will be used here.

Fast Lane Tip #68

To add a toolbar button

1. Click on **Tools**, or press **Alt/T**.
2. Choose **Customize**, then **Toolbars**. You will see the Customize dialog box shown in Figure 8-5.
3. Click on a category under the **Categories** column or use the **Tab** key and down arrow keys to choose a category. The buttons assigned to that category appear in the Buttons box.
4. To see a brief description of a button's function, click on that button, and a description will appear in the Description section. Choose categories, buttons, and their descriptions to identify those that you would like to appear on the toolbar.

The Complete Planning Guide for Microsoft® Project

5. When you locate a button that you would like to add, click on the button and drag it to the toolbar. (You can also click and drag buttons off the toolbar while the Customize dialog box is active.)

6. When finished, click on **Close** or press **Enter**.

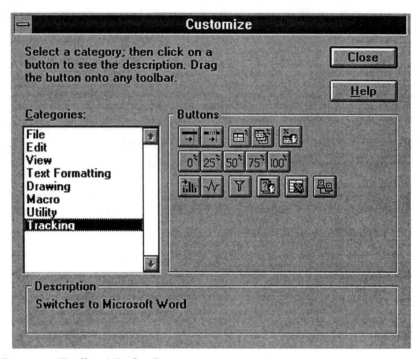

Figure 8-5. Customize (Toolbars) Dialog Box

Creating a New Toolbar Button

There are many commands that do not have a dedicated toolbar button. If you would like to access one of these functions quickly, you can rapidly create a button and place it on the toolbar. For example, let's say that you would like to add a button to close a file. Here's how.

Advanced Features

Fast Lane Tip #69

To create a new toolbar button

1. While holding down the **Ctrl** key, click on the location in the toolbar where you would like to position the new button. You will see the Customize Tool dialog box shown in Figure 8-6.

2. Move to the **Command** section beneath the Button Library, and use the scrolling arrow to locate and select **FileClose** (or other command).

3. Choose the blank button to start fresh and create a new button, or select an existing button to modify. You will see the Button Editor dialog box shown in Figure 8-7.

4. Click on each square that you would like to turn on or off. Each square box in the Button Editor represents a bit of information that can be turned on or off.

5. To change the color of any square, first click on the square, then on an appropriate color.

6. To inspect the new button, click on **OK** or press **Enter**. The new button will appear where you clicked while holding down the control key. Return to edit the button as necessary, using the above steps

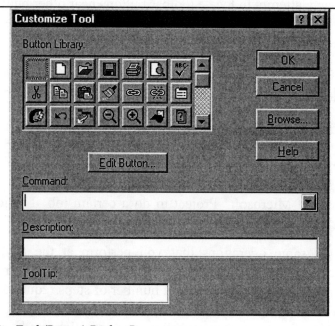

Figure 8-6. Customize Tool (Button) Dialog Box

The Customize Tool dialog box can be used to create a new toolbar button and to modify existing buttons.

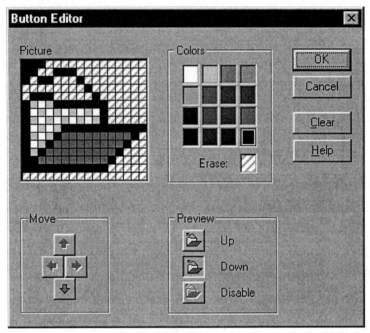

Figure 8-7. (Toolbar) Button Editor Dialog Box

In Figure 8-7, the FileOpen button was modified to create a CloseFile button.

As a general approach, attempt to locate toolbar buttons near other buttons that perform related operations, and near the related menu. This will reduce the time needed to locate a new button and to recall its function.

WORKING WITH MACROS

As you gain experience with Microsoft Project, you will sometimes find yourself doing the same jobs, the same way, over and over. In addition, there will probably be some jobs that you do infrequently, and that consist of a long series of steps that are difficult to remember. There is a solution for both—use a macro. A *macro* is a sequence of commands that instruct Microsoft® Project to do a certain job. The job is carried out automatically when you run the macro.

Macros perform the same operations that you perform at the keyboard. By using macros, you reduce errors, and the time it would take you to perform identical steps. With the existing macros, you can reduce the number of steps required to do many jobs in Microsoft Project to a simple click or a couple of keystrokes. By clicking on a button or pressing a couple of keys, you can perform an operation made up of almost any

Advanced Features

number of steps. Jobs like accepting status updates, batch printing a number of reports, switching to effort-driven scheduling, and creating optimistic, pessimistic, and expected schedules can all be performed using existing macros.

To accelerate your work with macros further, you can create a toolbar button, as described earlier in this chapter, to run any macro. You can also copy and use all or part of an existing macro.

The following sections will describe the macros that are currently available, and the functions they perform.

Available Macros

The macros displayed in the Macros dialog box in Figure 8-8 are available in Versions 4.0 and 4.1. The PERT macros are available, but will need to be installed. See the PERT Schedule Analysis section later in this chapter. A brief description of each macro is shown below. You may want to print a copy.

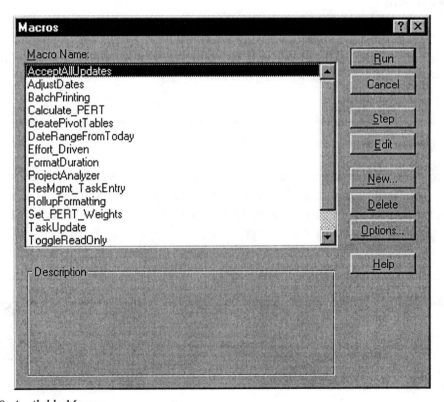

Figure 8-8. Available Macros

Accept All Updates

If you are working in a networked environment, and are using Microsoft Mail, this macro steps you through each inbox message. When you indicate yes, the macro automatically updates Microsoft Project with the message. Version 4.0 provides an example of VBAMAPI.DLL; Version 4.1 uses VBAMAP32.DLL to write to the messaging API.

Fast Lane Tip #70

To run the Accept All Updates macro

1. Click on **Tools**, or press **Alt/T**.
2. Choose **Macros**.
3. Select **AcceptAllUPdates** from the list of macros.
4. Choose **Run**. For each update message in your inbox you will be asked if you want the Microsoft® Project file updated. Respond accordingly.

Adjust Dates

This macro automatically changes schedule dates when you change the start date. Constraint dates are also changed to reflect the change. For example, if a task has a Must Start On date, and the project start date is moved by thirty days, the Must Start On date will also be postponed by thirty days.

Fast Lane Tip #71

To run the Adjust Dates macro

1. Click on **Tools**, or press **Alt/T**.
2. Choose **Macros**. You will see the Macros dialog box, as shown in Figure 8-8.

Advanced Features

3. Select **AdjustDates**, then **Run**. You will see the box shown in Figure 8-9 below.
4. Enter the new starting date and click on **OK** or press **Enter**. The dates will be changed.

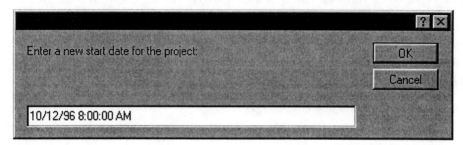

Figure 8-9. Adjust Dates Dialog Box

Batch Printing

This is a Visual Basic application (Version 3.0). If you need to print the same status reports every week, you can use this macro to create and print a number of views or reports. You use the Batch Printing dialog box to create one or more batches of views or reports that you would like to print.

Fast Lane Tip #72

To run the Batch Printing macro

1. Click on **Tools**, or press **Alt/T**.
2. Choose **Macros**. You will see the Macros dialog box.
3. Select **BatchPrinting**, then **Run**. You will see the Batch Printing dialog box shown in Figure 8-10.
4. Beneath **Print For** choose either **Active Project Only** or **All Open Projects**.
5. Choose **New** to create a new batch. You will see the Batch Definition dialog box shown in Figure 8-11.

The Complete Planning Guide for Microsoft® Project

6. Give a name to the batch of reports you are defining.

7. Choose **View** or **Report** and the scrolling arrow to choose the items that you would like to print. Choose a **Filter** if desired.

8. Choose **Add** to add each view or report to the batch. Use the **Remove** or **Remove All** buttons as necessary.

9. Choose **OK** when finished listing views and reports. You will see the Batch Printing dialog box again.

10. Choose **Print** or **Close** (if you wish to print later). You will be asked if you would like to save the batch file, and then be shown the Save Print Batch File dialog box shown in Figure 8-12.

11. Name the new batch file and choose **OK**.

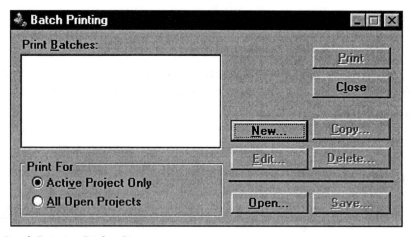

Figure 8-10. Batch Printing Dialog Box

The Batch Printing dialog box is used to create, edit, and open batches of reports and views.

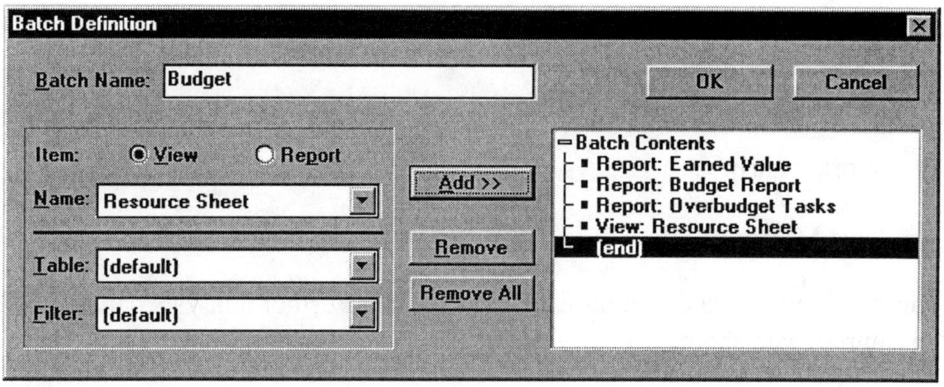

Advanced Features

Figure 8-11. Batch Definition Dialog Box

The Batch Definition dialog box is used to choose the views and reports that you would like to print.

Figure 8-12. Save Print Batch File Dialog Box

Create Pivot Tables

This macro is used to create resource-related tables in Microsoft Excel. The quickest way to create the pivot tables is to click on  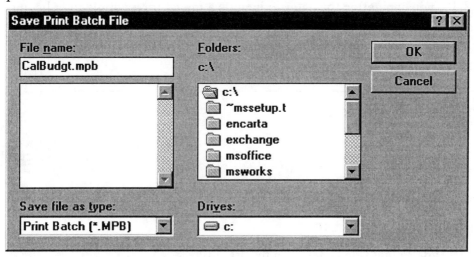, located on the resource management toolbar. In Version 4.1 this macro uses Microsoft® Excel Version 7.0 (Version 4.0 of Project uses Version 5.0 of Excel) pivot tables to create tables with resource information and other data from the active project. To run this macro in Version 4.0, you may need to first open Microsoft® Excel. The tables created include:

- Source Data

- Assignment Matrix
- Duration Matrix
- Work Matrix
- Cost Matrix

Each table is assigned a sheet in an Excel workbook. Further analysis can be performed using the Source Data sheet.

Date Range From Today

You can apply this filter to choose tasks and other data within a date range for which you know the exact dates. Using the Date Range From Today dialog box shown in Figure 8-13, you can define the dates to include a range, for example, that begins 0 days from today, and ends 15 days from today. For more information on filtering, see Chapter 7.

> **Fast Lane Tip #73**
>
>
>
> To run the Date Range From Today Filter Macro
>
> 1. Click on **Tools**, or press **Alt/T**.
> 2. Select **DateRangeFromToday** from the list of filters.
> 3. Choose **Run**. You will see the dialog box shown in Figure 8-13.
> 4. Indicate the number of days before and after today's date for which you would like to display tasks. If you would like a date range starting with today, leave Days Before Today's Date at 0. If you would like to go back in time, leave Days After Today's Date at 0.
> 5. Choose **OK** or press **Enter**. You will see a filtered list of tasks that are scheduled within the designated date range.

Advanced Features

Figure 8-13. Date Range From Today Dialog Box

Effort-Driven Scheduling

This macro enables you to add resources to a task without adding more work hours. If, for instance, you need to reduce the duration of a task, you can add another resource while keeping the number of work hours constant. Thus, task scheduled for 40 hours of effort between Monday and Friday, and one resource, could be accomplished by two resources in 20 hours (20 + 20). Note that this is not possible for every type of task.

Fast Lane Tip #74

To run the Effort-Driven Scheduling macro

1. Select the tasks for which you would like to add resources without increasing the amount of work hours.

2. Click on **Tools**, or press **Alt/T**. You will see the Macro Name List.

3. Select **Effort_Driven** from the list of macros.

4. Choose **Run**. You will see the Task Information dialog box opened to the Resource tab.

5. Add resources or make other changes in assignments.

6. Click on **OK**, or press **Enter**.

The Complete Planning Guide for Microsoft® Project

Format Duration

If you have entered the duration for some tasks in hours, others in days, and others in weeks, and you would like to use only one unit, such as days, this macro does the conversions. Note: rounding errors may occur.

Fast Lane Tip #75

To run the Format Duration macro

1. Click on **Tools**, or press **Alt/T**.
2. Select **FormatDuration** from the list of macros.
3. Choose **Run**. You will see the dialog box shown in Figure 8-14.
4. Enter the desired duration, such as **d** for days.
5. Click on **OK**, or press **Enter**.

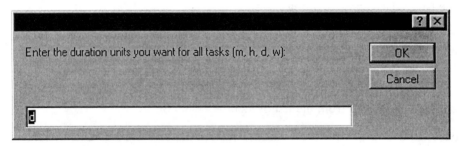

Figure 8-14. Duration Display Dialog Box

This dialog box helps you to choose a standard duration unit.

Project Analyzer

This is a Visual Basic application (Version 3.0). The project analyzer is useful for quickly analyzing one or more projects. If you would like to analyze your project data, this Visual Basic macro will help you locate:

- Slipped tasks sorted by finish variance

Advanced Features

- Resources with the highest cost variance
- Resources with the highest work variance

Fast Lane Tip #76

To run the Project Analyzer macro

1. Click on **Tools**, or press **Alt/T**.
2. Choose **Macros**. You will see the list of available macros.
3. Choose **ProjectAnalyzer**. You will see the box with the white background shown in Figure 8-15. Choose **OK**. You will see the Select Project dialog box.
4. Select a project, then choose **OK**. You will see the Microsoft Project Analyzer dialog box shown in Figure 8-16. The box shows three sections:
    - Slipped Tasks (by Finish Variance)
    - Overcost Resources (by Cost Variance)
    - Overworked Resources (by Work Variance)
5. Using the sort order, the highest variance is displayed in each box.
6. To see additional slipped tasks, overcost resources, or overworked resources, choose **More** beside any task or resource.
7. Choose **Select** if you would like to analyze another project.
8. Choose **Exit** when finished.

The Complete Planning Guide for Microsoft® Project

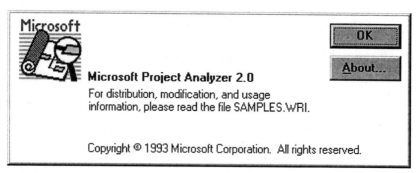

Figure 8-15. Introduction to Microsoft Project Analyzer 2.0 Screen

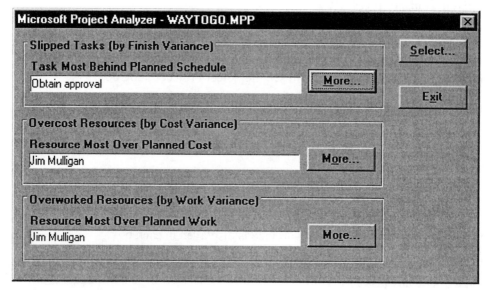

Figure 8-16. Microsoft Project Analyzer Dialog Box.

This box displays the item with the highest variance. To see additional variances in sorted order, choose the **More** button.

Resource Management Task Entry

This macro opens a combination view with Gantt chart and task entry table at the top, and the task form at the bottom. The task form displays:

- Resource Name and ID
- Units
- Work

Advanced Features

- Delay
- Start
- Finish

Rollup Formatting

This macro rolls up all task bars to show task bars for all summary tasks on one line. If you would like to reset all Flag 10 fields to alternate attached text on rollup bars from top to bottom, use this macro. This macro may be useful for reporting purposes when you have a large number of projects, for example fifty or more.

Task Update

This macro enables you to batch tasks to be updated. It shows the Update Tasks form for tasks that occur within a time period that you enter, from a filtered list, or for all project tasks. This macro can be activated by using [icon] on the Tracking toolbar.

Toggle Read Only

Use this macro to toggle between making access to the active file read only, and read and write. Use the [icon] button from the workgroup toolbar, or access the macro from the macro list. The macro saves the active file as read only or read write, depending on its last position. This macro code can also be used as part of larger macros.

PERT Schedule Analysis

This is a Visual Basic application (Version 3.0). When PERT was invented in the late 1950s, each task was analyzed to develop three time estimates: optimistic, pessimistic and most likely. Microsoft® Project uses "expected" in place of most likely. The expected estimate is given a weight of four, while the optimistic and pessimistic are each given a weight of one. You are given an option to change the weight distribution, however the sum of the weights must still be six. The six time estimates (4+1+1) are then divided by 6 to produce a time estimate based on the weighted average.

The method and macro are particularly useful when planning a "breakthrough" project, or other project with widely differing time estimates. Because overuse of this macro technique may result in "analysis paralysis", it is not recommended for projects that are very similar to previous projects.

Before using this macro you must install it. To install it, follow these steps:

The Complete Planning Guide for Microsoft® Project

> ## Fast Lane Tip#77
>
>
>
> To install the PERT Schedule Analysis macro
>
> 1. Open the **PERT.MPP** in the **Library** folder in either version. You will see a table that can be used to enter the three time estimates.
>
> 2. Click on **Tools**, or press **Alt/T**.
>
> 3. Choose **Macros** and select **Install_PERT_Analysis** from the list.
>
> 4. Choose **Run**. Three macros will be installed: Calculate PERT, Set PERT Weights, and Uninstall PERT Analysis. A new toolbar is also created.

Once the macros are installed, you will see a new PA PERT Analysis toolbar. Each button is briefly explained below.

 Display a column for entering optimistic time estimates.

 Display a column for entering expected time estimates.

 Display a column for entering pessimistic time estimates.

 Calculate PERT after estimates and weights are entered.

 Display an entry form to enter time estimates as shown in Figure 8-17.

Figure 8-17. PERT Entry Form

Advanced Features

This box enables you to enter the best/optimistic, expected/most likely, and worst/pessimistic time estimates for a task.

 Display weights form to make changes in weighted average.

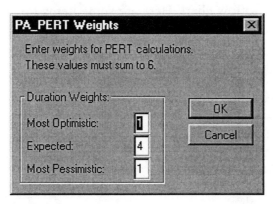

Figure 8-18. PA PERT Weights Form

With this dialog box, you can adjust the weights given to the three time estimates. The total of all three estimates must equal six.

 Display the analysis sheet as shown in Table 8-1.

Table 8-1. PERT analysis sheet

ID	Task Name	Dur	Opt Dur	Exp Dur	Pes Dur
	Way To Go Newsletter	61.75d	0d	0d	0d
1	Define Budget Requirem	3.5d	0d	0d	0d
2	Start project	0d	0d	0d	0d
3	Estimate production cc	20h	10h	20h	40h
4	Obtain budget approval	8h	4h	8h	40h

Additional macros exist that you may want to apply, including the Inflation Factors macro and Timesheet macro. To see a description of each macro and the steps required to run each one, open the samples.wri folder or directory in Microsoft Project.

Creating a Macro

You can easily create macros in Microsoft® Project. By creating macros, you not only make your work time more productive, you can also improve your ability to train someone else to use Microsoft Project. When macros have been created, someone with limited knowledge of the software can simply point and click, or press a couple of keys to use it to prepare reports, import a table of financial data from a spreadsheet, or do other work.

Preparing to Record a Macro

Plan and document the macro fully. By actually writing out the steps and other information before you begin to record a macro, you will make it much easier to create the macro, and make it easier to retrace your steps if and when surprises occur. Some find it useful to produce a flow chart. Here are some items to consider when preparing to record or create a macro:

- A descriptive name for the macro
- The exact sequence of commands
- The precise steps to perform
- The menu item to access
- The fields to select
- Pauses in the sequence for user entries
- Messages to display
- Choices to provide

When you describe the macro, be sure to explain where you should be within Microsoft Project, such as in a certain view or table, before running the macro.

Be very careful when using the cursor and Tab keys. One of the most important aspects of macro planning is the method of selecting items from lists, menus, and multiple-choice fields. These items are variable. Try to use the letter keys as much as possible when selecting menu items or when working in a dialog box. For example, if you choose a field in the task form by using the cursor and tab key, you must know the type and status of the task. Some tasks have fixed duration, which results in accessible fields that are different from other tasks; tabbing a certain number of times can take you to the wrong field.

If you work in a networked environment, some users may have modified their options, menus, or forms. As a result, some files may need to be altered to reflect differences in preferences.

To ensure that you are getting the right menu choice, always specify the full name of the menu item. To change task data, you may want to use a Gantt table with the desired columns and select and edit directly on the Gantt table instead of in a dialog box or form.

Advanced Features

If you divide your macros into easily understood (and easily entered) segments, they will be easier to record and troubleshoot. Some of these smaller macros can be general purpose, and may be useful in a variety of other macros.

Recording a Macro

While reading about macros, Chris realizes that she is frequently switching between views. She often needs to switch to the Summary table in the Gantt view from many other views and tables. She decides to create a macro to quickly switch to the summary table.

To create a macro, you actually perform a sequence of steps and record your actions. Chris follows these steps to record her steps in switching to the summary table. These steps are stored in Visual Basic® code.

Fast Lane Tip #78

To record a macro to switch to the summary table

1. Press **Alt/T** to see the Tools menu.
2. Press **R** to choose Record Macro. You will see the Record Macro dialog box shown in Figure 8-19. Give the macro a name. The macro name can include letters, numbers, and the underscore key. Do not use spaces or punctuation marks.
3. Press **Alt/O**. You will see an expanded dialog box, as shown in Figure 8-20.
4. Press **S** to show the macro in the macro list.
5. Press **K** to select a hotkey, and type a key to be used with the **Ctrl** key to invoke the macro.
6. Press the Tab key to move to the choice of saving the macro in the current file or in a global file. Press the letter **G** for global or **C** for current. Global is recommended.
7. Press the **Tab** key to move to choose **Absolute** or **Relative** row references. Make your choice by pressing the appropriate letter.
8. Press the **Tab** key to move to choose **Absolute** or **Relative** column references. Make your choice by pressing the appropriate letter.
9. Press **Enter** to indicate that you are finished. You can now perform the task while Microsoft® Project records the steps.

The Complete Planning Guide for Microsoft® Project

> 10. When finished recording the macro, press **Alt/T**, then **R** to stop recording.

Figure 8-19. Record Macro Dialog Box

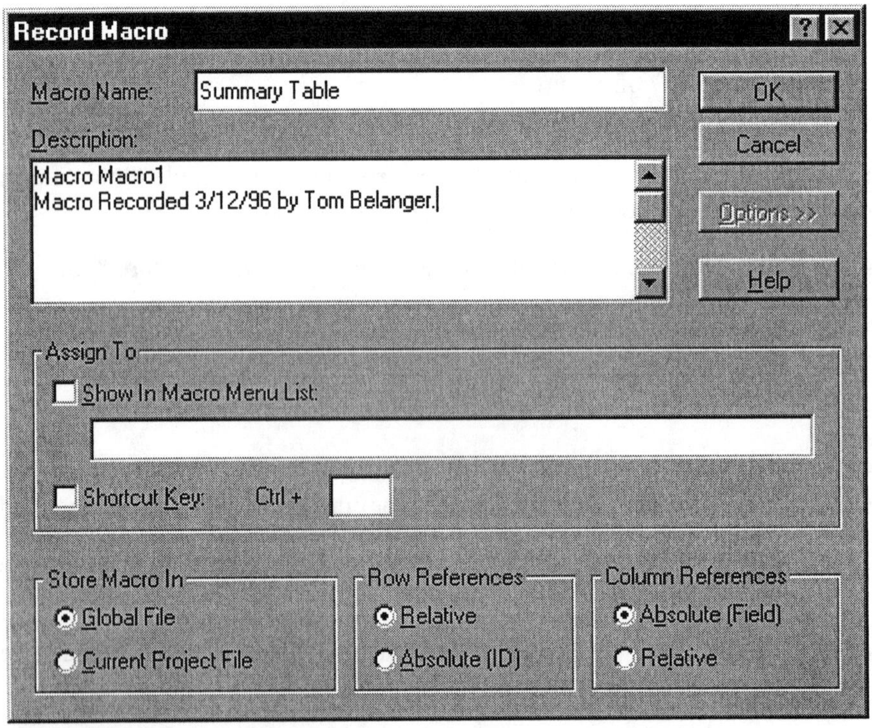

Figure 8-20. Expanded Record Macro Dialog Box

Store Macro In

You will need to decide whether to store the macro as a global file, and make it available to any other file, or limit its use to the current project file.

Row References

Choose **Relative** to begin your macro commands in the current cursor position.

Choose **Absolute** if you would like Microsoft Project to always begin at the same row that was used when you recorded the macro.

Column References

Choose **Absolute** to instruct the macro to perform its operation on the same fields that were specified when you recorded the macro. This choice will be honored even if the location of certain fields, such as Task Name, has changed.

Choose **Relative** to instruct Microsoft® Project to always begin at the same column position that was specified when you recorded the macro. For example, if you insert data into certain columns, the macro will always insert data into those columns.

Visual Basic®

For more advanced macro developers, Microsoft® Project has included a Version of the Visual Basic application and an accompanying toolbar that can be used. By using the Visual Basic application, you can record much more elaborate macros.

Macros can communicate with you by displaying explanatory messages and pausing for keyboard entry in dialog boxes, forms, and menu selections. It can also display menus to allow choices. A macro can invoke other macros or even itself.

For information about Visual Basic, you can choose **Help**, then **Find**, and enter **Visual Basic**. You will see a list of topics.

IMPORTING AND EXPORTING

Microsoft Project is, in effect, a very elaborate database of project information. The data is stored in records, one for each task and one for each resource. Using an appropriate table, you can import data to these records from a variety of applications as an alternative to manually entering it into Microsoft® Project. You can also export the data to other applications so that it can be manipulated and reported in a different format.

If you have already entered much project information into a spreadsheet, text document, or database, importing it into Microsoft Project can save hours of tedious reentry. If you are already using a spreadsheet as a data presentation or tracking tool, exporting Microsoft® Project data can help to integrate project data with other databases. For example, using spreadsheet software, you can show cost variance in a pie chart format.

Importing

To save data entry time, it is possible to open and import files from a variety of applications and file formats. You can import information from other project management applications, as well as spreadsheet, word processing, and database applications. You can also import files from different Versions of Microsoft® Project.

Microsoft can import (open) the following file (type) formats:

- MPX—Microsoft Project Exchange

- CSV—Comma-separated values

- TXT or ASCII—and other extensions used by some applications

- XLS—Microsoft® Excel

- WKS, WK1, WK3—Lotus 1-2-3®

- DBF—used by database applications that include dBASE III®, dBASE III Plus®, and DBASE IV®

- DBF—Foxpro database application

- MDB—Microsoft Access. See the DATABASE.WRI file

MPX is the recommended format. It works well with other project management applications because they include the information needed including default settings, tasks, resource assignments, and calendars, as well as base calendars.

To import data, you will first need to choose or customize a table in Microsoft® Project (the destination) so that it displays the same data and arrangement as that displayed in the source application file. Follow these steps to import a file.

Advanced Features

Fast Lane Tip #79

To import a file

1. Choose a table in Microsoft Project with columns identical to the columns in the source file. Customize Microsoft® Project and/or the source file as needed.

2. Click on **File**, or press **Ctrl/O**. The File Open dialog box opens.

3. Beside **Files of Type**, (**List Files of Type** in Version 4.0) use the scrolling arrow to choose a file type in a suitable format.

4. Choose the file to import.

5. Choose **Open** (**OK** in Version 4.0).

Fast Lane Tip #80

To add imported information to the end of a destination file

1. Create an ID column in the source file.

2. Enter numbers that are different from any ID numbers in the Microsoft Project destination file.

3. Import the file. The new rows of data will be appended to the end of the destination file.

Many companion applications to Microsoft® Project can easily be imported because they can save their files in the MPX format. Project files that are created in other applications, such as Project KICKStart and Milestones, Etc., can easily be imported. These and other companion products are listed at the end of this chapter.

Exporting

Exporting provides many advantages, such as decreasing data entry time and increasing flexibility. You can export Microsoft Project data to spreadsheet, word processing, and database software for inclusion in reports, proposals and presentations.

To export Microsoft® Project files to other files, save them in one of the following formats:

- MPX—Microsoft Project Exchange (recommended)
- CSV—Comma-separated values
- TXT or ASCII—and other extensions used by some applications
- XLS—Microsoft Excel
- WKS, WK1, WK3—Lotus 1-2-3®
- DBF—used by database applications that include dBASE III®, dBASE III Plus®, and DBASE IV®
- DBF—Foxpro database application
- MDB—Microsoft Access; See the DATABASE.WRI file

Fast Lane Tip #81

To export a file

1. Choose a table in Microsoft Project with columns identical to the columns in the destination file. Customize Microsoft® Project and/or the source file as needed.
2. Click on **File**, or press **Alt/F**.
3. Choose **Save As**. You will see the File Save dialog box in Version 4.1 and the Save As dialog box in Version 4.0.
4. In the **File name** box, you can leave the file name as it is displayed, or type a new name for the file.

Advanced Features

> 5. In the **Files of Type** section, (**List Files of Type** in Version 4.0), choose a suitable format.
>
> 6. Choose **Save** (Version 4.1) or **OK** (Version 4.0). The file can now be imported by another application.

Working with Incompatible Formats?

If you are unable to import or export data in a format that is compatible with Microsoft Project, here are some additional options that may work:

- Copy and paste or paste special—select the table in the source application, then copy and paste or paste special to the target file. You will need to create or modify tables with identical columns in each application.

- Use a conVersion utility that is provided by the source or target application.

- Use a third-party conVersion utility that will convert the data from the source application to a format that is compatible with the target application.

- Take a picture of the selected tasks. If you would like to display all or part of a Microsoft Project file in a Microsoft Word document, for example, click on .

OBJECT LINKING AND EMBEDDING

Linking and *embedding* are ways to bring an object that was created in one application into another. Objects can include a picture, graph, map, table, or an entire document. The *container*, or destination document, is the document or application that contains a linked or embedded object. The *server*, or source, is the document or application that provides information to a linked or embedded object in a container.

You may want to link or embed objects in Microsoft Project that were created in another application (the source). For example, you may want to embed a picture in the Gantt bar chart, or you may want to link tabular information from a spreadsheet. With linking, changes made in the source or server application are automatically reflected in the container application.

When you use object linking and embedding and have linked or embedded an object such as a spreadsheet in a word processing document, the spreadsheet functions are available, even though you are currently working in a word processing document. As a result, you can change the data and the spreadsheet makes the same calculations as if you were working in the spreadsheet application.

You may also want to link or embed objects that were created in Microsoft Project in another application. For example, you may want to link or embed a Gantt chart from Microsoft® Project into Microsoft® Word or other word processing application.

Because some fields of information, such as variances, are calculated in Microsoft Project, you cannot link or embed objects in these fields. For tabular data, choose columns that are user-entered only.

Linking and embedding can be used to insert and edit objects such as pictures, graphs, maps or columns of data. You cannot move or size an object in the task form or resource form. Objects can only be moved or sized in the Gantt chart bar section.

Linking and Embedding Objects from Another Application In Microsoft® Project

In some instances you may want to create a link between another application and Microsoft® Project, or embed this information in Microsoft Project. The type of information linked must be the same in both applications. For example, a text object in a sheet view must be linked to another sheet view, such as a Gantt table, task sheet, resource sheet, or the resource usage view. A text object from another application can be linked with Microsoft® Project if it supports OLE or dynamic data exchange (DDE).

When objects are linked to their server, dynamic updates to the container application are made automatically. For example, if a dollar amount changes in the server, the container application is automatically updated with the new dollar amount.

Note: Objects can be linked to, or embedded in a Microsoft® Project container by copying it to the task form, resource form or Gantt bar chart. Objects placed in the task form or resource form cannot be sized.

Fast Lane Tip #82

To link or embed a picture object in the resource form or task form

Prepare the Object

1. In the application where the object exists, the server application, save the object as a file.

Advanced Features

(You can also create an object in Step 7 below.)

<u>In Microsoft® Project</u>

2. Click on **View**, or press **Alt/V**.

3. Choose **More Views**, then **Task Form** or **Resource Form**.

4. With the task form or resource form open, choose **Format**.

5. Choose **Details**, then **Object**. The bottom of the form will become a large blank space that is ready to receive an object from a source. See Figure 8-21.

6. Choose **Insert**, then **Object**. You will see the Insert Object dialog box shown in Figure 8-22.

7. Choose **Create from File**, and use the **Browse** button to choose the file. (You can also choose **Create New** at this point if you haven't saved an object as a file.)

8. Check the **Link** box if you would like Microsoft Project to be updated when the source file changes. Leave this box blank if you would like to embed the object.

9. Choose **Display As** Icon if you would like to show the object as a small icon.

10. Choose **OK**. The object will be linked or embedded in Microsoft® Project.

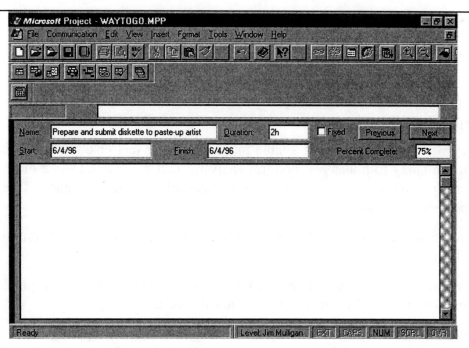

Figure 8-21. Task Form Prepared for New Object

The object will be inserted in the blank space at the bottom of the task form.

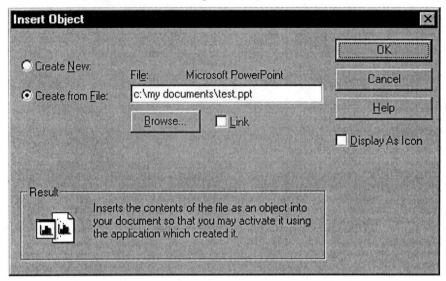

Figure 8-22 Insert Object Dialog Box

The Insert Object dialog box is used to choose:

- Whether to use an object that has been saved as a file, or to create an object
- Whether to insert the object as an icon
- Whether to link or embed an object

Linking or Embedding Objects from Microsoft® Project in Another Application

You may want to link or embed a table into Microsoft Excel or other spreadsheet so that you can apply formulas and perform analysis. You may want to link or embed a chart or table into a word processing package as part of a proposal or report. These jobs can be performed quickly.

Text information can be linked with another application if that application supports OLE or DDE.

Just as when you linked and embedded information in Microsoft Project, prepare the container and server applications to link or embed objects.

To display data that was created in Microsoft® Project in another application, you have several options. You can:

Advanced Features

- Copy and paste selected information (use Paste Special and the Paste Link command to create a link)

- Use the combination of Alt/Print Screen to copy a dialog box to the clipboard, then use the Paste command or button to paste the dialog box into another application

- Use the Copy Picture button to copy selected information

- Drag and drop Microsoft Project information into a container application

Both Versions of Microsoft® Project have extensive help on the topic of linking and embedding.

COMPANION PRODUCTS RELATED TO THIS CHAPTER*

CHARTS NOW!, software tool used to create work breakdown structures, flow charts, precedence diagrams; Foundation Microsystems, Inc. (510) 814-1695

GRANEDA Light, software tool used to create work breakdown structures, organizational breakdown structures, precedence diagrams and other charts; American NETRONIC, Inc. (714) 760-8642

Milestones, Etc., a software tool for creating a Gantt chart and project schedule; Kidasa Software, (512) 328-0168.

Project KICKStart, Software tool used to organize a project; Experience in Software, Inc. (510) 644-0694.

WBS Chart, Software tool used to create a work breakdown structure; Jim Spiller & Associates (707) 425-2484.

- Not all of these tools are designed for Version 4.1.

Appendix

Appendix A—Cue Cards available in Version 4.0

Appendix B—Keyboard Shortcuts And Available Function Keys

APPENDIX A

CUE CARDS AVAILABLE IN VERSION 4.0 FOR WINDOWS 3.1

These cue cards are not available as cue cards in Version 4.1. However, if you ask the Answer Wizard: "How do I ..." and finish the sentence with the cue card name, as listed below, you will see a list of related topics. These topics include procedures which perform the same function as a cue card in most cases. You can also ask the Answer Wizard to: "Tell me about...", and finish the sentence for a list of related topics and procedures.

The cue cards listed on the next page are available in Version 4.0.

The Complete Planning Guide for Microsoft® Project

1. Start a new schedule
2. Enter a task
3. Change a task to a milestone
4. Enter a recurring task.
5. Change a task duration
6. Delete a task
7. Organize your project using outlining
8. Use a work breakdown structure
9. Change working days and hours
10. Create and remove a task (dependency) relationship
11. Overlap or delay a task
12. Schedule a task to start or finish relative to a specific date
13. Learn about task (dependency) relationships
14. Create a resource list
15. Assign or remove a resource
16. Control when a resource starts work on a task
17. Set the working hours and days off for a resource
18. Assign a calendar to a resource
19. Assign a rate to a resource
20. Assign a fixed resource cost to a task
21. Assign a fixed cost to a task
22. Control how costs are accrued
23. View the cost per task
24. View total project costs
25. Learn about entering cost information
26. Evaluate your schedule
27. See steps for shortening your schedule
28. See steps for resolving resource overallocation
29. See steps for reducing project costs and managing cash flow
30. Print a view
31. Print a report
32. Scale a view proportionately for printing
33. Add a header, a footer, or a legend
34. Insert or remove a page break
35. Print columns in a sheet view
36. Set up a printer or plotter in Microsoft Windows
37. Print a custom view
38. Learn about choosing to print a view or report
39. Set a baseline or interim plan
40. Update schedule information
41. Check your progress
42. Learn about tracking progress
43. Learn about using views
44. Display a view
45. Work in a sheet view
46. Assign a resource to a task
47. Change the appearance of a view
48. Change the information displayed in a view
49. Work on the PERT chart
50. Work in a form view
51. Work on the calendar

APPENDIX B

KEYBOARD SHORTCUTS AND AVAILABLE FUNCTION KEYS

Available keys are shown in **bold** typeface.

Press	To Get These Results
F1	Help (works in any window or dialog box)
F2	Move to the entry bar
F3	Display all tasks or resources
F4	**No result; available for other uses**
F5	Edit Menu (Go To)
F6	Toggle back and forth in a combination view
F7	Activate the spelling dialog box
F8	Toggle Extend Selection mode on or off
F9	Calculate every open project
F10	Display the menu bar
F11	Open a new file
F12	Activate the Save As command
Shift/F1	Use the context-sensitive help pointer
Shift/F2	Activate the Task Information dialog box or Resource Information dialog box
Shift/F3	Sort by ID number
Shift/F4	Choose the Next button in the Find dialog box
Shift/F5	Activate the Find dialog box

Shift/F6	Divide the screen
Shift/F7	**No result; available for other uses**
Shift/F8	Toggle Add to Selection mode on and off
Shift/F9	Calculate current project
Shift/F10	**No result; available for other uses**
Shift/F11	Open a new project window
Shift/F12	**No result; available for other uses**
Alt/F1	**No result; available for other uses**
Alt/F2	Save As
Alt/F3	Show the Column Definition dialog box
Alt/F4	Exit the application
Alt/F5	Move to the next overallocation
Alt/F6	**No result; available for other uses**
Alt/F7	**No result; available for other uses**
Alt/F8	Insert resource assignment
Alt/F9	Apply update to all Dynamic Data Exchange (DDE) links
Alt/F10	**No result; available for other uses**
Alt/F11	**No result; available for other uses**
Alt/F12	**No result; available for other uses**

Appendix B

Ctrl/F1	**No result; available for other uses**
Ctrl/F2	Create a predecessor-successor link
Ctrl/F3	Reapply the filter
Ctrl/F4	Close the project window
Ctrl/F5	Reopen the project window
Ctrl/F6	Toggle between active project windows
Ctrl/F7	Move the project window
Ctrl/F8	Change the size of the project window
Ctrl/F9	Toggle Auto Calculate on and off
Ctrl/F10	Maximize the project window
Ctrl/F11	**No result; available for other uses**
Ctrl/F12	**No result; available for other uses**

Glossary

Accrual Method—the method used to determine when costs are charged to the project. Costs can be prorated according to percent complete, at the beginning or end of a task.

Actual Finish—the date on which the task actually finished.

Actual Start—the date on which the task actually began.

Arrow Diagramming Method—a method of expressing the precedence relationships among project tasks in which each task is represented by an arrow. This contrasts with the method used by Microsoft Project. See Critical Path Method.

Base Calendar—a standard project calendar that reflects holidays and other nonwork days for a set of resources or an entire project.

Baseline—a basis for comparison with actual project results. It normally includes schedule and cost baselines, and is a "stake in the ground" at a certain point in time. It may include some or all project tasks. In Microsoft Project, you may also save five additional interim baselines. See Interim (Baseline) Plan.

Calculated Field—a field that is tallied by Microsoft Project based on the information in related fields.

Calculated or Entered Field—a field in which you can either enter the value, or allow Microsoft Project to calculate it.

Children Tasks—subtasks.

Combination View—a display that contains a view at the top and a view at the bottom.

Communication Plan—a plan to facilitate ongoing communications among all stakeholders.

Constraint—a limit you can place on a task start date or finish date. Use with caution; constraints limit Microsoft Project's ability to calculate and adjust your project schedule.

Cost—an amount that represents project expenses and the consumption of other resources or fixed costs.

Critical Path—the path with the longest duration. Tasks on the critical path have no slack, and if delayed, can delay the project. (See Free Slack and Total Slack.) Zero durations in the total slack field indicate that the task is on the critical path.

Critical Path Method—a method of expressing the precedence relationships among project tasks in which each task is represented by a node or box. This is the method used by Microsoft Project.

Cue Card—a help screen that can display step-by-step instructions while you work.

Cue Card Author—a utility that allows you to create cue cards.

Dangling tTsk—a task without a predecessor or successor. This does not include the "start" or "finish" milestones.

Default—a setting that tells Microsoft Project how to act. For example, "As Soon As Possible" is a default setting for all project tasks.

Demote—to indent a task or subtask.

Dependency—an if-then relationship between two or more tasks. The most common type of dependency relationship is the Finish-to-Start relationship between a predecessor and its successor. See Task Relationship.)

Divider Bar—the vertical bar that divides the tabular information and the graphic representation on the Gantt chart.

Driving Resource—the resource that has the largest amount of effort assigned to a given task.

Duration—an amount of time necessary to accomplish a task. (See Elapsed Duration.)

Earned Value—the actual cost of work performed (ACWP).

Early Finish—the earliest date on which a task can end.

Early Start—the earliest date on which a task can begin.

Elapsed Duration—calendar time, includes the task duration plus non-working time.

Entered Field—a field in which you can type information.

Entry Bar—the bar on which you enter schedule information. It is located beneath the toolbar(s).

Expand—to display a task's subtasks.

Glossary

Filtering—a technique that is used to limit or highlight selected tasks, resources, or other data.

Fixed Cost—a cost that will not fluctuate with the number of hours or units. Sometimes used with fixed-price contracts.

Free Slack—an amount of time by which a task can be delayed without delaying the start of any successor task.

Gantt Chart—a chart that displays bars to represent each task's duration, and symbols to display milestones.

Goal—the project's ultimate endpoint. It is written in one sentence, and consists of the project's ultimate deliverable and a date.

Interim (Baseline) Plan—a baseline that is established after the initial baseline. It may include all or part of the project, and typically consists of cost and schedule data.

Lag—an amount of time by which a successor task begins after its successor begins. For example, a predecessor entry that shows 88SS+5d indicates that a predecessor (task 88) must have consumed five days before its successor begins.

Late Finish—the latest that a task can end without delaying any successor.

Late Start—the latest that a task can begin without delaying any successor.

Lead—an amount of time by which a successor task is delayed after its predecessor is complete. For example, a predecessor entry that shows 46FS+10d indicates that there must be a delay of 10 days after the predecessor is complete.

Menu Bar—the horizontal row at the top of the Microsoft Project window that displays the headings File, Edit, and so on.

Major Milestone—1) A project objective, representing a major category of project work. 2) A point in time that represents the accomplishment of a very important task.

Milestone—1) A point in time that usually indicates that a task has begun or ended. In Microsoft Project, tasks with zero duration are displayed as milestones. 2) A major category of project work

Negative Slack—a value that indicates the amount by which the task can delay the project.

Objective—see Major Milestone.

Parallel Path—a sequence of connected tasks that occur concurrently with one or more additional paths.

Parent Task—see Summary Task.

Path—a sequence of tasks that are connected by predecessor-successor relationships.

PERT Chart—a task network that displays all project task sequences.

Phase—a major category of project work, often composed of major milestones or objectives. Sometimes referred to as a "stage".

Predecessor—a task that immediately precedes one or more tasks. A predecessor-successor relationship is referred to as a "dependency relationship" or "task relationship".

Priority—the level of availability that is assigned to a task. Priority is used by Microsoft Project to resolve resource conflicts by delaying tasks with the lowest priority.

Project—a set of interrelated tasks designed to accomplish a specific goal.

Project Plan—a comprehensive document that is developed to manage a project. It typically includes the project scope, risks, schedule, technical, cost, and quality requirements. It is a working document that should be revised at key intervals during project execution.

Promote—to outdent a task or subtask.

Resource—a person, group, piece of equipment, machine, or other item that consumes and accumulates cost. See Fixed Cost.

Risk—the threat that an undesirable occurrence could jeopardize or delay the project.

Scroll Bars—horizontal and vertical bars that allow users to quickly move between locations. Do this by clicking on and dragging.

Slack—see Total Slack and Free Slack.

Sorting—a technique that is used to change the display order of tasks, resources, or other data.

Sponsor—a manager or a formal committee that has commissioned and approved the project.

Stakeholder—an individual or group who has an interest, or "stake", in the project.

Glossary

Status Bar—the row at the bottom of the Microsoft Project window that displays the current function and the status of the num lock, caps lock, and other keys.

Subproject—a component of a larger project, or master project.

Subtask—a component of a task.

Successor—a task that immediately succeeds one or more tasks. A predecessor-successor relationship is referred to as a "dependency relationship" or "task relationship".

Summary Task—a task that summarizes the duration, costs and other data from component tasks. Sometimes referred to as a "parent" task.

Task—a finite amount of work. Often a smaller component of an activity. Sometimes used interchangeably with "activity".

Task Relationship—a predecessor-successor relationship.

Timescale—the increments of time that appear above the task bars on the Gantt chart.

Toolbars—rows and clusters of icons that allow users to perform a function by pointing and clicking.

Total Slack—an amount of time by which a task can be delayed without delaying project completion. Zero durations in the total slack field indicate that the task is on the critical path.

Work Breakdown Structure—a decomposition of the project goal. When complete, it displays all of the levels of work in the project.

Bibliography

Arthur, L.J. *Improving Software Quality: An Insider's Guide to TQM*. New York: **John** Wiley & Sons, 1993.

Arthur, L.J. *Rapid Evolutionary Development: Requirements, Prototyping & Software.* New York: John Wiley & Sons, 1992.

Belanger, T.C. *How To Plan Any Project: A Guide For Teams (and Individuals).* 2nd ed. Sterling, MA: Sterling Planning Group, 1995.

Belanger, T.C. *Successful Project Management*. New York: American Management Association, New York, 1995.

Boehm, B.W. *Software Engineering Economics*. Englewood Cliffs, NJ: Prentice-Hall, Inc., 1981.

Boehm, B.W. *Software Risk Management*. Washington, DC: IEEE Computer Society Press, 1989.

Cave, W.C., and G.W. Maymon. *Software Lifecycle Management: The Incremental Method*. New York: Macmillan Publishing Co., 1984.

Cathcart, R.S., L.A. Samovar, L.D. Henman. *Small Group Communication: Theory and Practice*. Madison, WI: Brown & Benchmark, 1996.

Cleland, D.I., and R. Gareis, eds.*Global Project Management Handbook.* New York: McGraw-Hill, Inc., 1994.

Cleland D.I., and W. King, eds. Project Management Handbook. 2nd ed. New York: Van Nostrand Reinhold, 1988.

DeGrace, P. and L.H. Stahl. *A Catalogue of Modern Software Engineering Paradigms*. Englewood Cliffs, NJ: Yourdon Press, 1991.

Goldratt, E.M. and J. Cox. *The Goal*. Croton-on-Hudson, NY: North River Press, 1984

Lorenz, M. *Software Development: A Practical Guide*. Englewood Cliffs, NJ: Prentice-Hall, 1993.

Miller, H.W. "Creating The Evolutionary Model Software System". A Case Study. **Journal of Systems Management** (August 1990). 11–18.

Olson, D. *Exploiting Chaos*. New York: Van Nostrand Reinhold, 1993.

Rumbaugh, J. "Over the Waterfall and into the Whirlpool". Journal of Programming (May 1992).

Tran, P. and R. Galka. *"On Incremental Delivery with Functionality"*.. IEEE Software, (May 1991) 69–75.

Wellens, R.S., W.C. Byham, and J.M. Wilson. *Empowered Teams. San Francisco:* Jossey-Bass Publishers, 1991.

Index

A

About Microsoft Project, 42
Accept All Updates Macro, 244
    to run, 244
accrual method, 112
accumulating costs. *See* Costs
ACWP
    described, 205
Add Routing Slip. *See* File
    button, 166
Adding a New Task Network to the Menu, 235
address book
    icon, 98
Adjust Dates macro, 244
    to run, 244
Answer Wizard, 39, 40
Arrange All
    open projects, 177
ASCII, 260, 262
assessing risks
    loss of key resource, 111
Assignment Reports, 206
Available Macros, 243

B

BAC
    described, 205
Bar Styles
    in the Gantt chart, 139
    to show free slack, 144
Baseline
    described, 155
    saving/setting, 155
baselines
    interim, 155
Batch Definition dialog box, 247
Batch Printing macro
    to run, 245
BCWP
    described, 205
BCWS
    described, 205

Best Fit, 52
Bottom-up Approach
    planning, 62
box contents
    changing, 237
Box Styles dialog box, 242
Budget
    project, 119
Budget Report, 203
burden rate, 104
buttons. *See* icons

C

Calendar
    five day week, 128
    Text Styles dialog box, 131
calendar layout
    changing, 132
calendar rows
    decrease height, 128
    increase height, 128
calendar view
    creating a task, 129
    daily tasks, 129
    described, 126
change
    column heading, 53
    one or more views in a combination view, 101
Changing the Menu, 232
children, 73
Code, 113
codes
    subtasks, 73
Collaboration
    characteristic of a project, 125
column
    align, 53, 54
    definition, 74
    insert, 73
    width, 53, 54
Column Definition, 53

Column Heading,
    customizing, 53
combination view, 39, 101
Combine Resource Pools, 189
Communication menu
    creating a, 232
Communication Plan, 92
    elements, 93
competition criteria, 85
Completed Tasks Report, 200
completion criteria, 85, 161
Completion Example #1, 85
Completion Example #2, 86
Consolidate Projects
    button, 167
Consolidate Projects dialog box, 188
Consolidating Projects, 186
constraints
    remove, 100
Construct an Outline, 68
container
    defined, 263
Cost
    baseline, 121
cost information in the resource information
    dialog box, 112
cost per time period, 105
cost per use, 105
Cost Reports, 202
cost table, 121, 171
    resource Version, 173
    task Version, 171
Cost Tracking
    button, 225
Costs
    accrue at, 108
    fixed, 109
Create Pivot Tables
    box, 102
Creating a Macro, 255
Creating a New Toolbar Button, 240
Creating Custom Forms, 224
Creating Project Templates, 177
creating subprojects, 183
critical path
    definition, 146
Critical Tasks, 196

Crosstab Report, 215
CSV, 260
Cue Card icon, 47
cue cards, 10, 11, 46
Current Activity Reports, 198
Custom Forms
    button, 228,
custom forms toobar
    explained, 225
Custom Reports, 210
Customize Tool dialog box, 242
Customizing
    life cycle models, 59
    WBS numbers, 75
Customizing Menus, Toolbarsm and Toolbar
        Buttons, 232
CV, 205

D

Date Range from Today dialog box, 249
Date Range from Today Filter Macro
    to run, 248
DBF, 260, 262
default
    Gantt chart bars, 135
    wbs codes, 76
Define New Report Dialog Box, 211
Defining Information Requirements for reports,
    198
Delay
    only within slack, 116, 153
Delay field, 114, 115
demoting, 73
dependency, 149
Detailed Planning, 3
Dialog Editor, 225
Directory
    project, 95
Display Weights form, 255
divider bar, 63
double plus sign, 73
Duration, 78

Index

E

Earned Value Report, 205
Edit
    Copy, 28
    Cut, 27
    delete Task, 28
    Fill Down, 28
    Find, 28
    Go To, 28
    Link Tasks, 28
    Paste, 28
    Paste Special, 28
    Undo, 27
    Unlink Tasks, 28
editing
    cells, 72
Effort-Driven Scheduling Macro
    to run, 249
elapsed duration, 78
    described, 78
Electronic mail, 94
E-mail, 98
engineering, 125
Entry button, 225
Entry table, 63
estimating
    time, 77
expand
    summary task, 73
expected time estimates, 254
export
    a file, 262
Exporting, 262

F

Field Name, 53, 54
File
    Add Routing Slip, 27
    close, 26
    find, 26
    open, 26
    Page Setup, 27
    Post to Exchange Folder, 27
    Print Preview, 27
    Project Info, 26
    project information, 26
    properties, 26
    save, 26
    save as, 26
    save workspace, 26
    Send, 27
    Summary Info, 26
file
    start new, 11
File Menu
    description, 25
Filtering, 218
Filtering Resources, 219
Filtering Tasks, 218
finance, 125
Finish-to-finish
    task (dependency) relationship, 142
finish-to-start
    task (dependency) relationship, 142
Fixed Costs, 105, 109, 121
    assigning, 109
    creating a list, 105, 106
    identify, 104
fixed-price contracts, 109
flow chart
    for macros, 256
Format
    bar, 33
    bar styles, 35
    details, 35
    drawing, 36
    font, 33
    gridlines, 34
    layout, 35
    text styles, 35
    timescale, 34
Format Duration macro
    to run, 250
Format Menu, 33
Formatting toolbar, 36
free slack
    definition, 146
    to display on Gantt bar, 144
Funding
    project, 119

G

Gantt
    timing of tasks, 154
Gantt bars
    changing the appearance, 136
    changing the timescale, 137
Gantt chart
    described, 126
    editing, 135
    explained, 134
    wizard, 99, 141
Gathering Information
    status, 93
goal, 58
GoTo Overallocation button, 101
global file
    sharing common elements, 180
gridlines
    in calendar view, 137
    Gantt chart, 137
Gridlines Between Fields
    PERT boxes, 151
Group, 112
Guidelines
    project, 59

H

help
    in Version 4.0, 42
    search in Version 4.0, 44
    Version 4.1, 39
Help Menu, 3

I

Icons
    resource management toolbar, 98
import
    a file, 261
Importing, 260
Importing and Exporting, 259
Incompatible Formats
    for importing or exporting, 263
indenting. *See* demoting
Insert
    column, 32, 73
    drawing, 33
    object, 33
    page break, 32
    recurring task, 32
    resource assignment, 32
    task, 32
    task information, 32
    task notes, 32
Insert Menu, 31
Insert Object dialog box, 266
Inserting Columns, 51
interim baseline
    saving, 156

L

lag, 148
    to delay the start of a prececessor, 115
lag time
    described, 143
Layout
    Gantt chart, predecessor-succesor lines, 139
Lead time, 148
    described, 143
levels of indentation for project outlines, 72
Level Now, 115
    command, 153
Leveling Cue Cards button, 102
library
    template, 60
life cycles
    standard, 59
link or embed a picture object, 264
Linking and Embedding Objects from another application in Microsoft Project, 264
Linking or Embedding Objects from Microsoft Project in another application, 266
Links
    between any projects, 189
list
    task, 67

Index

M

macro
    definition, 242
Macros
    creating, 255
    explained, 242
major milestones, 68
Managing Many Projects, 176
Managing One Project, 160
manufacturing, 125
MAPI/VIM, 94
Max Units
    resource availability, 153
MDB, 260, 262
meeting
    team, number two, 62
    third team, 68
Menu Bar, 24
    customize, 37
Microsoft Project Analyzer dialog box, 252
milestone, 69, 71
    definition, 69
Milestones, 197
Milestones Report, 197
minus sign, 73
Monthly Calendar Report, 214
MPX, 262
    described, 260
Multiple Projects, 37
    project analyzer, 250
must start on, 116

N

negotiations, 160
new custom form
    creating, 229
new menu
    adding to menu bar, 233
Newness
    characteristic of a project, 125
node, 145
Non-Critical Tasks
    delaying or lengthening, 114
    described, 146
numbering

WBS. *See* outline levels

O

Object
    edit, 28
Object Linking and Embedding, 263
objectives, 68, 69
objects
    embedded, 28
    linked, 28
Open From Database
    button, 167
optimistic time estimates, 254
Organizer, 181
outdenting. *See* promoting
Outline levels
    expanding and collapsing, 72
    for a small project, 69
Overallocated Resources, 208
Overbudget Resources Report, 204
Overbudget Tasks Report, 204
overhead rate, 104
overtime
    rate, 108
Overview Reports, 193

P

Page Setup
    described, 221
parent tasks, 73
partitioning large projects, 184
path
    definition, 146
percent complete
    updating, 161
Permanence
    characteristic of a project, 126
PERT
    project flow, 154
    used with Gantt, 134
PERT Chart
    explained, 145
PERT task network
    modifying, 149
pivot tables, 98

in Microsoft Excel, 102
Planning Wizard, 19
    described, 141
plus sign, 73
practices
    project management, 58
predecessor
    definition, 142
Preparing to Record a Macro, 256
Print
    File. *See* File
Print Preview
    described, 221
Printing
    described, 222
priority
    levels, 116
Procedure Cards, 10
program, 2
Progress Marks, 152
project
    definition, 2
Project Analyzer macro
    to run, 251
Project Description, 17
Project Goal, 18
Project management
    definition, 3
project management terminology
    standardize, 69
project objectives
    newsletter, 69
Project Phases, 58
project schedule
    definition, 124
Project Scheduling, 124
    accuracy, 124
Project Statistics
    button, 162
Project Summary Report, 194
project summary task, 72. *See* goal
    creating, 71
    promoting, 73

Q

Quick Preview

R

Rate
    overtime, 108
    standard, 107
Record Macro dialog box, 258
Recording a Macro, 257
Report Categories, 193
requests for proposals, 105
Requests for Quotations (RFQ), 105
Requirements
    project, 4
    technical, 4
Resource
    eliminate overallocations, 114
    group, 107
    ID number, 107
    identifying needs, 104
    leveling, 113, 115
    maximum units, 107
    name, 107
    overallocated, 152
    removing, 118
    replacing, 118, 119
    split assignment, 115
Resource Allocation View, 98
    displayed, 98
Resource Assignment button, 101
Resource Assignment dialog box, 111
Resource Data
    changing, 112
resource details
    icon, 98
resource form
    for entering tasks, 109
Resource Graph, 116, 153
    display, 117
Resource Information Dialog Box
    resource Version, 112
    task Version, 113
resource leveling
    manual, 116
resource limitations, 147
Resource Management Task Entry macro, 252
Resource Name, 173

Index

Resource Pool
    developing, 105
resource-related tables, 30
Resource Report, 213
Resource Sheet, 105
Resource Usage Report, 210
Resource Usage View
    to see overallocation dates, 152
resources
    assigning, 109
    creating a list, 105
    manage, steps, 104
    managing and reassigning, 111
    reassigning, 114
    sharing with other projects, 182
Resources and Costs, 103
RFO, 105
RFQ, 105
right mouse button, 82
risk, 86
Risk Assessment, 86
Risk Example #1, 88
Risk Example #2, 88
Rollup Formatting macro, 253
row height
    increasing or decreasing, 65

S

Save Macro In, 259
Save Print Batch File dialog box, 247
Save to Database
    button, 162
Saving Several Projects as a Workspace, 179
scaling
    life cycle models, 59
Schedule
    finalizing, 152
Schedule Tracking button, 227
Screentips, 41
scope creep, 160
secondary mouse button, 25
Send Mail
    button, 167
server
    linking and embedding, defined, 263, 264, 266

Set Reminders
    button, 167
share resources among several projects, 183
Share Resources Dialog Box, 182
Sharing Common Elements as Global Files, 180
Sharing Resources With Other Projects, 182
Should Have Started Tasks Report, 201
Show Topics, 44
Size
    characteristic of a project, 125
skill level, 77
Slipping Tasks, 202
Slipping Tasks Report, 202
Sort dialog box, 218
Sorting, 216
Sorting and Filtering
    explained, 216
Sorting Resources, 218
Sorting Tasks, 216
sponsor
    definition, 3
stakeholder
    definition, 3
Stakeholders
    and information needs, 93
standards
    project, 58
standard project calendar
    changing, 15
standard
    rates, 107
Start-to-start
    (task dependency) relationship, 142
Start Variance, 171
statement of work, 18
status bar, 116
Status meetings, 94
submenus
    changes, 24
subproject
    controlling the start date, 186
    creating by inserting an existing project, 185
    creating from the active project, 184
successor
    definition, 142
summary reports
    preparing, 69

291

Summary Tasks, 73
SV, 205

T

Table
    create new, 53
    creating new, 53
Table Definition dialog box, 30
Task
    analysis, 82
    cut, 55
    Deleting, 54
    Editing, 55
    summary, 72
Task Analysis Worksheet, 83, 85
    described, 83
Task Assignment Table button, 102
Task Details Form, 76
Task Earned Value button, 226
Task Entry View, 100
    displayed, 99
task form, 63
Task Form Prepared for New Object, 265
Task Information
    dialog box, 113, 129
    editing in calendar view, 130
Task list
    newsletter project, 66
task network, 29
    creating with stickies, 147
    explained. *See* PERT chart
task notes, 18
Task Relationship button, 227
Task Report, 212
Task Update, 253
Task Usage, 210
Tasks
    entering, 65
Tasks In Progress Report, 200
Team Assign
    button, 167
Team Experience
    characteristic of a project, 125
Team Meeting
    fourth, 146
Team Status
    button, 167
Team Updates
    button, 167
teams, 125
template
    standard, 59
Template Wizard, 59
Templates
    available, 59
    for standardization, 58
    standard project, 59
Text Styles
    in the Gantt chart, 138
The Tools Menu, 36
time estimates, 78
Time Estimating, 77
Timescales
    calendar view, 127
Tip of the day, 42
Toggle Read Only, 253
Toggle Read Only macro, 253
Toggle Updates
    button, 167
Tracking Table, 168
Toolbar
    described, 47
    new, 48
    resource management. *See* resource management toolbar
toolbar button
    add, 239
    to remove, 239
toolbars
    customize, 37
Tools, 37
    change working time, 36
    customize, 37
    filtered for, 36
    multiple projects, 37
    options, 37, 71
    record macro, 37
    resource leveling, 36
    sort, 36
    spelling, 36
    tracking, 37
    workgroup, 37
top-down, 59-60

Index

Top-Level Tasks Report, 195
Total Costs, 121
Total slack
 definition, 146
Tracking, 37
Tracking button, 228
TXT, 260

U

Unstarted Tasks Report, 199
Up and Running Tutorial Vesion 4.0, 10
Update as Scheduled
 button, 163
Update Percent Complete
 buttons, 164
Update Read Only
 Button, 167
Update Resources
 button, 164
Update Task Range, 164
 button, 164
Update Tasks
 button, 164
Updating Project Status, 93
Using Resource
 dialog box, 101

V

Variance
 cost, 121
Variance Table, 169
view
 Calendar. *See* Calendar
 default, 29. *See also* defaults
 Gantt chart, 29
 more views, 31
 PERT Chart. *See* Task Network
 removing from view menu, 238
 reports, 31
 Resource Graph, 29
 Resource Sheet, 29
 Resource Usage, 29
 Table, 29
 Toolbars, 31
 Zoom, 31

View Menu
 description, 29
Views and Tables, 50
Visual Basic
 described, 259

W

WBS codes, 73, 74
WBS Numbers
 newsletter, 70
Weekly Cash Flow, 203
Weekly Cash Flow Report, 203
Weekly Titles, 127
Weekly To Do List, 208
Who Does What Report, 207
Who Does What When, 207
Window, 38, 39
 arrange all, 38
 currently open, 39
 hide, 39
Window Menu, 38
WKS, WK1, WK3, 260, 262
Wizard
 Gantt chart. *See* view---Gantt chart
Work Breakdown Structure (WBS) levels, 72, 124
work environment, 7
work hours
 actual, 77
work table
 resource Version, 175
 task Version, 174
Work Tracking button, 226
Workgroup
 toolbar button, 166
workgroup toolbar
 described, 166working days report, 198
working time
 changing, 96
Workload Reports, 209
workspace
 saving several files as, 179

X

XLS, 260, 262

CD ROM Contents

- Project Templates (created in Microsoft® Project Version 4.0)
- PERT Chart EXPERT™
- Three project management-related articles

A. Project Templates

The accompanying CD-ROM disk contains a wide variety of project template files (located in sub-directory CPGTEMPL) that can significantly reduce the time needed to scope and schedule your project.

1. Implementing bar code technology in manufacturing (cpgtempl\barcode.mpt)
2. Communicating (company) benefits (cpgtempl\benefit.mpt)
3. Providing a broadband network (cpgtempl\brodband.mpt)
4. Converging nine customer service phone lines into two (cpgtempl\convline.mpt)
5. Establishing a centralized customer support center (cpgtempl\custsupp.mpt)
6. Moving to a new facility (cpgtempl\facmove.mpt)
7. Manufacturing frequency converters (cpgtempl\freqconv.mpt)
8. Making renovations to the interior and exterior of a building (cpgtempl\intextre.mpt)
9. Renovating multi-unit housing (cpgtempl\multunit.mpt)
10. Developing multi-lingual instructions for a product (cpgtempl\multilin1.mpt)
11. Developing a network management tool (cpgtempl\netwmgt.mpt)
12. Buying a new home (cpgtempl\newhome.mpt)
13. Implementing a new LAN (cpgtempl\newlan.mpt)
14. Publishing a newsletter (cpgtempl\newsletr.mpt)
15. Converting to a centralized order management system (cpgtempl\ordersys.mpt)
16. Providing PC insurance (cpgtempl\pcinsure.mpt)
17. Establishing project management structure and training (cpgtempl\pmtrain.mpt)
18. Revising project management guidelines (cpgtempl\projguid.mpt)
19. Constructing a ranch house (cpgtempl\ranchose.mpt)
20. Opening a restaurant (cpgtempl\restrant.mpt)
21. Designing and developing a sales training program (cpgtempl\salestrn.mpt)
22. Selling hardware, software & support services (cpgtempl\techsale.mpt)
23. Reengineering processes for a training department (cpgtempl\trainree.mpt)
24. Planning to provide training (cpgtempl\tranplan.mpt)
25. Planning a summer outing (cpgtempl\summoutg.mpt)

B. A Demo for PERT Chart EXPERT™

A tool that quickly draws the PERT from a Microsoft® Project file. Jim Spiller & Associates, (707) 425-2484. (PERTCHRT)

C. Articles

The accompanying CD-ROM disk also contains three useful articles:
- Managing and Facilitating Project Meetings (articles\facskill.doc)
- Managing Creativity and Conflict in Projects (articles\creatcon.doc)
- How to Plan a Small Project (articles\verysmal.doc)

To see more about the templates, demo and articles, open "readme.txt".